K-POP: THE ODYSSEY

To. 수인누나
Always grateful for the love
ad support! 내가 놀러갈게
꽃은 보자 ~ ~

K-POP:
THE ODYSSEY

YOUR GATEWAY TO THE GLOBAL
K-POP PHENOMENON

WOOSEOK KI

NEW DEGREE PRESS

COPYRIGHT © 2020 WOOSEOK KI

K-POP: THE ODYSSEY
Your Gateway to the Global K-POP Phenomenon

ISBN

978-1-63676-643-0 *Paperback*
978-1-63676-169-5 *Kindle Ebook*
978-1-63676-175-6 *Digital Ebook*

For Mom, Dad, and Albert,

Thanks for the never-ending support. Congratulations for surviving my screams and shouts as I wrote this book while being quarantined with the family. 2020 shall be a year to remember. Dad also deserves credit for suggesting the title word, "Odyssey."

CONTENTS

———

AUTHOR'S NOTE

———

Welcome to the odyssey.

In Greek mythology, the *Odyssey* is the story of Trojan War hero, Odysseus, who after a ten-year war, encounters another decade of adventures and setbacks on his way home. I won't spoil the ending in case you want to check it out.

In a lot of ways, K-Pop has a parallel story; it has had no predictable progression of events but rather a series of trials and tribulations. A lot of things worked out but some just didn't. Unexpected game-changers happened frequently. The modern idea of K-Pop as we know it today spans at least two and a half decades, so how can a single news outlet condense all these fascinating stories into just a one-page article? Or just one YouTube video?

It's only relatively recently that we've seen Korean pop culture spread so vastly outside of its homeland; it started to make an impact in a major way during the late 1990s and early 2000s in Greater Asia. Initially, it was difficult for Korean pop culture to challenge the existing pop cultural paradigm because historically, the West has dominated this arena with staples such as Hollywood, Billboard, and the Grammys. Additionally, the nearby Chinese and Japanese markets had their own intricate pop cultural products: Chinese cinema, anime, and their respective pop industries. One way or another, however, K-Pop eventually spread and captured the global audience.

As a Korean American who has navigated both countries almost equally, I love seeing cultural diffusion. I get excited whenever I see people engage with and enjoy a cultural aspect or tradition that I hadn't expected them to. You can imagine my delight when I learned that my non-Korean classmates from places like New Jersey and Hong Kong had discovered and enjoyed K-Pop, either on their own or through a Korean mediator.

When I moved to the U.S. from Seoul as an eight-year-old, I missed seeing my favorite Korean singers on TV. The artists in my new country looked and dressed differently than Korean stars on music TV shows, and I could only memorize pop songs by their melodies because I couldn't understand the English lyrics. Even as I gradually began to embrace Western pop culture, I still wished for an Asian role model—a chill, trendy one that I could brag to my American friends about. Jackie Chan was my go-to for a while, since he was not only a badass but a household name. Yet, as great as the *Rush Hour* movies were, Chan is from Hong Kong, not South Korea. Plus, he was getting old! The fact that I had no Korean icon to automatically resort to was disheartening.

Fortunately, thanks to YouTube's popularity a few years later, I was able to reconnect with Korean pop music—which was newly heralded as K-Pop—and dive into a spiral of endless videos from acts like TVXQ and BIGBANG. I always wondered to myself, "What if these guys were to perform on a bigger platform like MTV or the Grammys?"

Years later, I started at UC Berkeley in Fall 2012 as a clueless freshman. Serendipitously, this was around the same time that a track called "Gangnam Style" was released. Then, things changed.

I had partied to this song all summer long on the streets of Gangnam District in Seoul right before my first semester at Berkeley. At karaoke bars, my friends and I would chant, "*OPPAN GANGNAM STYLE!*" before erupting into crazy dance routines, as everyone else did in Korea that summer.

Never did I expect to hear "Gangnam Style" blasting from a loudspeaker on my first day on the huge Berkeley campus.

What was going on here? Why were they playing this song in faraway America? The lyrics weren't even in English! But here in Berkeley, I saw people vibing, hopping along to the bouncy rhythm, and chanting, "*OPPAN GANGNAM STYLE!*" just like I had done in Gangnam.

Apparently, the "Gangnam Style" phenomenon was not only taking off—it was soaring. As its YouTube video view count kept rising, the singer, Psy, began to appear on American media like *The Ellen DeGeneres Show* and the *MTV Video Music Awards*. The term K-Pop became a frequent identifier on media headlines, and it increasingly attracted more and more global eyes. What I had imagined to be largely self-contained to Korea or maybe even to Asia was already being recognized by those all over the world. It was certainly fascinating to see K-Pop elevating to a global platform. At the same time, I thought, "Man, I wonder if we'll ever have something like 'Gangnam Style' again."

Since I attended a college with a student body of roughly 30,000 and a huge minority of Asian students—roughly 30 percent—it wasn't hard to find others interested in K-Pop. I was able to connect with many peers who celebrated the music and culture.

At the time, I thought it was only natural that K-Pop was becoming more global; members of the Millennial generation were living in the age of social media and heightened globalization. Thanks to the internet, it has become very easy to share music and content surrounding these K-Pop stars, and the Korean entertainment companies were very aware of this. More K-Pop artists like Super Junior, BIGBANG, and 2NE1 began to engage in worldwide tours, incorporated English lyrics or foreign-language-speaking members, and began working with international music producers and dance choreographers.

Things were certainly changing—the K-Pop stars of the 1990s and 2000s were mostly active throughout Asia. There were smaller, scattered communities of fans around the world who had discovered K-Pop on their own, but they weren't all connected in unison for the artists. Now, however, artists are producing content with the idea that the whole world will be watching.

Due to the success of "Gangnam Style" as well as many K-Pop artists' positive international reception, I knew that K-Pop was expanding outside of Asia, but I wasn't sure if I could call it global *mainstream* pop culture at all. After all, "Gangnam Style" singer, Psy, is still largely regarded as a one-hit-wonder. Was the world outside of Asia really ready to embrace music so fascinating yet so different? What about the language barrier? What did people outside of the existing K-Pop fandoms think?

With so many questions looming in my head, I continued to stay very invested in the K-Pop culture — dancing choreography onstage, keeping up with the latest music trends, and attending live events.

Several years later, in the latter half of the 2010s, a very special boy band named BTS rose to international stardom and captured both the East and the West. I began having flashbacks to Fall 2012 when I couldn't contain my excitement and confusion over hearing "Gangnam Style" in America. My hopes from ten years ago were reality—BTS were actual global superstars and were performing at the Grammy Awards! Could K-Pop keep soaring higher and higher? Should I stay on the edge of my seat for artists to shatter even more records?

* * *

Recent history has solidified the fact that K-Pop has evolved beyond just music from Korea; it's become a global pop-cultural phenomenon. I wrote this book because not only do I want to see K-Pop expand even more but also because I'm curious: Why and how has K-Pop become a global phenomenon? What about K-Pop appeals to non-Koreans worldwide? How many more groundbreaking milestones will it achieve?

This book isn't intended to be the end-all-be-all on K-Pop but rather a gateway; there's so much K-Pop content out there that I can't simply condense it into a singular book. Ultimately, it's up to you to decide with how much of it you want to engage.

Plenty of books, videos, academic articles, and theories analyze what has transpired with K-Pop over the years. Unfortunately, the internet is a maze—it may take you hours, days, or even months to become knowledgeable about what's really going on with K-Pop. For many global fans, a lack of understanding of Korean society leads many to only speculate about K-Pop's subtleties and nuances. Never fear! That's why I'm here.

First, in order to clarify any misconceptions about this book, here's a list of what this book **isn't**:

- **A history book**

A history of Korean pop music as a whole includes many larger themes such as geopolitics as well as a lengthy discussion of Korean history dating back to the 1950s. While such a discussion may be fruitful, I've determined that there's already a lot to take in and that there are better resources for such a purpose. Thus, I will not present history in a linear fashion throughout the entire book. Rather, we'll take a look at certain events and analyze their significance through the lens of K-Pop. This book definitely incorporates history in some chapters but isn't meant to be read exclusively for its historical content.

- **Journalistic or academic work**

No, I'm neither a journalist nor an academic scholar (a legal scholar, sure, but I don't have a Ph.D. in Korean studies or music). I'm a fan who's had relevant experiences and loves studying K-Pop. I'll be deferring to relevant resources when referring to studies, articles, or interviews. Many topical social issues and themes have warranted books and dissertations of their own, so you'll see me mention this idea repeatedly throughout the book.

- **An encyclopedia**

This book isn't meant to serve as the perfect compilation of K-Pop facts, nor will it analyze in detail one particular K-Pop artist the entire time. It's impossible to cover every single aspect of K-Pop. I can't discuss every single K-Pop artist or historical event like a Wikipedia article, and that's not what you want. You'll see some terms and figures mentioned throughout the book, but this isn't a biography of specific artists.

Instead, here's what this book **is:**

- **A buffet**

Treat this book like a buffet—it has steak, bulgogi, sushi, pizza, seafood, desserts, and more. It's not a steakhouse or a Korean Barbecue restaurant that focuses on one specific thing, but I guarantee you'll finish with a satisfying taste of everything. So, if I mention an interesting topic but don't analyze it deeply enough for your curiosity, I encourage you to go and explore further!

- **A gateway**

I intend this book to be your comprehensive gateway into K-Pop. It's meant to serve as a bridge to today's myriad K-Pop content today. There are fantastic books, YouTube videos, journalistic works, and academic papers if you want to dive deeper. Since it's sometimes difficult to distinguish between credible and non-credible sources, perhaps this book can serve as a reference.

- **A collection of thoughts**

This book includes my own thoughts as well as the insights of experts. Therefore, it won't be completely objective—it'll balance my thoughts and experiences of watching K-Pop develop while living in both Korea and the U.S. and also how I feel about certain successes and setbacks related to K-Pop as a topic. I will not openly criticize any particular company or artist, but I will definitely praise the ones that I deem influential.

So, my job is pretty straightforward; throughout this book, no matter how much you love or hate K-Pop, I'll help you think and learn about some of the key visions, people, and challenges involved in shaping the phenomenon. I'll guide you through historical events, expert testimonies, and discussions of the social issues underlying K-Pop's fascinating audiovisual experience. I'll also be showing you what's going on in South Korea, of course, with my two cents.

This book makes the most sense if you start it from the beginning, as I'll be referring to earlier content and terms in the later chapters. Read each "Part" or section of chapters, as its own mini-book within the larger context. Also, from here onward, whenever I say Korea, I mean *South* Korea.

Once you read all or part of this book, you'll be prepared to drop your new knowledge at cocktail receptions, on playdates and sleepovers, for school projects, or during conversations with Grandma.

I look forward to embarking on the K-Pop odyssey with you. Are you ready to go?

PART 1

WHAT IS K-POP?

How would I know? But it's awesome!

- **TABLO OF EPIK HIGH**,
ON NETFLIX'S *EXPLAINED* | K-POP[1]

---

1   *Netflix*. "K-Pop | Explained | Netflix," May 31, 2018, video, 0:45.

INTRO

Whenever a non-Korean asks me about K-Pop or whether I listen to it, I have never been hesitant to reply, "Yes!" As a dancer since high school, I was always dancing to K-Pop. However, I was dancing mostly to boy bands' choreography and was using K-Pop interchangeably with "idol pop" or "mainstream Korean music." I didn't think much of what K-Pop exactly encompassed or referred to until I started writing this book. Now, there's no going back for me.

Like I mentioned earlier, I was born into the Korean society and culture that created this phenomenon and was initially very surprised to discover that it was expanding outside of Asia. While growing up in the American suburbs, I remember being puzzled to learn that my Caucasian friend knew the group BIGBANG in 2007—a time when YouTube and Facebook were just getting started and Instagram and Tiktok didn't even exist. Apparently, her Korean friend had introduced her to some of their songs like "Last Farewell" (2007), and she really liked them!

I wasn't sure how this would happen, but nonetheless, I wanted more of my non-Korean friends to be exposed to

Korean pop culture. Not only would we be able to enjoy music together, but my non-Korean friends could learn more about where I came from. This childhood wish of mine has certainly started come true, thanks to K-Pop.

So, how and why did a global phenomenon spread? And what *exactly* is K-Pop?

Perhaps one of the reasons why you picked up this book was to seek out the ultimate answer to these questions. You may have even asked these questions to your excited friend or coworker who's been rambling on and on about K-Pop.

The short answer, according to the Merriam-Webster dictionary, is that K-Pop is "popular music originating in South Korea and encompassing a variety of styles."[2]

Helpful, right?

Just kidding. We both know you didn't pick up this book for a dictionary definition; you want a more comprehensive answer. There's so much more nuance and context to add to understanding the K-Pop phenomenon than "music from South Korea."

From my perspective, there are three ways to approach and discuss K-Pop: as **a music genre, an industry,** and **a culture**. By no means are these categories exhaustive, but subjectively speaking, a full comprehension of the phenomenon involves all three. Here we go.

---

2   *Merriam-Webster.com Dictionary*, s.v. "K-Pop," accessed August 21, 2020.

CHAPTER 1

K-POP AS A
MUSIC GENRE

———

I'll start by asking a fundamental question that scholars and fans have been debating for years: is K-Pop its own music genre, and if not, should it be one? The answer is much more complex than a flat-out yes or no; there are bigger implications at stake, and various schools of thought exist. Let's get started.

When discussing it as a music genre, scholars commonly define K-Pop as "Korean pop." Compare this to how we view "pop" music in general; "pop" is a shortened version of the word, "popular," and it's often synonymous with the mainstream. "Pop" refers to the songs you'd hear on the radio and at a venue like Coachella, the Grammy Awards, or a college frat party.

You may have heard of other "pops" like Latin Pop, Europop, Bubblegum Pop… the list goes on. So, isn't K-Pop basically the equivalent of Korea's "pop" genre? If so, would K-Pop then be a subgenre of just plain "pop" music like those other "pops" are? These are debatable questions that are more complex than you may think.

First, consider how you perceive songs from artists such as Beyoncé, Maroon 5, and Taylor Swift. Although they draw influences from other genres, most people would comfortably place these artists under the "pop" umbrella. Meanwhile, popular rappers such as Kendrick Lamar, Future, and Eminem tend to be grouped under the "hip-hop" genre, and groups such as Green Day, Foo Fighters, and U2 are perceived as rock bands. Could Kendrick Lamar and U2's hits be considered "pop music?"

Although those songs played on the radio and were also commercially successful, no one calls Kendrick Lamar a "pop singer." However, the "pop" label has become very fluid. Michael Jackson has been called the "King of Pop," but his music ranges from slow jam ballads to funky hip-hop dance tunes. Think about how flexible the word "pop" is. Then, imagine just how flexible K-Pop could be. Since even the "pop" part of K-Pop is fluid, let's hold off on calling all Korean songs K-Pop and automatically equating the label to mean "music from Korea."

K-Pop, as we know it today, doesn't just refer to all kinds of popular Korean music in a one-dimensional manner; there's an underlying industry, culture, and legacy. As a result, it's difficult to categorize K-Pop under a traditional music genre.[3] Let me explain the Korean music scene so you can understand why this is.

---

3   Gyu Tag Lee, "De-Nationalization and Re-Nationalization of Culture: The Globalization of K-Pop" (PhD diss., George Mason University, 2013), 84.

Contrary to the common perception, Korean pop music does not predominantly consist of boy bands and girl groups. In actuality, Korea's music industry is very diverse in terms of genres; Korean ballads have been popular for decades as well as hip-hop, rock, R&B, jazz, and indie/alternative scenes.

Now, let's compare and contrast how Korea and the rest of the world perceive K-Pop. The term K-Pop didn't actually come from Korea; to complement Japan's J-Pop, other countries in Asia used K-Pop to categorize Korean music.[4] In South Korea, mainstream music is called "*daejoong eum-ahk* (대중음악)," and, more specifically, "*gayo* (가요)" roughly refers to the popular, trending music that's distributed to a wide audience.[5] Within *gayo,* there may be a variety of different genres at the top of the charts, just as Beyoncé, Maroon 5, and Taylor Swift all have different musical styles but are often grouped together under the popular music label.

To Koreans, the term K-Pop is a subset of *gayo* and is comprised largely of music from "**idols**"— stars the fans look up to and cheer on. K-Pop idols are groups (boy bands, girl groups, and mixed gender groups) or solo acts that generally have a wide following among the younger generations, concrete fandoms, aesthetically pleasing visual appearances, synchronized dance choreography, and experimental sounds often

---

4   Suk-Young Kim, *K-Pop Live: Fans, Idols, and Multimedia Performance,* (Stanford: Stanford University Press, 2018), 8; Sungmin Kim, 케이팝의 작은 역사 [K-Pop's Small History], (Seoul: Geulhangari Publishers, 2018), 89.

5   *Encyclopedia of Korean Culture*, s.v. "Daejoong-Eumak" [Popular Music], accessed March 2, 2020.

influenced by global trends.[6] International media headlines on K-Pop often associate K-Pop with these idol stars.

There are plenty of non-idol acts like solo R&B singers or rappers who become very popular both domestically and internationally. However, in South Korea, the specific term K-Pop is commonly associated with "Korean idol pop for the global market," "young men and women singing along to synced choreography," or "idol multimedia performance."[7] This idol music is intended to be exported globally—previously just within Asia, but today all over the world.[8]

Idol music is actually quite diverse, and K-Pop idols have distinct styles that draw from a diversity of influences including dance-pop, hip-hop, EDM, R&B and alternative rock. Today, the abundance of readily accessible idol-related multimedia content like music, YouTube videos, live events, and merchandise makes it very difficult to not associate the term "idol" with K-Pop. There will be a subsequent section going in-depth into this idea of a "K-Pop idol" – this topic's intricacy comprises a world of its own. And no, it's quite different from *American Idol*.

---

6   John Lie, *K-Pop: Popular Music, Cultural Amnesia, and Economic Innovation in South Korea*, Oakland: University of California Press, 2015.

7   Kimjakga, "케이팝이란 무엇인가: Z-Girls, Boy Story, EXP 에디션 사례 연구를 중심으로" [What is K-Pop: Focusing on Research from Z-Girls, Boy Story, EXP Edition], *Donga*, June 28, 2019; Kim Jung-sook, "[글로벌 칼럼] 케이팝의 시작과 문제점은 무엇인가?" [Global Column: What Are the Beginnings and Problems of K-Pop?], *The Korea Post*, March 23, 2017; Kim, *K-Pop Live*, 9.

8   Mathieu Berbiguier and Young Han Cho. "케이팝 (K-Pop)의 한국 팬덤에 대한 연구" [Understanding the Korean Fandom of the K-Pop], *Korean Journal of Communication and Information*, Vol. 81 (2017): 273.

Interestingly, Korea didn't begin using the term K-Pop until the 2010s. After Hong Kong's media network, Channel [V], used K-Pop to generally refer to Korean music videos in 1995, it seemed like almost every other country but Korea seemed to start using the term as well.[9] When Korea did begin to use K-Pop, they used it to specifically refer to the pop music it exported; pop music columnist Shin Hyun-joon even describes the way that Korea originally used K-Pop as "music made in Korea for non-Korea."[10] Even today on Korean music streaming sites like Melon and Bugs, there is no specific K-Pop genre at all. However, Bugs does have an idol genre that consists of diverse songs from idols only.[11]

In contrast, both YouTube and Billboard added K-Pop categories for their respective pages and charts as early as 2011.[12] Today, on iTunes and Spotify, the K-Pop genre includes non-idol artists and songs that don't follow the idol formula. No one knowledgeable about Korean music would call the ballad legend, Shin Seung-hun, a K-Pop "idol," as his music is not representative of how idol music is produced. Yet, when Shin's new album released in 2020, it was featured on the iTunes front page under K-Pop!

---

9   Kim, *K-Pop Live*, 8.

10 Shin, Hyun-joon. 가요, 케이팝 그리고 그 너머 [Gayo, K-Pop and Beyond], (Paju: Dolbaegae, 2013), 31-32.

11 "한국대중음악" [Korean Mainstream Music], Melon, last accessed August 3, 2020; "국내 장르" [Korean Genres], Bugs, last accessed August 3, 2020.

12 Joongho Ahn, Sehwan Oh and Hyunjung Kim, "Korean Pop Takes Off!: Social Media Strategy of Korean Entertainment Industry," *2013 10th International Conference on Service Systems and Service Management*, Hong Kong (2013): 1.

So, does the rest of the world think that K-Pop is supposed to encompass any Korean popular music?

During a chat with CedarBough Saeji, Visiting Professor of East Asian Languages & Culture at Indiana University Bloomington, I learned that there are shared elements across genres on how the Korean music industry presents and exports music to an audience. Can one act, such as idol group EXO, be more K-Pop than another act like solo rapper Beenzino? Is Bruno Mars more pop than Jay-Z or Guns N' Roses? Should it be okay to subsume all Korean songs of diverse genres under the umbrella term K-Pop as long as they're all intended to be exported to a global audience?

To try to answer this question, I looked to the stars themselves. However, their answers differ. Jay Park and Eric Nam—two singers who are active in the Korean market—don't outright identify themselves as K-Pop artists anymore due to their unique respective trajectories and overseas careers.[13] Park and Nam perform R&B (also hip-hop, in Park's case) in the Korean scene and are also active in the U.S. market as artists independent of the K-Pop industry. Should we group these singers as K-Pop stars even when they don't necessarily see themselves as such? Other groups are more indifferent to how audiences classify them; according to Tablo, member of Korean hip-hop trio, Epik High, "There are debates online as to whether Epik High is K-Pop or not... We don't mind what we're

---

13   L. Singh, "Jay Park on K-Pop and Cultural Appropriation," *Vice,* November 29, 2019; Kat Moon, "Eric Nam Made It as a K-Pop Star. Now He Wants to Make It Back Home in America," *TIME,* November 26, 2019.

classified as."[14] In contrast, Jungkook, V, and J-Hope of boy band BTS have stated, "The genre is BTS."[15] Evidently, a discussion of K-Pop as a genre refers to something much more complex than the "popular music from Korea" idea.

The U.S. market also has posed a new problem as K-Pop acts have achieved greater Western mainstream success. For example, BTS's music has garnered international attention and fame; their 2019 track, "Boy With Luv," was certified platinum by the Recording Industry Association of America (RIAA), an objective measure of commercial success.[16] However, the 2019 MTV Video Music Awards (VMAs) grouped all Korean acts into a brand new "Best K-Pop" category, and none of the acts were nominated for the biggest awards like "Video of the Year."[17] Isn't this similar to what iTunes and Spotify are doing by lumping all Korean artists into the K-Pop genre, but with more negative consequences? Although the 2020 VMAs saw BTS's single "ON" be nominated under the "Best Pop" category with the likes of Justin Bieber and Lady Gaga as well as the "Best K-Pop" category, I think the initial backlash from the year before was justified.[18] We can consider MTV VMA's "Best K-Pop" category as similar to the "Best Latin" category.

14   Aria Chen, "'Korean Music Is Amazingly Vibrant.' Time Talks to Seoul Hip-Hop Sensation Epik High," *Time*, July 14, 2019.

15   John Ochoa, "BTS Talk New Album 'Map of the Soul: 7': 'the Genre Is BTS'," *Grammys*, February 22, 2020.

16   Tamar Herman, "BTS & Halsey's 'Boy with Luv' Goes Platinum," *Billboard*, June 24, 2019.

17   Alissa Schulman, "2019 MTV VMA Winners: See the Full List," *MTV*, August 26, 2019.

18   "Vote Now – Nominees for 2020 MTV Video Music Awards," MTV, accessed August 10, 2020.

Lumping all Korean acts into the K-Pop awards category brings up a larger discussion of power dynamics between Western and Korean pop cultures. As with the case of MTV, K-Pop as a perceived genre can be used to label and restrict certain music just because they're by Korean acts. Is there actually a shared musical component among these acts, other than the Korean lyrics and heritage of the singers?

Nonetheless, what's definitely clear is that K-Pop as a label notes a specific musical and cultural phenomenon exported from Korea. It's difficult to simply classify K-Pop as a music genre complying with existing musical frameworks because a discussion of the global K-Pop phenomenon implies the audiovisual elements of performance, music videos, and the underlying industry's production system.

Does K-Pop comprise a separate music category of its own, like Latin Pop does? Latin Pop also has a huge distinct culture that actually spans over numerous Spanish-speaking countries and combines specific sounds and melodies that define the genre. There are definitely similarities and differences between K-Pop and Latin Pop; the global landscape of K-Pop, however, is more distinguished by its exoticism than the distinct melodies in this comparison.[19]

Picture this—Cardi B's single "I Like It" (2018) is categorized as Latin trap, with a distinct Latin melody and salsa rhythms as she pays homage to her Latin heritage.[20] Yet if an

---

19   Gyu Tag Lee, 갈등하는 K, Pop [K-Pop in Conflict], (Seoul: Three Chairs Publishing Company, 2020), chap. 2.

20   Gary Suarez, "Cardi B, Bad Bunny, and the Perils of Latin Novelty," *Vice*, April 27, 2018.

Asian-American singer (independent of the K-Pop industry) releases a song with a supposed K-Pop sound in the U.S., there's bound to be questions whether this really fits under the K-Pop label. What exactly is this K-Pop sound to begin with and is there one?

This is why we often see online debates as to "_____ is/isn't K-Pop." I personally believe that K-Pop implies specific, systematic, industry-produced media that caters to both domestic and international audiences, not just any popular song in the Korean language. Korean indie and hip-hop songs can become popular, but they're often not a product of the K-Pop industry system.[21]

For this book, I'll be referring to K-Pop collectively as the industry-produced, global pop-cultural phenomenon and not just as a single music genre—you'll soon learn that K-Pop artists perform in a variety of different genres. When I refer to a K-Pop act or artist, I'm generally referring to idols for the sake of convenience and consistency, even though we shouldn't equate K-Pop to mere idol pop. This book covers the specific term K-Pop within the broader realm of Korean music, with a focus on idols. A book on Korean music's extended history or musicology would better address all types of Korean musicians and musical frameworks.

There are arguments to be made for both sides in the debate over whether K-Pop is a music genre. Ultimately, it depends on how you or the artist want to classify the music. Labels are

---

21 Gyu Tag Lee, 케이팝의 시대 [The K-POP Age], (Seoul: Hanwool Academy, 2016), 104.

just labels—they're for guidance and easy categorization. I see K-Pop as a made-up label just like Korean hip-hop or K-rock.

There's definitely an industry that supports K-Pop music production, but the music genre debate may be misguided. I think the real focus should be on the individual artists themselves and not necessarily on the overarching framework that leads people to lump all Korean acts under one umbrella of a music genre. We can't just contain the K-Pop phenomenon's complex elements into a single condensed category.

At the end of the day, music is fluid and often crosses over genres, especially with today's diverse collaborations. We should appreciate the artists for who they are without confining them to a single label. Whether it be girl group BLACK-PINK, R&B sensation Crush, modern rock band Hyukoh, or ballad vocalist Park Hyo Shin, please don't dismiss them all by saying, "K-Pop all sounds the same." Instead, explore the different artists, sounds, and the colors that comprise the popular music that Korea has to offer without adhering so strictly to labels.

Next, we're going to dive deeper into the industry behind the K-Pop phenomenon, so hold on tight.

CHAPTER 2

K-POP AS AN INDUSTRY

Music is showbiz, and there's no way around the fact that money talks in entertainment.

K-Pop, just like other forms of global entertainment, is an intricate, multi-billion-dollar industry. A 2018 Hyundai financial report found that the boy band BTS accounted for an average annual domestic economic effect (pure inducement plus added value) of approximately $4.93 billion USD, or 5.5 trillion Korean won.[22] That's more than some domestic midsized corporations' net sales and more than the 2018 Pyeongchang Winter Olympics, which generated 4.1 trillion won.[23]

The K-Pop industry is important because of its larger institutionalized mechanism—the entertainment company (*gihwaegsa/sosoksa;* 기획사/소속사), which usually serves as both agency (talent management) and label (music production) to produce both the songs and the artists. I want you

---

22 Moon-Hee Choi, "K-Pop Group BTS Induces Production Worth 4 Tril. Won per Year," *BusinessKorea*, December 19, 2018.

23 Tae Hoon Kim, "BTS 10년이면 경제효과가 56조원" [56 Trillion Won in Economic Effect for 10 Years of BTS], *Kyunghyang*, December 7, 2019.

to get familiar with the idea of the K-Pop industry—it exists to support and reinforce commercial music production, and this entertainment company system has been well in place for decades. For future reference, I'll be using "company" instead of just "agency" or "label" as the latter two are often kept separate in non-Korean contexts.

First off, let's discuss what the Korean music market looks like in relation to those of the rest of the world. According to the International Federation of the Phonographic Industry (IFPI), the organization that represents worldwide recording industries, Korea is the sixth-largest music market in the world as of 2019. The Korean market grew by 8.2 percent from 2018, while Asia's as a whole grew at a rate of 3.4 percent; Japan is still the largest in Asia at number two in the world, with China trailing behind Korea at number seven. The IFPI data accounts for physical sales, streaming revenues, digital downloads, performance revenues (money from playing songs in public venues), and synchronization revenues (playing a song in ads, TV shows, or films).[24]

Since other critical sources of revenue drive the K-Pop industry in addition to just the music-related sales this study analyzes, it's unclear whether K-Pop will be able to propel Korea into the top five of global music industries. One aspect this study doesn't measure is concert ticket and merchandise sales. K-Pop consumers, more than those of other types of music, are inclined to purchase concert tickets and affiliated official merchandise.[25] K-Pop is meant to be a complete audiovisual experience, so attending a concert is a must for any diehard K-Pop fan.

---

24 "Global Music Report: The Industry in 2019," IFPI, accessed June 13, 2020.

25 *The Korea Society,* "The Economy of Kpop." August 27, 2018, video, 42:43.

Now, let's compare the Korean and U.S. industry landscapes and how they differ in terms of the parties involved, including the artists and various companies. In the U.S., the management agencies (talent representation) and record labels (music production) are kept separate; the artist can work with a variety of professionals for music production, concert touring, promotional activities, and copyright ownership. The artist may employ separate agencies for different purposes such as PR and booking TV appearances. Ultimately, the artist and the manager have leverage in deciding with which agency to sign and partner, and thus have a high degree of ownership over with whom they work.

In contrast, the Korean music industry is dominated by entertainment companies that usually serve as both talent management agencies and record labels. This is significant for a couple of reasons. First, if one company does everything for the artists, there'll be a systematized process for producing and managing them. Second, the artist is signed exclusively to that particular company for a specific duration, during which they'll split profits. After contract expiration, the artist may re-sign for a better deal or freely entertain deals from competing companies.

Korean entertainment companies shoulder the responsibility of providing the services that U.S. artists can negotiate on their own, ranging from music production to partnerships with event promoters and music publishers to music distribution to platforms.[26] In Korea, rather than having the artists

---

26 Dong-gil Yoo, *K-POP* 뮤직 비즈니스의 이해 [Understanding K-Pop Music Business], (Seoul: AXIMU, 2017), 248-257.

sign deals with multiple companies for different purposes, one company generally does everything.

K-Pop idols are a product of this industry; today's popular idol acts wouldn't exist without the underlying industry model. There's a historical, institutionalized system of production that has proven to work. They produce idols through a trainee system in which companies recruit and train pre-teens and young adults, often for years pre-debut. The companies then oversee and manage all aspects of the idols' careers—their music, their schedule, and even their personal lives to an extent—which has been the discussion of international media, especially since it is largely a unique concept.[27] In my opinion, this very unique system puts the "K" in "K-Pop," from an industry perspective. But more on the trainee system and idol production process later.

Once industry executives realized that K-Pop's success had expanded outside of Asia, business strategies began to reflect the increased emphasis on K-Pop as a global export. In 2015, Park Jin-Young, the founder and mastermind behind JYP Entertainment explained:

> As the K-Pop industry expands farther outside of Korea, it's difficult to compete successfully against international entertainment companies without a company-driven [Korean] system. Unlike Japan that has a population of 100 million compared to Korea's 50 million, we have to expand internationally for

---

27   Elaine Chong, "'I Could Have Been a K-Pop Idol - but I'm Glad I Quit'," *BBC*, February 13, 2020; Julie Zaugg, "The Hothouse Academies Offering Kids a Shot at K-Pop Stardom," *CNN*, October 5, 2018.

growth. To do so, we need something that blends both the traditional Korean colors with what'd be received well internationally.[28]

But wouldn't it be sufficient for K-Pop idols to commercially succeed just in Korea? Possibly, but the producer-executives' desires to expand beyond the domestic market isn't a recent phenomenon. For decades, even prior to the social media age, the predecessors to the current generation of K-Pop artists engaged in a slew of international promotional activities. However, it was largely a trial-and-error process, and industry executives have built upon these past successes and failures to implement new export strategies. Today's industry experts better understand what generates revenue in Japan and China, two of K-Pop's early export markets. Even succeeding in the U.S. market, which seemed like a dream just ten years ago, is a reality as of 2020.

Recently, however, there have been discussions that challenge this existing industry framework. Does an artist need the K-Pop industry to gain exposure and release K-Pop music? Intuitively, upon our discussions surrounding the company-driven industry, you may think something along the lines of, "Obviously! Otherwise, how else can an independent, aspiring K-Pop star even compete with the skill level of trainees who have been trained for years?" You may be on to something.

---

28 *JTBC News,* "[인터뷰] 박진영 "기획사 시스템 아니면 해외경쟁 어려워"" [[Interview] Park Jin-Young "International Competition Difficult without Agency System"], May 5, 2015, video, 19:05.

The early 2010s saw the rise of Chad Future, an independent Caucasian male singer who labeled himself as America's first K-Pop star.[29] Future made YouTube covers of K-Pop songs in English and later debuted original music. Although none of his songs were in Korean, Future's music videos contained obvious K-Pop influences such as flashy dance choreography, dyed hair, specialized makeup, and video filming in the K-Pop style. Yet to this day, K-Pop fans criticize Future as an illegitimate replication of the K-Pop phenomenon. He was not officially produced by the K-Pop industry, didn't speak or sing in Korean, and never performed on Korean TV.[30]

I personally was shocked yet pleasantly surprised to see a Caucasian man perform in the K-Pop style, regardless of his talent or quality. Never had I expected it to even be possible! Yet, I wondered if he would actually make it in the market or if he was just a one-off? My skepticism was well-founded; we don't hear much from Chad Future in 2020, and his last video was uploaded in 2016.[31]

A few years later in 2017, EXP Edition, a "social experiment" of a four-member K-Pop boy band with no Korean members emerged. For a Columbia University graduate student's research project, EXP Edition was successfully recruited and crowdfunded to debut as a K-Pop act. Industry experts trained the members according to industry practices, and the group

---

29 *KCON TV*, "I Am Chad Future (Special)." April 8, 2014, video, 22:10.

30 Lee, 갈등하는 *K, Pop*, chap.4.

31 *Chad Future*, "What I Learned from Living in Korea - [CFTV] EP.10." September 24, 2016, video, 7:04.

proceeded to release a dual English-Korean single that did not chart domestically. They also performed on well-known Korean TV shows.[32] Similarly, 2020 saw the rise of Kaachi, a UK-based girl group that sings in Korean. Both Korean and Western media outlets heralded them as the UK's first K-Pop group.[33] Out of the four members of Kaachi, only one is Korean, and a UK label independent of the K-Pop industry trained the group members. International K-Pop fans have widely criticized both EXP Edition and Kaachi, as evident from their Twitter and YouTube comments.

I don't see Chad Future, EXP Edition, and Kaachi in the same way as I see existing K-Pop industry-produced acts. Thus, I find it unfair to impose the same expectations.

Whether a so-called K-Pop act formed independently of the Korean music industry and not predominantly comprised of Korean members can still represent the "K" in K-Pop is up for debate. Criticisms of cultural appropriation complicate this debate even more, as non-Asians enter and take up space in the once exclusively Korean K-Pop market.[34] Although legions of international K-Pop fans have criticized EXP Edition and Kaachi and questioned their legitimacy as K-Pop groups, such examples make me wonder whether we'll be seeing more examples of supposed K-Pop acts independent of the existing industry. Interestingly, Koreans don't seem to care much about the specific

32 Marian Liu, "Do You Need to Be Korean to Be K-Pop?" *CNN*, June 13, 2017.

33 Sara Lee, "유럽 최초 K POP 걸그룹 KAACHI, 런던에서 첫 데뷔" [Europe's First K Pop Girl Group Kaachi, Debuts in London], *NewsA*, April 30, 2020.

34 Lee, 갈등하는 *K, Pop*, chap.4.

gatekeeping criteria that forbid foreign acts from labeling themselves as K-Pop.[35]

Plenty of K-Pop industry-produced idols who are not ethnically Korean have achieved mainstream success, such as Thailand-born Lisa of BLACKPINK or Japan-born Sana of TWICE. For the time being, however, I find it very unlikely that non-industry acts will compete in the same field as K-Pop industry-produced idols in terms of commercial performance and skill level for quite a while. Yet, the existing industry paradigm continues to shift, as Korean companies have begun to produce Filipino and Japanese idol groups such as SB19 and NiziU, respectively. The aforementioned groups are primarily active in their domestic markets of the Philippines and Japan, but NiziU will also release Korean-language singles.

We can't fully comprehend K-Pop by focusing only on the music and ignoring the industry via the Korean entertainment company structure. Sure, we see idols in fancy music videos on YouTube, but how did they debut? How is their music written and produced? What determines their international business strategies? These are questions I'll answer throughout the book as we explore how the industry has evolved to keep up with heightened worldwide attention.

---

35 *DKDKTV,* "Is Kaachi Kpop? Koreans Define Kpop." August 8, 2020, video, 9:21.

CHAPTER 3

K-POP AS A CULTURE

———

To complete the K-Pop puzzle, we need to fit in the last piece: K-Pop culture. As it's commonly understood today, K-Pop has its own unique, distinct culture. However, "culture" is a broad term here; am I talking about the culture of the company-driven music business, K-Pop as a cultural export overseas, or even the culture of K-Pop fan communities? The fact that there are numerous discussion topics within K-Pop culture supplements my point that K-Pop is much more than the music.

K-Pop is, at its core, a pop-cultural phenomenon and a Korean export that certainly challenges existing notions of Western pop culture. During the initial *Hallyu* Wave or Korean Wave—the Korean pop culture phenomenon that began in the 1990s—Korea exported its films, soap operas (now known as K-Dramas), video games, and music throughout Asia and achieved commercial success. Music only comprised a fraction of the *Hallyu* Wave exports, however.

The music now referred to as K-Pop became a more influential component in the 2000s and especially in the 2010s.[36] The K-Pop phenomenon has been influential in strengthening aspects of Korean entertainment, Korean fashion, the Korean cosmetics industry, and tourism to Korea from all over the world. So, what exactly does it mean to be a K-Pop fan? How has K-Pop become a gateway to exploring what Korea has to offer? Most importantly, is it fair to say K-Pop is no longer just a subculture?

Hold up. You probably don't know the answers to these questions, so let's ask someone who does.

According to Moon Jae-In, President of South Korea, in 2019,

> The [media] content we've produced brings happiness to the world. Every time I speak with global leaders, the topics of K-Pop and K-Drama are always included. South Korea has evolved from a country that imports culture to one that exports it. The [media] content has transcended mere culture to an important industry revitalizing the Korean economy.[37]

The K-Pop phenomenon fits under the umbrella of the "content industry," the Korean equivalent for what we may generally address as media & entertainment content. In essence, the K-Pop

36   Byung-Chul Cho and Sim Hichul, "Success Factor Analysis of K-Pop and a Study on Sustainable Korean Wave - Focus on Smart Media Based on Realistic Contents," *The Journal of the Korea Contents Association*, Vol.13 No.5 (2013): 92.

37   Si-hyun Cho, "문재인 대통령 "우리 콘텐츠가 세계를 이끌게 될 것"" [President Moon Jae-In 'Our Content Business Will Lead the World'], *NewBC*, September 17, 2019.

culture and industry are symbiotic. What was once considered merely a form of domestic pop culture is now a proper channel generating both global revenue and exposure for the country. In 2019, *Hallyu*-related music content exports were estimated to have increased by 2.5 percent from $520 million USD in 2018 to $533 million USD in 2019, a greater increase than the metrics for TV shows, films, and animated characters.[38]

Although K-Pop is growing at a rapid rate, its overall content export revenues still fall behind those of the gaming (especially eSports) and character (IP licensing business like Pororo the Little Penguin) industries.[39] This serves to remind us that Korean pop culture does not equate solely to K-Pop. If anyone tries to falsely claim that K-Pop (or a particular artist) accounts for most of Korea's economic exports, kindly remind them of Samsung and Hyundai.

Nonetheless, K-Pop culture is taking on a new meaning of its own; it encompasses all aspects of K-Pop you already know about such as the music, events, teasers and videos, merchandise, IP, and much more.

Since K-Pop fans truly keep the culture alive, the K-Pop phenomenon is synonymous with the fandom culture. For example, fans participate directly in spreading the phenomenon by showing support for their favorite K-Pop acts online through social media or forums and offline at concerts and

---

38 Korea Foundation for International Cultural Exchange (KOFICE), *2019 한류의 경제적 파급효과 연구* [Research on Economic Ripple Effects of Hallyu]. (Seoul: KOFICE, 2020), 45.

39 Ibid.

events. Both on and offline, K-pop fans engage with fellow fans and consume content that drives exposure and revenue.

K-Pop fandoms are very community-driven. Think about how sports fans root for a particular team. There are special chants, official apparel, and a shared bond between fans. One example of this K-Pop community can be found on Twitter; K-Pop fans often work together to get specific hashtags trending to voice opinions about specific artists, such as #HistoryMakerV, which celebrated BTS member V's single reaching number one on iTunes in eighty-eight countries, and #blackpink-inyourarea, which is BLACKPINK's signature sound and catchphrase often used in BLACKPINK's songs.[40] Of course, Twitter hashtags are just one of the many diverse ways in which K-Pop fans participate in K-Pop related activities.

The fans are as critical to K-Pop as the artists and companies, as they directly contribute to the global K-Pop phenomenon by purchasing cool t-shirts and attending concert tours. I'm sure you're aware of the supply-and-demand principle, but there's an added sustenance component to a mere demand. Artists depend on the fans, and the fans look to the artists. Simple in theory but unique in application. A K-Pop artist, whether a solo or group act, has a fandom that illustrates this symbiotic relationship that I'll discuss later in the dedicated section.

When the industry produces K-Pop content such as a concert tour or a meet-and-greet event, excited fans will purchase

40   Wansik Moon, "빙탄소년단 뷔, 'Sweet Night' 아이튠즈 88개국 1 위..8년만 싸이 기록 경신" [BTS V, 'Sweet Night' #1 on iTunes in 88 Countries...Breaks Psy's Record in 8 Years], *Naver*, May 25, 2020.

tickets and merchandise either before or at the events. Thus, this is a participatory culture beyond mere recorded music consumption. For the fans who are unable to attend events in person, there are still plenty of ways to enjoy and create K-Pop content online, which we see in YouTube reaction videos, cover dance videos, Twitter threads, Instagram fan pages, and—amidst the coronavirus pandemic—virtual concerts. A fan of a particular K-Pop artist can engage with others on a variety of different channels to show support, which helps spread the K-Pop culture around the world.

Additionally, K-Pop fandoms have been a huge factor in driving global interest to the country of South Korea. According to a 2018 survey from the Korean Ministry of Culture, Sports, and Tourism (MCST) across 8,000 people from 16 countries, 22.8 percent said K-Pop was the core image they associated with the nation of South Korea. Further, 35.3 percent claimed that "pop culture including K-Pop, movies, and literature" was responsible for Korea's positive image.[41] Thanks to these statistics, the MCST has engaged in international efforts to further disseminate the K-Pop culture, such as plans to launch the official "K-POP ACADEMY" in 25 countries through which global fans may enroll in K-Pop vocal and dance classes from industry veterans.[42]

---

41   Young-mi Park, "문체부, 외국인 80% "한국 이미지 긍정적"…대표 이미지 한식·K팝" [MCST, 80% Foreigners 'Positive Image of South Korea'… Main Image Korean Food/Kpop], *Koreailbo*, January 22, 2019.

42   Hyung-won Kim, "문체부, 세계 25개국에 '케이팝 아카데미' 사업 추진" [MCST, Pursues 'Kpop Academy' Business in 25 Countries], *IT Chosun*, May 7, 2019.

I'm always fascinated and grateful whenever I meet global K-Pop fans who take the time to learn about broader Korean culture. I suppose that one thing leads to another; a thorough exploration of K-Pop involves an understanding of Korea to some degree. So, K-Pop's heightened attention has invited global fans to learn more about the "K" in K-Pop. Honestly, how else would you fully understand K-Pop without learning about Korea?

The world's youth, many of whom are K-Pop fans, are flocking to Korean universities to study; universities have reported a massive 40 percent increase in foreign students from 2007 to 2017. Now, approximately 123,000 foreign students are studying in Korea. Foreign student demographics have become more diverse to include students from Sweden, England, and France, the latter of which is the largest European population on Korean campuses.[43] Overseas, students have displayed a heightened interest in learning the Korean language and history upon K-Pop's success, with 14,000 students in American universities learning Korean.[44]

Amid these fascinating events and statistics, I pose a question: is K-Pop culture mainstream outside of the Asian context today? The West views K-Pop as a niche subculture, and despite its Asian success, K-Pop itself was not objectively well-known in the Western mainstream context arguably prior to Psy's "Gangnam Style" in 2012 or more so to BTS's international success in the late 2010s. But K-Pop was always

43   Korea Times, "K-Pop's Global Popularity Draws Foreign Students to South Korea Universities," *South Asia Morning Post*, April 18, 2018.

44   Matt Pickles, "K-Pop Drives Boom in Korean Language Lessons," *BBC*, July 11, 2018.

expanding and developing; we now have diverse viral K-Pop content, a larger talent pool, and more social media strategies than ever before. As a result, the debate today is whether K-Pop as a subculture is breaking out of its niche and into the global mainstream. It's still relatively recent that artists like BTS and BLACKPINK have become worldwide, popular monikers especially in the West. By now, is everyone ready to accept that K-Pop is no longer a niche subculture limited to a particular fan demographic?

Think about Asian representation in Western mainstream pop culture before K-Pop became a more recognized subculture. We had figures like Jackie Chan, Far East Movement, and Steve Aoki. Hmm… the list is actually quite finite. Where are all of the Asians in Western pop culture? More specifically, where are the Koreans? In a global entertainment landscape already lacking Asian diversity, the rise of K-Pop is a new, fresh source for Asian representation.

Coincidentally, global pop culture as a whole has begun to shift; with the growth of online channels and social media platforms that provide ample content, consumers no longer need to succumb to what's already mainstream. Instead, they can seek something that suits their individual preferences.

Fortunately, there is a plethora of K-Pop content for the consumer to explore; watching one YouTube music video leads you to watch another related video on the sidebar, and the process is endless. I could even start by watching the official "Gangnam Style" music video and eventually the YouTube algorithm may lead me to a fan compilation video of boy band SEVENTEEN's cutest moments.

The media and entertainment landscape has changed drastically in the last decade, fortunately for K-Pop. With more and more diverse K-Pop content produced and exported, the niche subculture has grown into a much larger phenomenon and has been acknowledged by both international media headlines and the general public much more frequently.

I still see obstacles for K-Pop to overcome in the cultural context, specifically in the Western world. Even though K-Pop is now recognized as a prominent, global pop-cultural form, there are still attempts to question K-Pop's legitimacy. Sure, K-Pop stars are now appearing on mainstream TV shows like *The Ellen DeGeneres Show* or *Jimmy Kimmel Live!*.[45] However, let's not forget how the 2019 MTV VMAs lumped all Korean acts into one K-Pop category and none were nominated for the biggest awards. Let's not forget how iTunes and Spotify both established a K-Pop genre in which it grouped all Korean artists.

K-Pop is also rarely played on U.S. radio stations; BTS was only played 83,000 times in 2019 even though they had a platinum-certified single, compared to Taylor Swift and Post Malone who were played a massive eighteen and twenty-seven times more, respectively. Much to the dismay of BTS's fandom ARMY that spent an exhaustive and collective effort reaching out to radio stations, BTS's new single "ON" was played only once during its release on Feb. 21, 2020, and never again as of March 30, 2020, on KIIS-FM and Z100, two of

---

45   Dam-young Hong, "How K-Pop Is Becoming Mainstream on Us Talk Shows," *The Korea Herald*, March 27, 2020.

iHeartMedia's largest radio stations.[46] The song proceeded to peak at number four on the Billboard Hot 100, which considers radio airplay as a major criterion for chart rankings.[47] What if radios had played "ON" just a little more as they did for BTS's all-English single, "Dynamite," which finally hit number one in Summer 2020?

The U.S. radio industry is still very traditional and lacks influential East Asian figures. In this industry, objective sales or popularity don't determine which songs get played; rather, the "radio is about maintaining the audience," which supposedly involves songs that are easy to sing along to and remember. BTS's Korean lyrics definitely didn't do them any favors.[48] It's crazy to think that so many radio listeners in the U.S. are being blocked from accessing K-Pop.

I asked Tamar Herman, K-Pop expert and frequent contributor for Billboard and *Forbes*, about the future outlook on K-Pop's prevalence and cultural significance in the U.S. According to her, whether the radio industry and possibly the larger global market as a whole is completely ready for new cultural exchange is up in the air. She notes,

46 Brian Patrick Byrne, and Ahir Gopaldas, "Radio, Why Won't You Play BTS?," *NowThisNews,* April 3, 2020.

47 Gary Trust, "BTS Sets New Career Best on Hot 100 as 'on' Blasts in at No. 4; Roddy Ricch's 'the Box' Rules for Eighth Week," *Billboard*, March 2, 2020.

48 Byrne, and Gopaldas, "Radio."

The industry is supposed to protect the dominant culture. Entertainment creates and reflects culture. For this industry to be open to change and to let go of the tight, existing framework is tough.

Language barriers and even xenophobia are very real and manifest themselves in both overt and subtle ways. If people unfamiliar with K-Pop believe it deviates too much from an expected cultural norm, there's no doubt there will be efforts to police its dissemination.

However, considering how all radio stations around the world frequently played "Gangnam Style" and "Despacito" during and after their Billboard peaks, maybe progress for K-Pop cultural exchange isn't impossible. I do believe there's still much more to be done, however.

Furthermore, the rise of misinformed Western journalism focusing specifically on the negative stereotypes of the K-Pop industry is a major problem. Articles on K-Pop posit terms such as "dark rise, robotic, manufactured" that perpetuate stigma and otherness.[49] The tendency to focus only on the problems related to K-Pop in such media content reinforces the need for accurate representation. If I want to read an article about K-Pop's fandom culture, I should not be bombarded with the flaws of the idol production system or Korean beauty standards.

---

49   Hyun-su Yim, "Is There a Media Double Standard for K-Pop?," *The Korea Herald,* June 18, 2020.

At the end of the day, good music—regardless of background—appeals to everyone. Unfortunately, K-Pop cultural dissemination is policed and mediated by an intermediary, which is a dilemma for all K-Pop fans to consider and challenge together.

OUTRO

_____

After reading this section, I hope you now understand that K-Pop isn't just random "music from Korea." Going forward, when you think about the K-Pop phenomenon, picture it as a wonderful culmination of the three components in this section: the music and artists, the industry and entertainment companies, and culture and consumers.

We will begin the rest of this book by taking a look at some bigger themes and answering, "How did K-Pop get here?" We'll discuss how this phenomenon expanded from Korea out to the rest of the world by observing its failures and successes, and we'll explore the importance of social media in this expansion.

We shall then proceed to the specifics of the K-Pop idol system to observe and analyze the question, "Who does K-Pop involve?" in terms of the music, the business, and the fandoms. Finally, I will conclude with the question, "Where is K-Pop headed?" and offer some of my own speculations.

PART 2

GLOBALIZATION

We still cannot believe we are standing here on this stage at the Billboard Music Awards. Oh my gosh.

- **RM OF BTS**

AT THE 2019 BILLBOARD MUSIC AWARDS[50]

---

50   *Billboard Music Awards,* "BTS Wins Top Duo / Group - BBMAs 2019," May 1, 2019, video, 1:26.

INTRO

Get ready, because I'll be dropping a lot of facts in this section. Globalization is an overarching theme in K-Pop, meaning that you'll see it come up again throughout the rest of this book. In this section, we will explore where the K-Pop phenomenon stands with respect to the rest of the world. Through important case studies, you'll realize K-Pop's global popularity didn't happen overnight. These chapters will be largely rooted in historical events and their implications on K-Pop today. Let's get started.

CHAPTER 4

STARTED FROM SOUTH KOREA, NOW WE HERE

———

Whenever famous international celebrities visit South Korea, Korean journalists have always asked them a variation of "Do you know _____ (insert Korean icon here)," which usually warrants confused or awkward responses. In the 2000s, the reporters would usually ask them if they knew *kimchi* (the national food), Rain (a singer), Kim Yuna (a figure skater), or Park Ji-sung (a soccer player). In the 2010s, however, journalists began to ask newer variations in "Gangnam Style," BTS, or K-Pop.

Korean journalists received a lot of ridicule and criticism online for unprofessional questions like these, but I understand where they were coming from. After all, South Korea is a small country with a lot of talent and a unique culture. If superstars like Robert Downey Jr. or Jamie Foxx expressed some type of fondness for a Korean artist or cultural product, it would be a big deal in the Korean media. To understand why, we must discuss globalization, a central theme to how the K-Pop phenomenon came about.

First of all, South Korea is a country similar to the size of Minnesota. Take a second to locate it on a map. And no, North Korea is a very different place. South Korea (again hereinafter as Korea for convenience's sake) is densely populated with more than 500 people per km² and 99 percent ethnically homogenous, meaning that almost everyone in Korea is of Korean ethnicity.[51] Now think about the fact that for some reason, people all over the world are interested in or even obsessed with Korean pop culture. Plenty of people don't even care about their own country's pop culture, so why and how did K-Pop grow exponentially on a global scale?

Despite this exponential growth, the global K-Pop phenomenon didn't just happen overnight. Successful Korean stars have always existed, just largely contained within the Asian market until relatively recently. When I grew up in Korea as a kindergartener in the late '90s, flashy idol groups like Shinhwa and S.E.S were often on TV executing flawless on-sync dance choreography in conjunction with rhythmical ad-libs. Solo vocalists like Kim Gun-Mo and Jo Sung-Mo were selling a million records domestically. The singers would also appear on non-music TV programs known as "variety shows," where they would entertain the audience in talk shows, comedy skits, and even sports competitions.

Korean pop culture—especially the music industry—has always been forward-looking. Both the artist and companies continued to evolve and reinvent their musical direction

---

51 "South Korea Population 2020 (Live)," World Population Review, accessed April 2, 2020.

and concept (roughly meaning the public image and artistic direction for the artist and album).

Even before their international presence, K-Pop artists and the industry experienced Korean consumer criticism, both constructive and unfounded. For example, there were many cases of Korean artists plagiarizing J-Pop in the 1990s, and many online critics have discussed this issue's severity at the time.[52]

Many dance-pop singers and the early idol groups lip-synced on stage. The public ridiculed them for not singing live, calling them '*boong-uh* singers' (which roughly translates to 'carp singers') because they looked like fish, just opening and closing their mouths on stage.[53] After receiving such feedback, the industry worked on systemizing their artist production. They decided that trainees would be recruited and trained under a formula to improve and showcase skills for their debut. This isn't to say lip-syncing and poor live performances don't exist today, but now the Korean public has much higher expectations, especially for idols.

Today, plenty of idol acts can dance and sing live flawlessly and have begun to increasingly take part in their own music production rather than delineating everything to industry executives. Plus, recent vocal competition programs such as *Immortal Songs*, *Hidden Singer*, and *King of Masked*

52 Sungmin Kim, 케이팝의 작은 역사 [K-Pop's Small History] (Seoul: Geulhangari Publishers, 2018), 73.

53 Sunghyun Kim, "댄스음악이 케이팝의 전부 아냐.. 또 한번 진화할 것" [Dance Pop Isn't All of K-Pop...it Will Evolve Again], *Chosun*, February 24, 2020.

Singer—exported to the U.S. as FOX's *The Masked Singer*—placed greater emphasis on artists' vocal skills. This is creative progress.

If Korea is a small country with a distinct pop culture and industry of its own, then how would non-Koreans find out about all this if they didn't live in Korea? During the analog era, TVs, phones, and radios were the primary channels of media dissemination. These early years before social media involved a lot more work on behalf of the artists to reach the fans. As a result, artists would travel abroad to perform shows and meet with producers on site, among other tasks.

Therefore, it was difficult for the fans to stay up to date on their favorite acts without relying almost exclusively on journalists. During those days, whenever a Korean artist did pretty much anything overseas, it was a huge deal. In contrast, today, American stars like Ariana Grande and Pharrell Williams give public shoutouts to Korean stars BTS and G-Dragon, respectively. Singer Grimes even recently confirmed that Gowon of idol group LOONA was her newborn son's godmother.[54]

---

54   Palmer Haasch, "Grimes Says That X æ a-XII's Godmother Is a K-Pop Idol She Collaborated with in 2018," *Insider*, May 26, 2020.

CHAPTER 5

KNOCKING ON NEIGHBORS' DOORS IN GREATER ASIA

———

In its early days, Korean pop music was generally contained within the Korean domestic market and East Asian countries like Japan and China where Korean artists found international commercial success. Some artists enjoyed great success in Japan through a localization strategy that consisted of commercial activities like releasing songs and albums in Japanese, appearing on Japanese variety shows, and performing at Japanese venues.

SM Entertainment, known as one of the "Big 3" companies with YG and JYP Entertainment, targeted the Japanese market with this strategy in 2000 and successfully produced BoA, a Korean female solo artist who debuted when she was only thirteen years old. BoA became a big star in both Korea and Japan since SM Entertainment marketed BoA as both a K-Pop and J-Pop star. She released Japanese studio albums, spoke

Japanese fluently, built up a Japanese fanbase, and became known as the "Star of Asia."[55]

Let me try to analogize BoA's success. Canadian Justin Bieber and British Ed Sheeran are both active in the American music market. Do they both participate in their respective markets? Sure. Now, think of them having to learn an entirely new language and understand cultural differences while trying to make money in a foreign country. It takes *a lot* of work.

In the 1990s and 2000s, a pop-cultural phenomenon called the *Hallyu* Wave (Korean Wave) was happening. Korean media content such as dramas (soap operas) and motion pictures were gaining massive popularity throughout Asia, which catapulted top Korean celebrities into international superstardom. Japan even heralded Korean actor Bae Yong-Joon from the popular drama *Winter Sonata* (2002) as *Yon-sama*, a Japanese honorific.

Is the K-Pop phenomenon part of the *Hallyu* Wave? Well, the latter accounted for a variety of different forms of Korean pop culture. It originated in the late 1990s as Korean dramas gained popularity in China and later in Japan. K-Pop, however, didn't actually take a more prominent role in the movement until the mid-late 2000s.[56] This makes sense too, as it would've been much easier to understand and watch Korean TV shows because of subtitles on the screen rather than trying to comprehend Korean lyrics in a song.

---

55   ""The Star of Asia' BoA, the Star of Asia, Unveils a Teaser Image That Makes a Difference! Focus Your Attention!" SMTOWN, last modified June 1, 2019.

56   Byung-Chul Cho and Sim Hichul, "Success Factor Analysis of K-POP and A Study on sustainable Korean Wave - Focus on Smart Media based on Realistic Contents," *The Journal of the Korea Contents Association*, Vol.13 No.5 (2013): 91

Despite the initial international focus on Korean dramas and films, K-Pop persevered and succeeded in the Asian market. In light of the earlier *Hallyu* Wave in Asia, I'd like to dive deeper into K-Pop's historical developments in key Asian regions. These nearby markets provided the consumer demand that contributed to K-Pop's early globalization.

JAPAN

I can't overstate the importance of the Japanese market for K-Pop's global progression. Japan was and still is a main international customer—it's the second-largest music market in the world and Korea's geographical neighbor. After seeing BoA's success in the early 2000s, SM Entertainment would later attempt the same localization strategy again with boy band TVXQ, promoting and marketing them in Japan under the Japanese name *Tohoshinki*. Already a top act in Korea, TVXQ had to start over in Japan by touring local venues and consistently releasing Japanese albums for years before eventually reaching number one on the Oricon Daily Single Chart—Japan's Billboard counterpart—in 2007.[57] TVXQ, performing under the name *Tohoshinki*, would launch a successful 2013 Japan Dome Tour, a feat only achievable with 30,000 to 50,000 concertgoers per show.[58]

With a successful business strategy and positive international reception in the early 2000s, entertainment companies such as SM, DSP, and JYP Entertainment promoted artists

57 Myungshin Kim, "동방신기, *'Purple Line'* 오리콘 싱글 차트 1위!" [TVXQ, 'Purple Line' Oricon Single Chart #1!], *Hankookkyungjae*, January 17, 2008.

58 Kim, *History*, 104-105.

in both Korea and Japan going forward. Groups such as BIGBANG, KARA, Girls' Generation, and 2PM began to release Japanese albums during their off-season from K-Pop. Even today, many artists have achieved greater international recognition and commercial success by concentrating on Japanese activities.[59]

I also see K-Pop's Japanese success as meaningful in light of political tension. If you didn't know, Korea and Japan have a complicated history. Recent tensions have been especially dire, with company boycotts and hate speech coming from both countries. However, this hasn't been a deterrence for Japanese consumption of K-Pop; K-Pop in Japan is cemented as a legitimate pop-cultural form already, and they no longer view K-Pop artists who sing in Japanese merely as subsets of J-Pop. Yes, K-Pop acts promote in Japan, but they're a strong force on their own without succumbing to existing Japanese frameworks.

Take JYP Entertainment's girl group, TWICE, for example. TWICE has three Japanese members who appeal to Japanese audiences. When TWICE releases Japanese singles, the three aforementioned members take the helm in promotions. As a result of JYP Entertainment's strategy, TWICE has reached number one on the Oricon Daily Singles chart multiple times, including in February 2018 for the Japanese-language single, "Candy Pop." Yet later in the same year, their Korean-language mini-album *What is Love?* ranked number two on the Oricon Weekly Albums chart.[60]

---

59 Ibid.

60 Mikyung Sun, "[공식입장] TWICE, 韓 앨범으로 日 오리콘 차트 2위...'원톱인기'''" [[Official] TWICE, Korean Album Charts #2 on Japanese Oricon Chart...'One-Top Popularity'], *Chosun*, April 18, 2018.

Here, I see K-Pop artists transcending national barriers. Japanese fans want more, no matter whether the songs are in Japanese or Korean, and artists like TWICE continue giving them what they want.

GREATER CHINA

Korean pop music's relationship with Greater China dates back to the earlier success of dance duo Clon in Taiwan in 1998 and subsequently boy band H.O.T.'s Beijing concert in 2000. As a result of the larger *Hallyu* Wave, both idol and non-idol acts became popular here, including TVXQ, Super Junior, BIGBANG, and Wonder Girls. Notably, in 2015, BIGBANG's Chinese leg of the "MADE World Tour" stopped in eleven Chinese cities, the most for any K-Pop act in mainland China to this point. After attracting an audience of 180,000, BIGBANG would launch another international fan-meeting tour in early 2016 that focused heavily on the Chinese market, stopping at eight cities and drawing more than 180,000 attendees once again.[61]

What were the early K-Pop strategies for Greater China? With the Chinese market in mind in 2005, SM Entertainment debuted a Chinese trainee named Hankyung (*Han Geng*) as a member of the thirteen-member boy band, Super Junior. With Hankyung as a focal point, SM would later produce the sub-unit Super Junior-M, consisting of both Korean and

61 Sukmin Yoon, "빅뱅, 한국가수 최다 중국 11개도시 18만명 동원 투어 성료" [BIGBANG, Korean Artist Record for Biggest Chinese Tour with 11 Cities and 180,000 Attendees], *Hankookkyungjae*, August 31, 2015; Eunyoung Yoo, "빅뱅, 3월 중국 투어...총 8개 도시 18만 2 천 관객" [BIGBANG, March Chinese Tour... Total 8 Cities, 182,000 Attendees], *Busanilbo*, February 5, 2016.

Mandarin-speaking members.[62] We'd later see more Chinese talent debut in K-Pop idol groups like f(x)'s Victoria Song and with Miss A's Meng Jia and Wang Feifei. In 2012, the Mandarin unit of EXO known as "EXO-M," even debuted four Chinese members out of the group's six. This localization strategy of recruiting non-Korean members for an idol group continues to be effective today in Asia but must be simultaneously accompanied by effective promotions.

As a side note, we have seen even greater Asian ethnic diversity in K-Pop recently, including idols from Greater China, Japan, Thailand, and Indonesia. So once again, it's certainly inaccurate to dismiss all K-Pop acts as pop music made by Koreans—there are more layers to it than just "music from Korea."

In 2016, the Terminal High Altitude Area Defense (THAAD) incident led to heightened political tensions between South Korea and China. As a result, China essentially restricted all Korean cultural content imports, which was a critical hit to the Korean entertainment industry as a whole.[63] Artists of Korean ethnicity could not perform on Chinese television or tour, and thus many K-Pop artists had to resort to promoting and performing in other Asian countries. For clarity, this didn't affect non-Korean stars like Jackson Wang or Lay Zhang who were already active in the Chinese market as solo artists.

---

62 Kyungran Lee, "슈주 차이나, 8일 중국서 데뷔 무대" [SuJu China, Chinese Debut Stage on the 8th], *Joongangilbo*, April 8, 2008.

63 Daegeun Im, "중국의 '뒤끝 작렬' 한한령, 한류의 미래는 있는가" [China's Holding Grudge *Hanhanryung*, Does Hallyu Have a Future?], *Joongangilbo*, February 26, 2019.

Experts assessed that the restrictions may be loosening in 2020, but nothing is for certain.[64] I hope Chinese fans can soon watch their favorite K-Pop stars live once again.

SOUTHEAST ASIA

I want to emphasize just how crucial the market comprised of countries such as Thailand, Indonesia, Vietnam, Malaysia, and the Philippines is to K-Pop's global success.

Korean pop cultural content spread to this region initially during the *Hallyu* Wave in the early 2000s. Take a look at the chart below with data from a survey of 500 people from various countries in 2019.[65]

Survey - K-Pop's Reputation in Southeast Asia

	Thailand	Indonesia	Vietnam	Malaysia	Japan	U.S.
Associating Korea's National image with "K-Pop"	24%	40.60%	17.20%	31.40%	17.20%	24.90%
Positive stance towards S. Korea after cultural content consumption	73.60%	77%	62%	69%	22%	64.20%
K-Pop defines "Hallyu"	57.80%	78.80%	62%	77%	67%	60.20%

64   Sun-hwa Dong, "K-Pop Artists' China Virus Gig Invite No Ban Lift: Experts," *The Korea Times*, April 2, 2020

65   Korea Foundation for International Cultural Exchange (KOFICE), *2020 해외한류실태조사* [2020 Research on Hallyu's Global Reality]. Seoul: KOFICE, 2020

Korea has already been exporting content to Southeast Asia for nearly two decades and received positive reception. Thailand, for example, is an absolutely crucial K-Pop market in terms of influence on neighboring countries such as Myanmar, Laos, and Cambodia. Although *Hallyu* content spread initially in Thailand with Korean dramas, since 2007, the domestic company, GMM Grammy, has officially distributed K-Pop albums.[66] Thai K-Pop idols such as Nickhun from 2PM, Lisa from BLACKPINK, and BamBam from GOT7 are massive national stars who have secured numerous Thai endorsements.

Korea and Vietnam have experienced rising trade relations and goodwill between the two countries that have helped K-Pop form a big presence there. Vietnam even hosted Korean music TV programming and events including a part of the large-scale *Mnet Asian Music Awards* in 2017.

YouTube has proved crucial to the spread of K-Pop throughout Southeast Asia. Consider this YouTube view count data for two popular groups, BLACKPINK and BTS:

---

66 Korea Creative Content Agency (KOCCA), "Content Industry Trend of Thailand (2019 Vol.9)," Naju, KOCCA: 2020.

BLACKPINK
Where people are listening
Top countries

1. Indonesia 106M views	6. United States 34.9M views
2. Philippines 66.8M views	7. India 34M views
3. Thailand 62.9M views	8. Mexico 32.6M views
4. Brazil 57.8M views	9. Malaysia 31.1M views
5. Vietnam 55.3M views	10. South Korea 26.9M views

Top cities

1. Bangkok 31.1M views	6. Surabaya 11.4M views
2. Jakarta 23M views	7. Seoul 9.97M views
3. Kuala Lumpur 18.3M views	8. Phnom Penh 7.74M views
4. Quezon City 13M views	9. Hanoi 7.47M views
5. Ho Chi Minh City 11.9M views	10. Lima 7.47M views

[67] BLACKPINK YouTube View Count Regional Demographics

BTS
Where people are listening
Top countries

1. Indonesia 93.6M views	6. Mexico 43.1M views
2. India 59.2M views	7. Philippines 42.1M views
3. Brazil 55.1M views	8. Thailand 32.1M views
4. United States 50.5M views	9. South Korea 30.9M views
5. Japan 44.6M views	10. Vietnam 23.5M views

Top cities

1. Jakarta 19.8M views	6. Phnom Penh 9.58M views
2. Bangkok 15.4M views	7. Kuala Lumpur 8.95M views
3. Seoul 10.4M views	8. Quezon City 7.96M views
4. Lima 10.1M views	9. Mexico City 5.76M views
5. Surabaya 10M views	10. Semarang 5.45M views

[68] BTS YouTube View Count Regional Demographics

These YouTube view counts from Southeast Asia are incredible. For BLACKPINK, eight of the top ten cities that generated the most YouTube views are in Southeast Asian countries. Indonesia tops the list for both artists and by a wide margin, almost doubling the views from the runner-ups in the Philippines

---

67   "Music Charts & Insights - BLACKPINK," YouTube, accessed August 25, 2020.

68   "Music Charts & Insights - BTS," YouTube, accessed August 25, 2020.

and India (for BLACKPINK and BTS respectively). Of course, certain artists have higher view counts from Southeast Asia than others. For popular K-Pop girl group TWICE, the number one city is Seoul with 5.67 million views.[69]

With this much demand just via YouTube streaming, think of how many eager fans would attend concerts and purchase merchandise should K-Pop acts tour in Southeast Asian countries.

WRAP-UP

Long story short, K-Pop is huge in Asia.

Yet while the *Hallyu* Wave was occurring in Asia, our Western neighbors farther away had to rely on Korean friends, visit or live in Korea, search through websites like Soompi, or frequent local Korean video rental shops to get a taste of Korean pop culture. Today we take YouTube for granted; those were more challenging times! If you were one of those OGs, you deserve all the respect and have earned the right to clap-back with, "I knew them before they were famous" to whoever tries to argue about K-Pop with you.

---

69   "Music Charts & Insights - TWICE," YouTube, accessed August 25, 2020.

CHAPTER 6

WESTWARD BOUND

———

In 2005, when I lived in New Jersey, I saw a poster for the Korean singer, Rain, on the wall of a *soondubu* (soft tofu soup) restaurant, ironically on a rainy afternoon. He had a concert coming up titled, "Rainy Day," in New York. At that time, I didn't really know who he was, but I assumed he was a big deal. When I got home, I searched up *Bi*—his Korean stage name and the Korean word for "rain"—on Korean websites. I found out that news articles called him a modern-day "world star." I thought, *Wow, Koreans are really branching out here!*

Later I learned that Rain was the product of hit singer-songwriter, Park Jin-Young, whom we've discussed before as the mastermind behind JYP Entertainment. I noticed Park was different from other executives and artists in the industry; he has lived abroad in the U.S., attended the prestigious Yonsei University, and excelled at singing, dancing, and songwriting. His creative mindset led him to form JYP Entertainment, the company behind many K-Pop stars like Rain, *god,* Wonder Girls, 2AM, 2PM, Miss A, GOT7, DAY6, TWICE, Stray Kids, and ITZY.

Upon Rain and *god* becoming Korean superstars in the early 2000s, Park ventured to the U.S., much to the dismay of JYP Entertainment stockholders. He'd spend all day traveling through Hollywood to sell his songs to American producers while composing music at night. He visited the labels' front desks every day to deliver his CDs and was never invited upstairs until Will Smith's team finally reached out.[70]

Park's determination to succeed in a bigger market eventually led him to produce songs for American artists like Will Smith, Mase, and Cassie. In a 2014 interview, Park recalls his Will Smith collaboration, "I Wish I Made That," as his most rewarding moment.[71]

Objectively, however, Rain did not make a huge impact in the Western market with his U.S. concert tour and his superstardom stayed largely within Asia. Keep in mind that Rain was popular in an era before social media when Korean journalists printed even the smallest gossip or news in entertainment. In hindsight, I don't think the "world star" moniker should've been taken too literally, but there weren't many other ways to gauge what was happening on the other side of the world without relying on hearsay or journalism. Today, we have social media resources to confirm exciting news like when artists give public shoutouts, take spoiler pictures in the studio, and even confirm or deny rumors.

70 Joonho Maeng and Youngmok Lee, "세계를 깜짝 놀라게 한 작곡가 박진영" [Songwriter Park Jin Young Who Shocked the World], *Joongangilbo*, April 13, 2005.

71 Jinyong An, "박진영 "윌 스미스에 곡 줄때 가장 행복했다"" [Park Jin Young "Giving My Song to Will Smith Was My Happiest Moment], *Munhwailbo*, November 5, 2014.

Lee Soo-Man, the founder of SM Entertainment, had a different plan to tackle the U.S. market. In 2008, SM Entertainment had gathered a team of famous American managers, agents, and choreographers alongside Lee serving as executive producer for BoA's U.S. debut. At her initial press conference, BoA emphasized how important localization would be in the U.S., just as it had been for her in Japan.[72] From the onset, it was a big deal in Korea for BoA to debut on MTV's *Total Request Live*.[73] The year after, in early 2009, BoA also cracked the Billboard Albums Chart at number 127 with her U.S. debut album. Unfortunately, however, BoA experienced a plethora of schedule cancelations, miscommunications, and a lack of ample promotional opportunities in the U.S to make her presence known. Eventually, BoA and Lee returned to Korea after an abrupt halt to her planned U.S. concert tour.[74]

JYP Entertainment also embarked on the U.S. venture once again during this period. With his self-produced girl group, Wonder Girls, Park solidified himself once again as a star producer and songwriter in the domestic market; the group's legendary songs, "Tell Me," "So Hot," and "Nobody" became mega-hits domestically. Park attempted to use this momentum to prepare for Wonder Girls' U.S. debut. The English version of "Nobody" entered the Billboard Hot 100 at number 76 in 2009 after Wonder Girls opened for a series of the Jonas Brothers' nationwide concerts.

---

72 Hyerin Lee, "보아 "미국진출, 난 물 만난 고기였다"" [BoA 'US Promotions, I Was a Fish in the Water], *AsiaKyungjae*, September 10, 2008.

73 Sang-hee Han, "BoA to Make US Debut through MTV," *The Korea Times*, November 30, 2008.

74 Eunwoo Kim, "[미국음악일기] 보아·세븐·원더걸스, 3대 기획사의 미국 진출 실패담" [[US Music Diary] BoA, Se7en, Wonder Girls, the Big 3 Labels' Failed US Promotions], *BizHankook*, November 9, 2017.

However, performing in the U.S. required nationwide traveling on tour buses and handing out flyers to potential attendees, something they'd never have to do in Korea.[75]

In contrast to Lee's strategy for BoA, Park relied on in-house production of an existing Korean single instead of assembling a U.S.-based team. Yet, Wonder Girls also did not make a huge impact in the U.S. market; for two months there were no opportunities, and their single albums were distributed to children's apparel stores instead of record shops.[76] American audiences didn't bite, and Wonder Girls lost the top position in the Korean market when they returned. On a TV talk show in late 2009, Wonder Girls member Sunmi confessed:

> I was lonely [in the US]. I had no idea how to get adjusted or to live in this foreign environment.[77]

Could BoA and Wonder Girls be considered Western successes in light of such shortcomings?

I think it depends on how we view success. Although these attempts didn't make much pop cultural impact in the U.S.,

---

75 *MBCEntertainment*, "[라디오스타] 이제는 말할 수 있다! 박진영의 미국병 (?) 해명 20200812" [[Radio Star] He Can Say It Now! Park Jin Young's US-Fever (?) Explanation 20200812], August 12, 2020, video, 2:59.

76 Kyudae Ko, "원더걸스 사태로 본 아이돌 가수 미국 진출의 실상" [The Reality of Idol Stars' US Promotions, from the Wonder Girls Incident], *Donga*, March 03, 2010.

77 Ibid.

I believe they made greater steps toward a goal outside of Asia. These early attempts show producers' desires to launch K-Pop onto newer grounds, which became a clearer reality a decade later.

At the same time, the reliance on localization strategies, which had succeeded in the Japanese market, proved largely futile in the U.S. BoA's hip-hop-based musical style in her U.S. debut album had deviated from her previous Korean and Japanese hits that creatively blended dance-pop. For K-Pop to truly take off in the West and for a K-Pop artist to not only be commercially successful but also widely recognized, what were the executives supposed to do?

Social media offered a solution to this dilemma; not only did social media allow easier communication with Western executives, but the K-Pop artists and companies could also communicate directly with both global artists and fans, which would be critical to international business strategy.

After social media became more prominent and helped connect the world, we indeed began to see a lot more global interactions. Stars or companies could directly reach out to each other upon seeing something interesting on social media. They could just type, *Hey, that was sick! Wanna collab?* This type of interaction actually happened between Scooter Braun, a well-known entertainment executive who discovered Justin Bieber, and Psy, which led to the "Gangnam Style" phenomenon in 2012.

CHAPTER 7

PSY AND "GANGNAM STYLE"

———

Oh, boy, remember this?

When you think of "Gangnam Style," it would be hard not to immediately conjure up the image of a stout Asian man in sunglasses, the horse dance that mimicked a rider on a horse's saddle, and the catchy chorus. "Gangnam Style" had the entire world following in a frenzy in 2012, and this is not an overstatement. People were doing the horse dance all over the globe, and the music video's YouTube views continued to skyrocket until they finally propelled it to the "Most Viewed Video" at that time in 2012. It was the first video on YouTube to reach one billion views and even reached 3.8 billion views by 2020.[78] Yet this was even before K-Pop became a household keyword as it is today; who was this guy and why was this happening?

---

78 "Psy - Gangnam Style M/V," *officialpsy,* July 15, 2012, video. 4:12.

Even before "Gangnam Style," Psy was already very well-known in Korea for his catchy dance tracks, vibrant stage performances, and proficient musicianship. He defied conventions from the onset—in his debut album, he was actually fined by the Korean government for inappropriate lyrics and performances. He strayed far from the popular visual tropes and donned sleeveless shirts while flying around the stage with no signs of exhaustion.

Though the public viewed him as a brat, Psy achieved a domestic breakthrough with his hit track "Champion," which coincided with the 2002 Seoul World Cup. He'd proceed to consistently release his own albums and produce music for other artists before completing his mandatory Korean military service from 2004 to 2006. Yet, the government redrafted him for negligent duty the first time around. By 2012, Psy had spent four out of his nine years in the industry doing military service.[79]

After his second discharge, Psy resumed his career with positive reception. "Gangnam Style" was the lead single from his sixth full-length album, which dominated the streets of Gangnam in Seoul as well as all amusement parks that summer. The Gangnam district is a metropolitan hotspot—from high-rise buildings, bustling atmosphere, and packed nightlife. Compare it to the likes of New York or Beverly Hills.

---

79 Jiwon Yang, "싸이 "군대를 두 번 간게 아니고 훈련소 두 번"" [Psy 'I Went to the Army Training Facility Twice, Not the Army Itself Twice], *Joongangilbo*, April 8, 2010.

Psy's horse dance was simple and catchy enough for people of all ages to dance along. It seemed like Psy would conclude his album promotions successfully in Korea once again. Strangely enough, the "Gangnam Style" music video view count soared while both the song and video spread organically. A worldwide craze was underway, and it would've been a shame not to capitalize on it.

With the help of talent manager Scooter Braun, Psy officially embarked on a series of U.S. promotions.[80] Psy appeared on prominent American media programs like *The Ellen DeGeneres Show* and the *MTV Video Music Awards*. The song was frequently played on the radio and eventually peaked at number two on the Billboard Hot 100 chart. Psy's year of success even concluded with a performance at the Times Square New Year's Eve Countdown, making him the first Korean artist ever to do so. This was unlike anything Korean popstars had done before.

A few months later in 2013, Psy followed up with the single "Gentleman," which incorporated the successful elements of "Gangnam Style": a simple chorus, a catchy dance, and witty lyrics. However, "Gentleman" did not overtake its predecessor as it eventually only peaked at number five on Hot 100. In a speech at Harvard University, Psy admitted:

80 Melena Ryzik, "His Style is Gangnam, and Viral Too," *The New York Times*, October 11, 2012; *officialpsy*, "Public Announcement - Scooter Braun Regarding PSY," September 3, 2012, video, 1:23.

My only goal with Gentleman was being Top 10 of Billboard and making 100 million views to YouTube… I was so surprised that I [was] disappointed [at] number 33 on Billboard. I was so shocked! Are you crazy? Number 33 on Billboard? I'm so spoiled. That's huge, more than huge.[81]

Psy eventually wrapped up his U.S. activities and returned to Korea. If "Gangnam Style" taught us anything, it would be how crucial YouTube—as well as other social media platforms—are to disseminate music. Not just for K-Pop but for global music entertainment.

Keep in mind that Psy is not an idol and didn't have a core fandom or sustained popularity like many K-Pop acts do today. I've discussed "Gangnam Style" extensively because I believe a broader view of K-Pop's globalization requires understanding this song's significance; after Psy's success, global media began to pay greater attention to the term K-Pop as a whole, and the industry realized how crucial YouTube would be going forward.

Psy achieved enormous success both commercially and culturally. The world has since moved on, but his legacy remains. If I was to hear "Gangnam Style" today, I'd still be tempted to bust out the horse dance, anytime, anywhere.

---

81 *Harvard University*, "'Gangnam Style' Singer PSY Visits Harvard," June 19, 2013, video, 1:18:36.

People still debate whether "Gangnam Style" was just a meme or an anomaly. How did K-Pop become better understood as a pop-cultural form today? Let's unravel some more.

CHAPTER 8

THE 2010S: A DECADE OF POSSIBILITIES

────

I'll never forget my first K-Pop concert experience. It was absolutely spectacular. I was fortunate enough to attend the first-ever SMTown World Tour in Summer 2010 featuring all of SM Entertainment's top idols like BoA, TVXQ, Super Junior, Girls' Generation, SHINee, and f(x). The kickoff began in Seoul—where I was at the time—then traveled to cities including Paris, Los Angeles, Shanghai, Tokyo, and New York. This tour was a historic moment that would cement the export of K-Pop from Korea.

Let's look at what was going on during the 2010s as a whole. "Gangnam Style" spread all over the world and the K-Pop industry was blossoming with the advent of a new generation of idol groups. The 2010s welcomed a flood of idols, so the scene was not only becoming more diverse but very competitive. To provide some context, an enormous total of thirty-eight girl groups debuted in 2012, *but only one—AOA—* was still active in 2020.[82]

We started to see a variety of international events dedicated to spreading the K-Pop movement like the SMTown World Tour. At the time, I was mind-blown that a K-Pop tour of SM Entertainment's top artists visited not only Asia but the U.S. and Europe as well. Today, global K-Pop events happen all the time—most notably, KCON LA.

In 2011, Korea's Ministry of Foreign Affairs began hosting the annual K-Pop World Festival—a jam-packed event featuring international contestants showcasing their skills by singing and dancing to well-known K-Pop songs—in the city of Changwon. The organizers conducted a global audition tour of sixteen countries, after which the selected contestants would compete against each other in front of a live audience of 10,000 people.[83] The TV music program, *Music Bank,* also launched a series of world tour programming in 2011 that showcased live K-Pop idol performances in Japan and eventually in countries such as France, Turkey, Mexico, Vietnam, Brazil, and more.[84]

2012 marked the first of the famous KCON conventions in Los Angeles, sponsored by the mega entertainment company

---

82   Yoosub Im, "지난 10년간 데뷔한 걸그룹 들서 살아남은 그룹들" [The Debuted Girl Groups of the Past Decade That Are Still Active], *Joongangilbo*, February 27, 2017.

83   "K-Pop 월드페스티벌 2011 창원서 열려" [K-Pop World Festival 2011 Commences in Changwon], Ministry of Sports, Culture and Tourism, last modified December 12, 2012.

84   August Brown, "K-Pop Brings Superfans and Diversity to KCON L.A. 2019," *Los Angeles Times*, August 18, 2019.

CJ E&M. This fan-centered event includes performances by K-Pop stars, panels featuring industry experts, dance contests, meet-and-greets, and more.[85] If you have friends or kids who want to get involved in the K-Pop culture, KCON would be the place to take them. Today, the convention has expanded into multiple international hotspots including New York, Japan, and Thailand. As a friend of mine who worked as an annual KCON volunteer told me, "It's crazy in all ways possible."

When I saw these early global events specifically celebrating K-Pop in the early 2010s, even before "Gangnam Style," I realized there was legitimate international demand for K-Pop. The numbers supported my realization; SM Entertainment's 2011 tour in Paris attracted a crowd of 14,000 over two days, with over 70 percent being European fans.[86] Also, BIGBANG won Best Worldwide Act at the 2011 MTV European Music Awards, a category that fan votes decide.[87]

In early 2012, the girl group, Girls' Generation, performed on *The Late Night Show with David Letterman*.[88] With achievements like this that departed from a figurative "world tour" just a few years prior, it was clear that K-Pop's reach was expanding. Experts didn't know whether this phenomenon

85 Eunkyung Song, "KBS '뮤직뱅크' 다음달 두바이서 열려...백현.트와이스 등 출연" [KBS 'Music Bank' to Launch in Dubai Next Month... Baekhyun, TWICE, Etc. to Perform], *Yonhap*, February 1, 2020.

86 Wooyoung Cho, "SM 파리 공연 후 1년..가요계 빅3가 말하는 K팝" [1 Year after SM's Paris Show... K-Pop as Told by the Industry 'Big 3'], *eDaily*, June 11, 2012.

87 Yoon-mi Kim, "Big Bang Wins Best Worldwide Act," *The Korea Herald*, November 7, 2011.

88 Jeff Benjamin, "Girls' Generation Makes Big U.S. Debut on 'Letterman': Watch," *Billboard*, February 1, 2012.

would be sustainable, and figuring out how to further cater to global fans was a new challenge.

All of the global K-Pop events begged the question, "Did K-Pop *actually* have a legitimate chance of mainstream success outside Asia?"

Let's recap. We knew K-Pop artists already succeeded in the Japanese and Southeast Asian markets. Some of our only U.S. evidence came from Rain's U.S. concert as well as BoA and Wonder Girls' debut projects, which were all lackluster. We also knew there were global fans thanks to social media and concert tours. Given all the evidence, experts were skeptical in 2011. Even within Asia, K-Pop was largely confined to major cities like Tokyo, Hong Kong, and Taipei, specifically among a teenage demographic.

During this time, I thought it was also a stretch to call K-Pop a mainstream phenomenon in Europe, seeing as the world tours attracted just a small group of K-Pop enthusiasts. The label of K-Pop was considered nothing more than grandiose and less than already established phenomena like Hollywood, J-Pop, or Bollywood.[89] Understandably, while the Korean media hyped up every global K-Pop event, big or small, industry experts remained cautious about declaring K-Pop a global success. There were objective measures of commercial success like the Wonder Girls single, "Nobody," ranking in the Billboard Hot 100, but it was still difficult to gauge if the average American citizen even knew what K-Pop was. Did David Letterman

---

89   Ho Jae Jung, "유럽소녀 흥분 그 후 케이팝의 불편한 진실" [K-Pop's Inconvenient Truth after European Girls' Excitement], *Donga*, July 8, 2011.

even know who Girls' Generation was or how big of a deal their performance on his show was in Korea?

A 2013 Korean study analyzed the fourteen different Korean documentaries that aired on national TV from 2011 to 2012 that touted K-Pop's global scope and success. All of the documentaries could be categorized into three types: ones with a focus on K-Pop's global success, ones that focused on the artist, or ones that focused on the fandom. All of the documentaries depicted similar scenes of long lines of global fans cheering on K-Pop idols at concerts and all interviewed both Korean and foreign experts.

The documentaries directly asked global K-Pop fans to choose their favorite idol, discuss why they love K-Pop, and other topics in the same vein. The foreign experts consulted were mostly various journalists who merely weighed in on the K-Pop phenomenon's longevity and success rate, not industry executives or musicologists.[90]

I remained keen and skeptical when I watched these documentaries live. Sure, they depicted a large audience of non-Korean fans, but it was hard to say if they accurately depicted the extent of K-Pop's global success. After all, it was hard to gauge whether K-Pop would succeed in the larger sense by observing a niche subculture. Global K-Pop fans were plentiful, but outside of Asia, these fans comprised a small minority. How diverse were these concerts' audiences? Testimonies

---

90   Sooah Kim, "K-POP 과 신한류의 대한 텔레비전 담론" [Television Discourse on K-Pop and K-Pop Idol Stars' Passion], *Seoul National University Journal of Communication Research,* vol.50, no.1 (2013): 67-73.

from SM Entertainment's Los Angeles tour reported that most audience members were of Asian ethnicity.[91]

Despite the questions, it was hard to deny that K-Pop was expanding. In 2012, top K-Pop acts BIGBANG and Girls' Generation-TTS cracked the Billboard Albums Chart organically at numbers 150 and 126 respectively. Neither group engaged in any U.S. promotional activities for these albums, which marked a huge difference from past industry attempts.[92] I was very intrigued and proud—I didn't expect it, but something interesting was happening.

Social media platforms—particularly YouTube—were a critical tool in solidifying and legitimizing K-Pop as a pop-cultural phenomenon globally. K-Pop content generated tons of exposure and spread easily, thanks to the accessibility of K-Pop content on these platforms. The fans' collective actions even earned Girls' Generation single, "I Got a Boy," the Video of the Year award at the first YouTube Music Awards in 2013.[93]

With K-Pop's rising success, I wondered if venturing outside of Asia was really about seeking some form of Western validation. In contrast, what if industry executives just wanted to capitalize on the demand for K-Pop artists around the world?

91 Gyu Tag Lee, 케이팝의 시대 [The K-POP Age], (Seoul: Hanwool Academy, 2016), 195.; Dongyeon Lee, "SM 엔터테인먼트 LA 공연의 진실" [The truth behind SM Entertainment's LA show], *Pressian*, January 25, 2012.

92 Jeff Benjamin, "Girls' Generation Splinter Group Enters Billboard 200," *Billboard*, May 4, 2012.

93 Jeff Benjamin, "Girls' Generation Reacts to YouTube Music Awards Win, Talks New Music: Exclusive," *Billboard*, November 4, 2013.

I was genuinely surprised when I first learned that K-Pop fandom communities existed outside of Asia. I didn't feel that K-Pop needed to be validated by the West, per se, but I was very curious, nonetheless.

K-Pop became a more mainstream discussion topic after "Gangnam Style," which—given YouTube's influence in spreading the song—proved that a well-crafted social media strategy would be a crucial tool for global success. Also, if K-Pop was going to expand and cater to larger audiences, artists and companies need to give the fans what they want. There now was actual demand, in contrast to the exploratory "I hope they'll like it" strategy of the 2000s.

The current K-Pop industry clearly implements the "give them what they want" business strategy. Here's an example scenario involving localization for you. I mentioned how K-Pop idols are very popular in Southeast Asia, especially in Thailand. If you were to produce a new K-Pop girl group to capture that specific market, how would you cater to the Thai fanbase? Should the group release songs in Thai, and would you train the Korean members to speak it? For that matter, why not just recruit a talented Thai trainee and have her debut as a K-Pop idol? The girl group BLACKPINK decided to use this strategy by adding a Thai member, Lisa, who is massively popular all across Southeast Asia. This is a localization strategy that the Southeast Asian fans can relate to because it's authentic.

As for the U.S. market, however, only idealistic theories from the past formal attempts of BoA and Wonder Girls existed. The demand from the niche demographic of K-Pop fans within the American landscape was still a small drop in the ocean.

Should Korean companies continue to "give them what they want" by doing concerts there? How would they organically grow the existing fanbase? Would that generate sufficient revenue? I still wondered whether an artist would appeal to a much wider audience than a perceived small subculture in K-Pop.

My questions were answered in 2017 when BTS won Top Social Artist at the Billboard Music Awards.[94] Experts assess that a synergy of the artist's quality music performance, authentic fandom communication on social media, and their company BigHit Entertainment's astute business strategy catapulted boy band BTS into the global mainstream.[95] Of course by no means was this a blueprint, because BTS's trajectory is completely unique apart from any other K-Pop act with unprecedented success.

Instead of dedicating an excerpt section on BTS like I did for Psy, I'll be explaining specific aspects of the group's success throughout the entire book. BTS is a current phenomenon—they're still setting records, creating new historical milestones, and capturing the world as I write this book. Thus, it would only be right for me to discuss their ongoing influence on the topics in this book rather than dedicate a section in reflective hindsight.

---

94 Jason Lipshutz, "BTS Thanks Fans for Top Social Artist Win at Billboard Music Awards 2017: Watch," *Billboard*, May 21, 2017.

95 Yoochang Yang, "'빌보드 1위' 새 역사 쓴 방탄소년단의 4가지 성공 비결" ['Billboard #1' The 4 Success Strategies of History-Writing BTS], *MK*, May 29, 2018; Joohee Kim, "美 타임지, 방탄소년단 글로벌 성공 비결 집중 조명..."가장 중요한 건 음악"" [US Time, Sheds Light onto BTS's Success Factors...'the Most Important Is the Music'], *Seoul Kyungjae*, October 10, 2019.

BTS and their company BigHit Entertainment successfully used numerous strategies to achieve well-deserved mainstream recognition. Remember BigHit wasn't mentioned in my previous discussion of the "Big 3," because their recent successes have clearly disrupted the industry; perhaps it's time to retire the term. However, since BTS's global success is an outlier, some even suggest that BTS should be viewed apart from the label, "K-Pop;" Western media has increasingly been referring to BTS as "K-Pop artists" or as the "South Korean sensation," which actually serves to restrict and downplay BTS's music and achievements in this context.

To understand this argument, recall how the Western media like the MTV VMAs uses the label, K-Pop; undoubtedly, BTS is from the K-Pop industry, yet their success invites newer discourse on how we discuss K-Pop in the Western context. As more K-Pop acts achieve Western mainstream success, there should be more emphasis placed on the artists themselves rather than on restrictive labels. Fortunately, now the global K-Pop phenomenon has grown to the point where we can have these discussions more often.

There's another reason why BTS is important in terms of globalization. Sure, they are the first Korean act to achieve a number of accolades including ranking number one on the Billboard Hot 100, performing at Wembley Stadium, and setting the Japanese Oricon Chart record for the most first-week record sales by a foreign male artist.[96] The list goes on.

---

96 Gary Trust, "BTS' 'Dynamite' Blasts in at No. 1 on Billboard Hot 100, Becoming the Group's First Leader," *Billboard*, August 31, 2020; Mark Savage, "BTS Are the First Korean Band to Headline Wembley Stadium," *BBC*, June 2, 2019; So-yeon Yoon, "BTS Sells Most Records

More importantly, in terms of the bigger picture, BTS has shown us that it's possible for an act produced by the K-Pop industry to stand at the top of the global pop music scene for an extended period. We now engage in optimistic speculation regarding "how much farther can they go?"

So much has changed in this decade of possibilities and achievements. Thanks to technological advances, it has become apparent that K-Pop fans exist on every continent and desire more content. Today, K-Pop acts generally dedicate ample time for both Korean and international promotions simultaneously. We'll be exploring the artists', companies', and fans' contributions to K-Pop's globalization throughout the book. Stay tuned!

for Male, Foreign Act in First Week of Release: Oricon," *Korea JoongAng Daily*, July 21, 2020.

CHAPTER 9

A NEW ERA: 2020 AND BEYOND

___

As we wrap up the discussion on globalization, I wanted to clear up one potential source of confusion regarding the Western context.

Korean media has a tendency to equate globalization with Westernization, especially in terms of pop-cultural exports. For example, the Korean media constantly referred to Rain—who was mostly popular in Asia—as a "world star," especially after he performed a show in the U.S. Rain later appeared on *The Colbert Report* and fan votes ranked him number one multiple times on *TIME's* Most Influential People.[97] I think context matters when we evaluate the exactness of the "world."

The aforementioned K-Pop documentaries from the early 2010s focused mostly on the Western world despite

---

97 Megan Friedman, "Korean Pop Star Rain Wins Time 100 Poll — Again," *TIME*, April 15, 2011.

analyzing K-Pop's global success, which brings into question whether "global" in the K-Pop context should be taken literally or not.[98] International media's insistence on terms like "global" and "world" often refer to the West, despite K-Pop's already successful commercial performance in Asia. Even further, globalization in the pop-cultural context was also used synonymously with "Americanization" because American influences and trends are often perceived as the most dominant in the world.

South Korea exported its pop culture successfully to Greater Asia during the *Hallyu* Wave, but terms like "global" or "world-class" in Korean media headlines imply validation from the West as well. In a discussion with Gyu Tag Lee, Assistant Professor at George Mason University and K-Pop scholar, I learned that the early K-Pop strategies of localization like those of BoA and Wonder Girls also reflect this underlying idea of seeking Western validation.

Today, however, the Korean elements of K-Pop such as the underlying industry and the Korean lyrics, visuals, and performance style no longer need to be completely abandoned for artists to be successful in the West. In fact, these very elements are what made K-Pop successful in a foreign context and are now celebrated worldwide. Professor Lee posits:

98   Kim, Television Discourse, 67-73.

No longer does the K-Pop act need to start over as a rookie American pop act and attempt a crack at the American industry for exposure. The landscape has vastly changed, and K-Pop has evolved outside of South Korea. K-Pop is produced with the intention of spreading globally and has achieved success by maintaining the very unique elements that comprise it.

It seems that at this point, the focus of the K-Pop industry and their acts may be on Western recognition rather than validation.

From the K-Pop industry's perspective, there would be no reason to ignore global demand. The Korean phrase, "*gang-je jin-chool* (강제진출)," roughly meaning a "compulsory foray" into Western markets, is appropriate today; neither Psy nor BTS debuted in Korea with the sole intention of cracking the Billboard charts. Once there was a possibility of overseas demand, however, both acts capitalized on it successfully. They listened to their audience.

The previous localization strategies have been modified for current global success. For example, through their international members fluent in foreign languages like English, Mandarin, and Thai, groups like BLACKPINK and NCT appeal to worldwide audiences without having to adopt a new musical direction like BoA or leave Korea for an unpredictable journey overseas like Wonder Girls did.[99] Thanks to social media, the artists can stay true to their direction and concept while catering to international tastes simultaneously.

Quite often, when I discuss my Korean ethnicity with non-Korean colleagues today, they ask me what I think about K-Pop. During my days on a competitive dance team, my teammates even labeled me the "K-Pop star," as I was the only Korean on the team. Just to clarify, I frequently taught them K-Pop dance moves, so by no means was this label stereotypical in any way. Nonetheless, I realized that K-Pop had become a common icebreaker question and pop-cultural discussion topic.

This is a huge change from the days when a Korean had to ask, "Do you know K-Pop?" Now the question is reversed! I wonder if K-Pop's ubiquity will open doors for more Korean cultural dissemination and awareness.

There are still questions and issues we must tackle as K-Pop gains greater mainstream exposure in the West; for example, Western journalists repeatedly ask K-Pop acts questions that center the West, such as, "Will you release an English album?" or "Where'd you learn English?"[100]

There's also more complex discourse on K-Pop now than ever before. Ten years ago, I would've been excited to see

---

99 Youngdae Kim and T.K. Park, "What the Rise of Black Pink and BTS Says about the Future of K-Pop," *Vulture*, August 28, 2018.

100 Raisa Bruner, "BTS Explains Why They're Not Going to Start Singing in English," *TIME*, March 28, 2019; SCMP Reporter, "BTS Singer RM's English Skills Criticised by the Times. BTS Army Go on the Offensive on Social Media," *South China Morning Post*, October 9, 2018.

any positive Western media headline, such as, "The K-Pop sensation from South Korea." Now, however, things have changed and most people in 2020 at least have heard of the term K-Pop in some form—even in the sociopolitical context of 2020 anti-Black hashtags and police brutality in the U.S., in which K-Pop fans generated mass media coverage for their online collective action.[101] So, do we still need to question K-Pop artists in such a way when they've already generated global success and attention? When will the othering—viewing and labeling K-Pop artists as oriental, foreign, etc. through a stigmatized lens—stop? I still have many questions, and I'm sure you do too.

We're also seeing newer variations in the K-Pop production model. For example, SM Entertainment launched project supergroup, SuperM, in 2019, intentionally targeting the U.S. market. The group is comprised of seven individual members from four different popular SM groups—SHINee, EXO, NCT, and WayV—and have secured the number one spot on the Billboard 200 Albums Chart with their debut album.[102]

Now, even foreign idol groups import and undergo the K-Pop idol trainee system; recently, Korean companies' idol trainee system and formula produced Filipino idol group SB19 and Vietnamese idol group D1Verse.[103] Recall NiziU, a 2020 JYP

---

101   Alicia Lee, "K-Pop Fans Are Taking over 'White Lives Matter' and Other Anti-black Hashtags with Memes and Fancams of Their Favorite Stars," *CNN*, June 8, 2020.

102   Keith Caulfield, "SuperM Debuts at No. 1 on Billboard 200 Albums Chart with 'the 1st Mini Album'," *Billboard*, October 13, 2019.

103   Youngwoon Kang, "한국인은 아니지만…"우리도 K팝 아이돌"" [Not Korean…'but We're Also K-Pop Idols'], *MK*, February 28, 2020.

Entertainment-produced girl group in collaboration with Sony Music Japan. While this group is comprised of all Japanese members and is primarily active in the Japanese market, they'll be managed by JYP Entertainment for Korean promotions, and Park Jin-Young even wrote the debut single.[104] The management of groups like NiziU implies that it's not impossible in the near future for Korean companies to branch out to non-Asian areas like the U.S. and Europe to produce groups according to the K-Pop idol formula. How much "K-Pop" groups like NiziU are is a separate discussion.

As I'd like to reiterate, K-Pop really is something more than just music from Korea. Ultimately, maybe there'll come a day when K-Pop artists will blend seamlessly into the global mainstream so that they can be appreciated everywhere for their musical identity and talents rather than just be noticed for singing in a different language or being from Korea. The globalization of K-Pop shall continue to march forward, but its success and reception also hinge on media portrayals' orientalism and otherness. We're increasingly going to be having more complex K-Pop discourse, but I'm optimistic for K-Pop's global expansion.

---

104 So-yeon Yoon, "JYP's Newest Girl Group NiziU Release Pre-debut EP," *Korea JoongAng Daily,* June 30, 2020.

PART 3

ONLINE TECHNOLOGY AND CONTENT

K-Pop loves Twitter, and Twitter loves K-Pop.

- **JACK DORSEY**,

CEO OF TWITTER, AT 2019 SEOUL PRESS EVENT[105]

105 *YonhapNewsTV*, ""K팝 좋아요"…트위터·인스타그램 CEO 방한 / 연합뉴스TV (YonhapnewsTV)" ['I like Kpop'… Twitter ·Instagram CEO Visits Korea / YonhapNewsTV]. March 22, 2019, video, 1:52.

INTRO

One day in my tenth-grade biology class, my teacher showed us a YouTube video titled "Battle at Kruger," which featured a herd of buffaloes protecting a little one from a lion attack. This 2007 video currently has an astounding 82 million views.[106] My teacher concluded the video and said, "What did we do before YouTube existed?" I truly don't know.

Our lives have changed for the better since the advent of social media, right? Social media is a key driver in disseminating content in the entertainment industry. It's hard to imagine music not being promoted on YouTube or Instagram today, either directly from artists or indirectly from the users. Music industry companies prioritize social media data for their business strategy expansion, so the music business and technology have now become inseparable.

We've also entered into an era in which third-party users produce original creative content that propels them to online stardom. Whether you've decided to start a YouTube channel

---

106 *Jason Schlosberg*, "Battle at Kruger," May 3, 2007, video, 8:24.

or make unique Tiktok videos, the creative opportunities on social media are endless. The advent of online viral culture has brought generations together and has also propelled K-Pop to unprecedented heights. Technological developments and social media platforms are critical components in K-Pop's growth. How else would K-Pop be a truly global phenomenon without an online mediator?

Combined with the diverse array of content for audience consumption—music videos, dance practices, behind-the-scenes looks, online contests, etc.—the K-Pop phenomenon only grows bigger. In this section, we'll be exploring markets, applications, content creators, and upcoming developments within the K-Pop realm.

CHAPTER 10

THE ONLINE VS. OFFLINE STRATEGY

———

In 2006, I curiously searched up Korean artists on iTunes so I could purchase songs for my brand-new iPod Nano. Needless to say, there were no results. I was sad about my shortage of options to listen to and purchase Korean music in the U.S. So, I had to turn to YouTube to see if someone had uploaded an unofficial music video. Fortunately, today this isn't the case.

K-Pop is distributed simultaneously both online through MP3s and streaming services as well as offline in physical CDs. In an internet-dominated world today though, one mode may be better than the other. In order to decide, let's learn about both.

In South Korea, physical CD sales had been decreasing steadily since the International Monetary Fund (IMF) financial crisis in 1997. Because of a foreign exchange shortage, the IMF stepped in to restore the economy.[107] The Korean

———

107 Eun-hyung Kim, "빈곤한 가요, 무너진 시장" [Poor *Gayo*, Crashing Market], *Hangyeorae*, January 20, 2000.

government responded by heavily emphasizing growth in the IT sector, which allowed not only rapid advances in the internet but also in MP3s. Domestic file-sharing sites such as Soribada, Bugs, and many other illegal pathways thrived. Before plummeting even further, the physical sale-driven music industry was forced to acknowledge and adapt to the shift toward the digital age.[108] Under industry pressure, websites like Soribada and Bugs began to operate under legalized, commercialized means, and digital sales became the main driver in the domestic market.

Korean music sales reflected the switch to digital sales; in a 2013 governmental report from the Korea Creative Content Agency (KOCCA), South Korea reported an average of 87 percent online and 13 percent offline sales from 2006-2012 compared to the U.S.'s 38 percent to 62 percent and Japan's 21 percent to 79 percent.[109] Note this ratio discrepancy occurred even before social media took a more pivotal role in entertainment.

By 2019, however, global music industry revenues have gradually turned away from both physical and digital sales altogether in favor of online streaming.[110] Yet, in the Korean market, digital downloads (MP3s) actually increased by 31 percent in 2018 as opposed to streaming, which only increased by 6 percent.[111]

---

108 Sungmin Kim, 케이팝의 작은 역사 [K-Pop's Small History]. (Seoul: Geulhangari Publishers, 2018), 124-126.

109 Patrick Messerlin and Wonkyu Shin, "The Success of K-Pop: How Big and Why So Fast?" *Asian Journal of Social Science* (January 2017): 4.

110 "Global Music Report: The Industry in 2019," IFPI, accessed June 13, 2020.

111 "국내 음악시장 현황" [Status of the Domestic Pop Market], GAON Chart, last modified March 5, 2019; Korea Creative Content Agency

2018 Korean Streaming/Downloads Top 400

Unit: %

Total Yearly Streaming Top 400

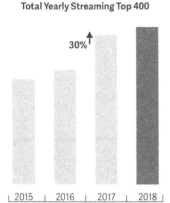

30%

| 2015 | 2016 | 2017 | 2018 |

Total Yearly Downloads Top 400

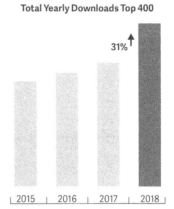

31%

| 2015 | 2016 | 2017 | 2018 |

112

I expected streaming to increase exponentially and make digital downloads obsolete, but clearly that's not the case here. The 2019 KOCCA report accredits this to idol fandoms' activities. For example, prior to 2020 amendments, Korean online music platform Melon used to determine online chart rankings by allocating 60 percent to digital downloads as opposed to streaming's 40 percent. This meant that the more digital downloads than streams, the higher likelihood that a particular song will earn higher points for cumulative online

(KOCCA); "*2019 Eumahk Sahnup Baekseo*" [2019 Music Industry White Paper] (Naju, KOCCA: 2020), 35.

112 KOCCA, *2019*, 38.

sales to climb up the charts.[113] Fans want their idols to succeed and are constantly monitoring the online charts to ensure they performed well. If digital downloads comprise a bigger portion of online chart performances, then you bet fans would rush to download MP3s. Such is an anomaly in the K-Pop market when considering the notion that MP3s are now outdated.

Contrary to the global decline in physical CD sales, the Korean market has experienced a huge resurgence. According to the second graph, there's actually an increase in Korean physical sales whereas those in the U.S. have been steadily decreasing.

Korea & US Total CD Sales

Unit: 1 CD

142.8M

119.9M

97.6M

21.54M

16.93M

87.6M

10.80M

7.37M   8.38M

52.0M

2014   2015   2016   2017   2018

—○— S. Korea   --□-- US

114

---

113 Ibid.

114 KOCCA, *2019*, 42; Seungjun Yang and Jung-geun Song, "아이돌 파는 상술 덕에 CD시장 '웃픈' 부활" [CD market's bittersweet revival after trick of the trade via idol sales], *Hankookilbo*, December 18, 2018; "RIAA 2018 YEAR-END MUSIC INDUSTRY REVENUE REPORT," Recording Industry Association of America (RIAA), last modified 2020, accessed September 2, 2020.

In the midst of declining physical sales worldwide, K-Pop idol fandoms' collective action have caused another anomaly.

Since today's Korean physical album sales are largely fandom-driven, generally idol groups with large fanbases have recorded the highest global physical sales in the past decade. For example, in 2019, BTS's global physical sales accounted for 42.1 percent of the Korean music industry's physical sales with 3,718,230 copies, followed by SEVENTEEN's 9.7 percent and EXO's 8.7 percent. The rest of the top ten are also popular idols' albums.[115]

According to the Korea Music Content Association, in 2020 alone, idol boy band acts with strong core fandoms including BTS, Baekhyun (of EXO), and SEVENTEEN recorded over one million physical sales each, whereas the top digital sales were from less fandom-driven solo acts such as Zico, Changmo, and IU.[116] This is an interesting dichotomy in today's market. Clearly, a combination of factors such as the music, mainstream appeal, fandoms, and viral content.

I see this dichotomy of top physical versus digital sales a topic for the industry to discuss and strategize over because K-Pop is posing an anomaly in the global pop music landscape. Physical sales are fandom-driven and concentrated around the top artists, so how can new rookie artists survive? If I were an executive producing a new K-Pop artist, I'd not only try to build a solid core fandom that would generate physical sales but also reach

115 KOCCA, *2019*, 44.

116 Hyojung Kim, "날개 단 음반 판매...상반기에만 밀리언셀러 3 팀" [Physical Sales Soar...3 Million Seller Acts in First Half Alone], *YonhapNews*, July 2, 2020.

wider audiences that are more likely to stream online. To accomplish both, social media marketing would be absolutely critical.

Despite K-Pop artists' massive physical sales, many of you readers rely more on online channels like streaming, so I'll elaborate more on that now.

In the past few years, K-Pop built up a following through global online channels, with early instances like BoA's U.S. single being released on iTunes in 2008.[117] Today, the world recognizes K-Pop's success and is actively seeking strategic partnerships with Korean entertainment companies.[118] With platforms like YouTube and Spotify, Korean entertainment companies can negotiate licensing agreements to have the artists' music be available for streaming overseas in specific regions. As a result, even though I live in the U.S., I have access to an entire K-Pop library for streaming on Spotify. In South Korea, domestic services like Melon and Genie dominate the online channels instead of global counterparts.

Yet, the Korean music industry is a company-based landscape in which artists are small fish in a big pond, even if they market their songs directly to consumers as some independent musicians do.[119] On Korean online music platforms, service

---

117   Kim, *History*, 126.

118   *"More K-Pop Artists Team up with U.S. Labels to Expand Careers," YonhapNews*, March 11, 2020.

119   Ingyu Oh and Hyo-Jung Lee, "Mass Media Technologies and Popular Music Genres: K-Pop and YouTube," *Korea Journal*, vol. 53, no.4 (Winter 2013): 34-58; Ingyu Oh and Gil-Sung Park, "From B2C to B2B: Selling Korean Pop Music in the Age of New Social Media." *Korea Observer* 43.3 (Autumn 2012): 365-397.

providers like Melon and intermediary distributors take 49 percent of the generated revenue, the production company takes 35 percent, and the producer and songwriter take 10 percent, leaving the musician only the remaining 6 percent.[120] Of course, the more high-profile, popular artists negotiate better distribution deals with their company.

It will be interesting to see if Spotify will make a splash and compete with YouTube Music in Korea, especially given Apple Music's unsuccessful licensing deal with major Korean publisher, Kakao M.[121] Nonetheless, consumers benefit the most from a plethora of platforms to choose from, hence the old Korean idiom, "The customer is the king (or queen)."

By the 2010s, the music industry worldwide had largely shifted from B2C (business to consumer) to B2B (business to business); online platforms such as YouTube and Spotify derive profits from advertisement revenues. In exchange for displaying ads before or during a YouTube video, companies such as Samsung pays royalties, which are then disbursed to YouTube and the entertainment company.[122] In 2019 alone, YouTube recorded an ad revenue of $15 billion USD, roughly 10 percent of owner Alphabet Inc.'s overall $162 billion USD.[123]

---

120 Pogeuni Kim, "1곡 재생때 0.4원…이효리도 "음악으로 먹고살기 힘들어"" [0.4 Won for 1 Song Played…Even Lee Hyori Says "It's Hard to Make a Living off of Music"], *Hangyeorae*, November 12, 2017.

121 Yujin Baek, "[혼돈의 음원시장]①글로벌 공룡이 달려든다" [[Chaotic Digital Music Market] ① Global Dinosaurs Are Coming], *BusinessWatch*, March 3, 2020.

122 Oh and Lee, "Mass Media," 34-58.

123 Paige Leskin, "Finally: Google Just Revealed YouTube's Ad Revenue, 14 Years after Acquiring It, and the Video Site Brought in $15 Billion Last Year," *BusinessInsider*, February 3, 2020.

That's a lot of money going to intermediaries while the artists receive only small amounts.

Let's admit, no one likes annoying YouTube ads. But what if the ads were a bit more enjoyable?

Many K-Pop music videos are actually promoted through paid YouTube ads. This method has proven to increase the official view count, since many are ad-generated views. Historically, K-Pop idols have starred in online ads for a special sponsorship, like when boy band Monsta X endorsed Pepsi in the video, "Pepsi For The Love of It."[124] These YouTube ads show a short snippet of the video, which both promotes the product and increases the artist's exposure to the wider YouTube audience. The ad-generated views are then accumulated for the official view count at 9.8 million for the Monsta X video.

Some artists promote official music videos through these online ads during the comeback season. According to a study by the "K-Pop on YouTube" webpage, popular groups such as Red Velvet and BTS that have been around for a while generally display a similar viewership curve: there's a sharp peak on the release day followed by a drop to a regular plateau and a gradual decline. In conjunction, the "likes" display a similar but less severe curve after the initial release date.

---

124 *StarshipTV*, "[MV] Monsta X – Pepsi For The Love Of It (Korean Version)," September 9, 2019, video, 2:45.

Red Velvet's "Zimzalabim" pretty standard normal view curve

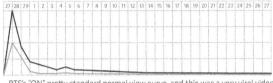

BTS's "ON" pretty standard normal view curve, and this was a very viral video

125

In contrast, for a newer group such as Stray Kids, the duration of the peak for their song, "Levanter" (2019) lasted two days before experiencing the natural decline. Yet, after the YouTube ad promotions started, a rise to a second peak began, which eventually overtook the first. Interestingly, the video's likes don't correlate with the views as they normally would for a K-Pop video; instead, the "Levanter" video's likes declined to a flat curve after the first peak.[126] Because Billboard charts and Korean music TV program charts now reflect YouTube view counts, rookie groups especially benefit greatly from this added exposure.

125 "K-Pop - YouTube Ads Spell the End of Meaningful View Counters," Aoimirai's KPOP, last modified May 2, 2020, accessed May 15, 2020

126 Ibid.

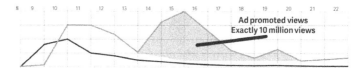

8 9 10 11 12 13 14 15 16 17 18 19 20 21 22

Ad promoted views
Exactly 10 million views

Stray Kids "Levanter" with the AD portion highlighted, based on the clear discrepancy between views and likes

127

K-Pop online ads are not only strategic but also beneficial for both the artists' exposure and for the potential fan to discover new artists and songs. Consider turning your Adblocker off next time—the ads might just lead you to discover your new favorite K-Pop group.

127 Ibid.

CHAPTER 11

THE TECHNOLOGY EVOLVED, AND SO DID THE FANS

———

According to **Lenzo Yoon**, co-CEO of BigHit Entertainment,

> The company is always thinking of ways to deliver meaningful content to the consumers. Not just music but also what consumers want, what's going through the young generation's minds, and what would be a new experience for them.[128]

The plethora of diverse BTS-related content today, including animated characters and video games, exemplifies Yoon's point. A lot of the content is generated online, where global fans come together to support their favorite idols.

---

128 Joonhyung Park, "빅히트 대표 "정답은 콘텐츠입니다"" [Bighit Rep 'the Answer Is Content'], *MK*, April 19, 2020.

People overseas often discover K-Pop either directly through social media platforms or indirectly via another person. If they're in Korea, they may have watched K-Pop acts live on TV and chatted about them with peers the next day. But how did the earlier generations of global fans get involved with the K-Pop culture when it wasn't as widespread?

By analyzing K-Pop's general trend throughout the decades, we can see that global expansion is symbiotic with the growth of social media and communications technology. During the *Hallyu* Wave in the 1990s, China and Japan were the main countries for K-Pop exportation.[129] Fans used TVs, videotapes, radios, and landline phones to support their stars, whether it be through pre-ordering albums at the local record shop or voting for weekly TV charts by phone.

As we progressed through the mid-1990s and everyone started to own personal computers, the internet became a crucial mode of communication. Landline-based network services facilitated online communities collectively known as "PC *tong shin* (PC통신)," in which users could discuss music together.[130] By the early 2000s, we were seeing the rise of online communities and forums—the precursors to modern social media—which helped fans organize fandom activities and gather information regarding the stars' schedules, music, and media headlines.

---

129 Ingyu Oh and Gil-Sung Park, "From B2C to B2B: Selling Korean Pop Music in the Age of New Social Media." *Korea Observer* 43.3 (Autumn 2012): 366-367.

130 Gyu Tag Lee, 케이팝의 시대 [The K-POP Age], (Seoul: Hanwool Academy, 2016), 71.

Idol groups like TVXQ had their official online fan clubs in the form of "fan cafes," which were something like a Facebook group today. TVXQ's fan club, Cassiopeia, even earned a Guinness World Record in 2008 for the largest number of officially registered members—800,000—in an online fan club.[131] As successors to the earlier fan clubs like Club H.O.T., those of the early 2000s were highly centralized and institutionalized, helping give everyone the chance to assemble online in collective action.[132]

Thanks to their online communities, the fandom culture evolved as Korean fans further diversified their activities that supported their idols. The stars would sometimes even visit the fan cafes to write a personal message to the fans by saying hello, updating them about marriage plans, or confessing struggles.[133]

While the industry was already exporting K-Pop into Greater Asia through promotional activities amidst the *Hallyu* Wave, it was still very difficult for global fans to join these insular and domestic communities. Not everyone could attend the Korean events and were lucky if their favorite artist was traveling internationally, even if they mostly stayed within Asia or visited Los Angeles. Furthermore, not everyone could purchase official merchandise, as it was distributed mainly in Korea and would not only need to learn the Korean language but also keep up with insider slang to comprehend Korean

131   "TVXQ in Guinness World Record," *KBS World*, March 24, 2009.

132   Jinwoong Park, "아이돌 팬덤, 당당한 문화로 자리잡다" [Idol Fandoms Confidently Find Own Cultural Ground], *KUNews*, May 12, 2019.

133   Hyemyoung Park, "팬클럽과 팬문화" [Fanclubs and fan culture], *cine21*, November 9, 2006.

fandom activities. Japan and China had their respective fan-bases for K-Pop acts that toured there, but Korea was naturally still the heart of fandom operations.

So how did global K-Pop fans eventually come together on Twitter and Instagram?

Enter YouTube in the mid-2000s. If you were there in the early days of YouTube, there weren't a lot of official videos from the global music industry. Rather, there was comparatively more user-created content like "Evolution of Dance" by Judson Laipply, as well as unauthorized uploads of music videos and TV programs.[134] For example, SM Entertainment only officially uploaded TVXQ's music video for "Rising Sun" (2005) in 2009, four long years after its release.[135]

But it was better late than never; the K-Pop industry executives eventually realized that YouTube was a viable way of officially connecting with global fans who already listened to K-Pop via the aforementioned unauthorized uploads. Even though I lived in Korea in 2009, this meant I could easily share a video link to my friend in New Jersey who wouldn't be as exposed to Korean pop culture. Anyone around the globe could learn and engage with K-Pop idols by watching YouTube videos at any given time without having to type in Korean.

Global fans who previously gathered on early online forums such as Soompi to discuss *Hallyu*-related news could now

134 *Judson Laipply,* "Evolution of Dance," April 6, 2006, video, 6:00.

135 *SMTOWN,* "TVXQ! 'Rising Sun' MV," November 23, 2009, video, 5:19.

engage with audiovisual content even more easily.[136] The easy transfer of information and accessibility across computer and mobile platforms aided tremendously in spreading K-Pop content. I could watch a YouTube video while simultaneously reading and writing comments, thereby engaging with others regarding the video in question.

In the mid-late 2000s, as we saw with TVXQ, the industry began to embrace YouTube's strengths. Major entertainment companies created their own YouTube, Facebook, and Twitter accounts to upload official content.[137] The data analytics from the social media platforms would then be used to determine and brainstorm effective, innovative content to get the fans excited.

The K-Pop industry's expansion via social media and its subsequent global reception distinguishes it from the Japanese and Chinese music markets, which relied substantially more on traditional routes like via TV and CDs.[138] The internet allowed for unique, personalized experiences that traditional outlets simply couldn't provide; for example, if Indonesian fans made up a large percentage of viewers of a particular K-Pop video on YouTube, the artist could upload a special video message for them in Indonesian or devise some exclusive

---

136 "Interview with Susan Kang, founder of 'Soompi'," Korean Foundation for International Cultural Exchange (KOFICE), last modified March 15, 2017, accessed April 3, 2020.

137 Hyein Lee and Heejin Ko, "SNS 중심에 있는 그들, 한류의 중심이 된다" [Those at the Center of SNS, Become the Center of Hallyu], Kyunghyang, December 31, 2017.

138 Ingyu Oh and Hyo-Jung Lee, "Mass Media Technologies and Popular Music Genres: K-Pop and YouTube," Korea Journal, vol. 53, no.4 (Winter 2013): 42.

artist merchandise for Indonesian distribution. Once again, give the fans what they want.

By the third generation of K-Pop acts in the early 2010s, many social media platforms were already thriving overseas, especially Facebook and Twitter. Third-party communities like Soompi and allkpop facilitated forum discussions while translating Korean news articles for fans to engage with. Not only was online content a core part of business strategy, but it was also a necessity; it was the primary way for global fans to encounter K-Pop. Upon "Gangnam Style's" success from YouTube, the importance of online content became more important than ever before.

Today, K-Pop idols don't need to stay confined to TV programs; there's just not enough room for everyone on TV. Fortunately, alternative online platforms not only exist but are effective. So, the next question is, which ones?

CHAPTER 12

WHERE, WHEN, AND HOW: SOCIAL MEDIA PLATFORMS

———

In entertainment, exposure is critical; the more talk and hype around a K-Pop act and its content, the more gateways to commercial success. Here's what I've noticed about each of the major social media platforms and how they have helped K-Pop gain exposure.

YouTube

Undoubtedly, YouTube has been the most critical social media platform for K-Pop's dissemination. Ninety-five percent of internet users frequent YouTube, and one million users visit the site on a daily basis. For Korean YouTube content, only 20 percent of the viewership actually comes from Korea; the rest is from worldwide viewers.[139] It's the most widely used

———

139   Jongmo Baek, "방탄소년단·싸이는 왜 유튜브에 영상을 계속 올리나" [Why Do BTS/Psy Continue to Upload YouTube Videos?], *DailySmart*, July 1, 2018.

platform in Korea, as Koreans have reportedly spent 46 billion minutes watching YouTube videos in a single month.[140] With more K-Pop content being produced as part of the *YouTube Originals* series, such as TWICE's *Seize the Light* documentary, YouTube continues to grow as a platform and keeps propelling the K-Pop phenomenon to newer heights.[141]

In addition to official music videos and teasers, third-party K-Pop content also thrives on this platform. These creators don't directly work in the industry and create K-Pop-related content that caters to fans of existing artists. More on third-party creators later.

Fun fact: "Gangnam Style" is the oldest video as of 2020 in the top ten most trending view counts.[142]

Instagram

Most idol groups have official Instagram accounts that post important announcements and updates for comebacks, tours, trailers, and other materials. Companies usually allow more experienced idols to create their own individual accounts, as all five of Red Velvet's members recently did. Groups like BTS and TWICE still don't have individual accounts as of late 2020. This may be a strategy to maintain undivided attention on the groups themselves rather than establishing personal accounts for individual members. There are definitely advantages for

140 Kyung-jin Kim, "Koreans Spend Hours Plugged into YouTube," *Korea JoongAng Daily*, September 11, 2019.

141 *TWICE*, "Ep 1. First Step Towards Our Dream | TWICE: Seize the Light," April 29, 2020, video, 15:46.

142 "YouTube Viewcount," KpopRadar, last modified August 24, 2020.

having individual accounts, as it would drive exposure to a particularly popular member which, in turn, would help boost the group activities or even a solo career.

Another way that Instagram has helped K-Pop's expansion is that it allows fans to comment on pictures and even create their own fanpage accounts to post content of their favorite idols from TV shows, performances, and fancams. Instagram CEO, Adam Mosseri, visited Korea in 2019. He noted that Instagram was a "global platform for spreading Korean culture around the globe," and recognized K-Pop as one of the most popular Instagram content categories.[143]

Twitter

Twitter's effects are similar to those of Instagram but with an even more widespread community. Fans can retweet from official group accounts or from the idols themselves and may get direct responses if they're lucky. Fans often post short GIF files of their favorite idols in comments to show appreciation and engage with fellow fans, non-fans, and fans from other fandoms in thread discussions. Sometimes they'll be good-spirited, and other times they aren't. In 2019, Twitter CEO Jack Dorsey said that the most-liked Tweet in Twitter history was BTS-related and that there were 5.3 million K-Pop-related tweets in a year.[144] In fact, the highest retweet of 2019 was a video of BTS member

143 Ilyong Kang, "SNS, 케이팝에 빠지다" [SNS Is Obsessed with Kpop], *AjuKyungjae*, April 9, 2019.

144 Ibid.

Jungkook dancing, surpassing a million to beat the previous record holder.[145]

In the same year, Twitter extended its existing "In-Stream Video Sponsorships" to include official Twitter-produced K-Pop content.[146] Furthermore, the recently launched "Topics" feature, through which users can subscribe to Tweets of particular interest, offered K-Pop and sports as the first examples.[147]

Tiktok

Tiktok is the most talked-about platform of 2020. Users create videos involving music or funny meme content to deliver a certain message within a short timeframe. K-Pop artists now utilize the platform for promotion—like BTS did for their "Map of the Soul: 7" comeback promotions —or to take part in or start dance challenges such as Baekhyun's #CandyChallenge.[148]

Especially when everyone was quarantined at home during the early days of the COVID-19 pandemic, Tiktok provided a creative outlet for many new users. Using this situation as momentum

---

145 Jack Lau, "BTS Army Makes Jungkook Video Twitter's Most Retweeted Tweet in 2019; 'World Record Egg' Well and Truly Beaten," *South China Morning Post*, December 11, 2019.

146 Yeonjeong Kim, "In-Stream Video Ads and Sponsorships to Include K-Pop Content Worldwide," *Twitter* (blog), *Twitter*, February 7, 2019.

147 Junhyuk Cho, "트위터, '케이팝' 내세워 전 세계 3억 유저 사로잡는다" [Twitter, Captures 3 Million Worldwide Users with 'Kpop' at Forefront], *HankookKyungjae,* November 7, 2019.

148 Ashley King, "Did Tiktok Crash during Its 30-Second BTS Exclusive?" *Digital Music News*, February 21, 2020; Marah Ruiz, "EXO's Baekhyun performs "sweet" and "spicy" versions of 'Candy' in live showcase," *GMA Network,* May 27, 2020.

for growth, Tiktok is becoming a strong player in social media marketing in the entertainment context. It's only a matter of time until we see even more K-Pop content on the platform.

Facebook

K-Pop fans have largely relegated Facebook to the proverbial backseat, although pages like Mnet or M2 post official idol fan-cams or dance content, and third-party news sites such as allkpop post translated news articles for the fans to comment on. Many users still do create Facebook groups in which they discuss and support idols. Despite Facebook's success and social media dominance in the late 2000s and early 2010s, the emergence of strong competitors and alternatives has left Facebook trailing behind.

* * *

The discrepancies across the important platforms—YouTube, Instagram, Twitter, Tiktok, and Facebook—provide different usages and goals for both the audience and the companies. According to a 2014 study analyzing the K-Pop audience's consumption behaviors across both YouTube and Twitter, the popular clips shared on Twitter reflected greater personal inclinations and diversity than did YouTube, on which users mainly focused on official music videos with high view counts. In other words, Twitter better reflected the audience's individual cultural consumption with thoughts and commentary, whereas YouTube data emphasized music content.[149]

---

149 Yong Hwan Kim, Dahee Lee, Nam Gi Han and Min Song, "Exploring characteristics of video consuming behaviour in different social media using K-Pop videos," *Journal of Information Science*, Vol 40(6) (2014): 806-822.

One amazing thing about this online distribution through YouTube is that there aren't as many restrictions as there are with offline modes, such as spending greater time and money on CDs and concert tickets.[150] I can now freely engage with content by watching K-Pop music videos and concert footage all day from the comfort of my sofa. I don't need to go out to a store or order a concert DVD and wait days for it to arrive. Plus, I can quickly search for any song I want on streaming platforms like Spotify and play them immediately instead of purchasing an MP3 file and waiting for it to download. Everything is covered in my monthly membership.

Ingyu Oh and Gil-Sung Park believe that the "offline camaraderie" is a result of communication; the viewer can engage with a like-minded audience when watching a YouTube video by writing comments, liking or disliking the video, and sharing it to another platform like Twitter for more discussion.[151] Let's say I'm enjoying a YouTube video of singer Crush singing his hit song, "Beautiful." I proceed to comment, *More people need to see this*, which receives a series of upvotes from like-minded, English-speaking users. If I type the same comment in Korean, chances are I will get some Korean replies in agreement.

The entertainment companies' increased emphasis on You-Tube and other social media platforms have reduced the overwhelming need for popular idols to frequently appear on TV programs for exposure. Real-time alternatives to cable TV

---

150 Ingyu Oh and Gil-Sung Park, "From B2C to B2B: Selling Korean Pop Music in the Age of New Social Media." *Korea Observer* 43.3 (Autumn 2012): 372-376.

151 Ibid.

like YouTube, Tiktok, Facebook Live, and V Live—a Korean app which I'll discuss soon—provide ample business opportunities for companies to branch out and reach global audiences. However, the Korean TV industry is still important; building exposure and a solid fanbase by appealing to a broader audience on TV music programs and variety shows is critical, especially for rookie idols. Think about it: if roughly 1000 individual idols debut in a year, these rookie idols must do everything they can to become known.[152]

With the increasing amount of artists today, we need more platforms on which they can thrive. According to Lee Soo-Man, founder of SM Entertainment, at the 2019 World Knowledge Forum:

> When the IT industry expanded, I imagined cultural content would be next. I learned to think that cultural creation is a form of technology and was determined to create an entertainment source based on cultural technology. In the future, audiences will experience content beyond the mere audiovisual limits—there will be no barrier between the real and the virtual space.[153]

I find his word choice in "barrier" fascinating; it implies there are even more advancements to come. But haven't we been breaking many barriers already?

---

152 Sungho Moon, "데뷔 확률 0.1%, 그들이 아이돌에 도전 하는 이유," [Debut possibility 0.1%, the reason why they continue to try become idols], *SeoulTV*, March 10, 2020.

153 Dakyeom Lee, "'세계지식포럼' 이수만이 꿈꾸는 미래 #CT #슈퍼엠 #컬처 유니버스(종합)" ['World Knowledge Forum' the Future Lee Soo Man Envisions #Ct #Superm #Culture Universe], *StarToday*, September 26, 2019.

Consider live streaming on social media with your favorite stars, which was previously unimaginable. Social media facilitated a more live view of K-Pop in that fans are treated to enhanced, real-time experiences. Instagram, YouTube, Facebook, Twitter, and Tiktok offer live-streaming capabilities, through which artists can communicate directly with the audience.[154] During the stream, fans can ask artists how they're doing, tune into exclusive vocal performances, or even get a behind-the-scenes look at the studio.

Korean mobile application, V Live, makes it even easier for K-Pop fans to engage with stars by offering more than 1,300 specific channels, each dedicated to a celebrity.[155] Loyal fans tune in during a specific time to watch stars make major announcements or share their daily activities live, as well as watch officially produced programming such as "MMMTV (Mamamoo TV)" or "GFriend's Memoria." Such programs often show the stars' off-stage personalities, an authenticity that fans find appealing. In 2019, Naver—Korea's most popular online platform and search engine, a.k.a. Korea's Google—launched "Fanship" under V Live, a premium paid feature providing exclusive videos, advance concert ticketing privileges, special merchandise, and fan usage analytics to help expand the artists' global activities.[156]

V Live is essentially an application that incorporates all of the fun aspects of existing live-streaming platforms but is

154 Jefferson Graham, "Coronavirus: From Facebook to YouTube, Live Video Is Back. How the Apps Compare." *USA Today*, March 26, 2020.

155 "Channels," V Live, last accessed May 3, 2020.

156 Heejeong Ahn, "네이버 브이라이브, 글로벌 유료 멤버십 '팬십' 출시" [Naver Vlive Launches Global Paid Membership 'Fanship'], *ZDNet Korea*, March 26, 2019.

dedicated exclusively to K-Pop star programming and communication. With strategic partnerships launching in Japan, Thailand, Vietnam, and Indonesia, V Live is evolving into a strong force in Asian entertainment technology.[157]

Some of the V Live app content is concurrently uploaded to official YouTube channels, but when I downloaded V Live on my phone, I was pleasantly surprised to see both exclusive and cross-platform content neatly organized on each artist's page. I could also tune in during an exclusive V Live live stream while browsing a large catalog of video content.

So, is V Live supposed to be the end-all-be-all for exclusive K-Pop video content? Possibly for some fans, but there are additional alternatives. For example, BigHit Entertainment produced its own application through a subsidiary beNX called "Weverse," which features both BigHit artists like TXT and BTS, and non-BigHit artists like CL and Henry Lau. Fans can join Weverse and communicate directly with the stars or amongst themselves and gain access to exclusive, official content.

Although similar to V Live in that nature, Weverse provides a heightened sense of community amongst the fandoms while further emphasizing the bonds between the artists and the fans.[158] On Weverse, like on Twitter, the idols communicate directly with the fans by uploading their own written posts,

---

157 Daeun Shin, "동남아 공략하는 브이라이브...현지 연예인과 맞손" [VLive targeting Southeast Asia... collaborations with local celebrities], *Hangyeorae*, June 27, 2019.

158 Jaehoon Lee, "세븐틴, BTS 소속사 '빅히트'가 만든 위버스 입점" [Seventeen Enters BTS's company BigHit's WeVerse], *Newsis*, March 12, 2020.

selfies, and questions. In contrast, V Live serves as more of a video catalog and fan forum. So, not only does Weverse provide an insular, exclusive channel for media content, it also heightens the fan experience by allowing them to comment directly on BTS or CL's posts. The stars might not always respond directly to me, but it still feels more authentic than commenting on a YouTube video. I think we may see V Live and Weverse eventually competing for the upper hand in attracting users with exclusive content.

Social media platforms are shaped both for and by the users, implying that perhaps someday it won't be a stretch to see apps like V Live or Weverse branch out to include other global stars known for their fandoms. If Justin Bieber ever decides to try something new with his fandom, the "Beliebers," maybe he can take a page out of K-Pop's playbook for a fresh approach.

CHAPTER 13

THE "UNTACT" ERA

I wrote this book during the 2020 coronavirus pandemic. It's interesting how such an unfortunate situation actually shed light on newer implications for online K-Pop video streaming. This is the age of the "Untact," which Koreans use to refer to contactless interactions.[159] I didn't coin it so don't quote me on that.

BTS's South Korean leg of their world tour for their new album, "Map of the Soul: 7," scheduled for April 2020, was unfortunately canceled due to safety concerns. As a substitute, on April 18-19, 2020, BigHit Entertainment hosted its initial "Bang Bang Con," a YouTube live stream featuring unreleased past concert and fan-meeting footage from 2015 to 2018 as well as new intermission clips. BigHit elevated the interactive experience by implementing Bluetooth technology to light up the official BTS glow-up sticks "Army Bombs," in sync with the Weverse app and YouTube concert audio.[160] At the peak, 2.24 million viewers tuned in live

---

159 Jinyong Jeon, "언택트 시대 온다?" [Is the Untact age coming?], *NextEconomy*, April 6, 2020.

160 Kyungwon Min, "전 세계 아미 방구석 찾아간 BTS 방방콘…이틀간 5059 만뷰" [BTS BangBangCon Visits Worldwide Army...50.59 Million Views], *JoongangIlbo*, April 20, 2020.

and over 50 million watched the stream over that weekend.[161] The fan reaction to this event was overwhelmingly positive. Sure, it wasn't the same as an in-person experience, but this implied huge future event opportunities.

SM Entertainment took a different approach by conducting a live concert on April 26, 2020, that featured the group SuperM on the V Live app. The concert was tailored specifically for online streaming, featuring AR/VR technology and 3D graphics for an enhanced virtual experience at home.[162] Picture that! Perhaps the home IMAX experience is coming soon to K-Pop as well.

SuperM kicked off SM and Naver's joint project, the "Beyond Live" series. The idol groups, WayV, NCT Dream, and NCT 127 hosted their own concerts in the following weeks.[163] The price was approximately $30 USD, which generated over $1 million USD in sales and attracted 75,000 concertgoers from 109 countries.[164] SM and Naver entered into an official partnership to expand the "Fanship" feature with SM's artists going forward.[165]

---

161   Isobel Lewis, "BTS: More Than 50 Million Tune into Bang Bang Con Virtual Concert Series," *Independent*, April 20, 2020.

162   Hoyeon Lee, "[HI★리뷰] "팬들과 함께 있는 듯" 슈퍼엠, 신개념 온라인 콘서트 성료" [[HI★Review] "Feels like we're with the fans" SuperM, Successfully Completes Innovative Online Concert], *Hankookilbo*, April 26, 2020.

163   Bin Woo, ""슈퍼엠이 연다"…SM X 네이버, 라이브 콘서트 스트리밍 서비스 시작" ['SuperM the Opening Act'... SM X Naver, Starts Live Concert Streaming Service], *10asia*, April 21, 2020.

164   Tamar Herman, "SuperM's Virtual K-Pop Concert Sees Major Earnings," *Forbes*, April 26, 2020.

165   Seohyun Shim, "브이라이브 강화하는 네이버, 이번엔 SM과 '언택트 팬관리'" [Naver Strengthening V Live, This Time with SM 'Untact Fan Management'], *Joongangilbo*, April 14, 2020.

On June 14, 2020, BigHit also launched a live paid concert titled "Bang Bang Con: *The Live*" featuring BTS. The concert attracted a massive 750,000 viewers from 107 countries for ninety minutes, during which BTS performed a medley of their hits live.[166] Fans experienced heightened filmography and could choose from six different camera angles.[167] Similarly, the 2020 KCON titled "KCON:TACT" was also filmed and held remotely without a live audience in Korea. From June 20-26, KCON featured a continuous, twenty-four-hour stream of "live and pre-taped content" that included concerts, meet and greet sessions, panels, and other exclusive content.[168]

In August 2020, SM Entertainment and JYP Entertainment—two of the top K-Pop companies—announced a strategic alliance to form the Beyond LIVE Corporation, further expanding the aforementioned "Beyond Live" series. JYP Entertainment artists like girl group TWICE would also launch their own online concerts on the V Live platform. With actions like these, it's apparent that the industry is adapting, collaborating, and investing heavily in streaming technology platforms, all during 2020. Will streaming live concerts be the norm going forward?

To address this, Korean entertainment company executives gathered to discuss the standard guidelines for overseeing

---

166 Seung-hyun Song, "K-Pop Powerhouses Ask for Financial Support from Government," *The Korea Herald*, June 21, 2020.

167 Jeongyeon Lee, "방탄소년단 첫 온라인 콘서트 '방방콘 더 라이브'...전 세계 아미들 열광" [BTS first Online Concert 'BangBangCon the Live'... ARMYs Enthusiastic Worldwide], *Donga*, June 15, 2020.

168 "KCON:TACT 2020 Summer Brings KCON to Fans Worldwide," KCON, last accessed June 1st, 2020.

future in-person concerts with the Ministry of Culture, Sports, and Tourism. While details will be contingent upon how Korea manages the pandemic for a safe, in-person concert experience, the industry must develop online alternatives for now.[169] Many planned in-person concerts were canceled in 2020, so the Ministry discussed ways to support the industry via tax incentives and subsidies for the time being.[170]

Think about it again: 750,000 people watching live at once! Although the concert experience must be modified, the industry is adapting to the changing landscape. As terrible as the pandemic situation has been, the alternatives to in-person concerts present new implications for the future of online content and the concert industry. Of course, I'd like to be vibing to K-Pop with my fellow fans in a large stadium, but once in awhile, I wouldn't mind an online concert. When will we be able to enjoy massive K-Pop concerts again? Perhaps long after this book is released, but I'm confident that we'll be streaming more online concerts in the near future as well.

---

169 Jisun Kim, "K팝 기획사들 "오프라인 공연 못해 어려워"…문체부 " 하반기부터 준비"" [Kpop Companies 'Difficult without Offline Performances'… MCST 'Preparation Starting Second Half of Year'], *KBS News*, June 19, 2020.

170 Song, "K-Pop Powerhouses."

CHAPTER 14

DIVERSITY OF CONTENT: THIRD-PARTY CREATORS

———

"Gangnam Style" inspired an onslaught of fan-created You-Tube videos in the form of dance covers, parodies, and flashmob footage. Various figures and institutions around the world created their own "_____ Style," including MIT's "Chomsky Style," Mitt Romney, and my alma mater.[171] The dance was a critical component of the phenomenon, and YouTubers who put their own twist on it helped the video's circulation.

Fans and creators become advocates by producing an array of online K-Pop content that propels the culture far beyond the limit that the companies can reach. There are no creative restrictions online—as long as it's legal—so the amount of online K-Pop content multiplies tremendously for all to enjoy.

---

171 *MIT Gangnam Style*, "MIT Gangnam Style," October 27, 2012, video, 5:02; *CollegeHumor*, "Mitt Romney Style (Gangnam Style Parody)," October 8, 2012, video, 2:51; *and2jw*, "Berkeley Style: PSY- Gangnam Style Global Parody Cover Full [J.Won.K]," August 25, 2012, video, 4:11.

In 2017, I was working at YouTube's headquarters, getting a behind-the-scenes look at how they moderated online video content. I was surprised to see a lot of K-Pop-related videos reported for copyright violations. Was someone reporting every single K-Pop video? As it turned out, there was; the K-Pop production companies were aware that creators were using their music online and wanted to protect it. The videos ranged from vocal and dance covers to reaction videos to K-Pop commentaries. YG Entertainment initially even wanted to remove my dance video to G-Dragon's "Light It Up."

Just like how I made dance videos, creators all over the world were incorporating K-Pop into their content. During the 2010s, when there was a surge of active K-Pop idols—remember, thirty-eight girl groups debuted in 2012— third-party online content began to really thrive. K-Pop stars such as Ailee began their careers through YouTube cover videos, which would later be revisited after their debuts.[172] SM Entertainment hosted a series of "cover contests," inviting fans from all over the world to upload themselves singing or dancing to an SM idol's song to win prizes. The cover culture later influenced the official Korean TV program *Stage K* in 2019 where international cover dancers competed and performed together with K-Pop idols.[173]

YouTube channels like ReacttotheK and DKDKTV commented on the latest K-Pop songs with their own twists, Korean Unnie taught Korean using K-Pop lyrics, and former

---

172 *[Ailee OFFICIAL] aileemusic*, "Ailee Singing the Climb by Miley Cyrus," August 7, 2009, video, 3:51.

173 "StageK," JTBC, last accessed April 2, 2020.

industry insiders like GRAZY GRACE weighed in on behind-the-scenes gossip. What does this plethora of diverse content imply for K-Pop as a whole? It means more exposure for the artists, more feedback, and more creativity overall in the scene. If you have an innovative idea, just go with it. Who knows? You might just become a viral sensation.

This rise of K-Pop adjacent industries, as Professor Cedar-Bough Saeji of Indiana University Bloomington suggests, is very important to K-Pop's global dissemination.[174] Adjacent, in this context, refers to a parallel lane of creators who don't work directly for K-Pop entertainment companies but still create K-Pop content on their own. As companies experimented with how to attract the global audience, third-party creators already proceeded to cater to them directly. Curious fans, who were disappointed by the lack of variety or the slow speed at which official content was uploaded, were delighted to find that third-party YouTube channels were already conducting interviews and filming games and challenges with their favorite stars.

I didn't have to wait for companies to upload formulaic interviews of the girl group EXID or for them to appear on generic Korean TV programming; I discovered that EXID played a game of "Would You Rather" on the YouTube channel Buzzfeed Celeb. Through the video, I could see a new, more personal side of my favorite idols.[175] My life is absolutely

---

174 *GW IKS,* "CedarBough T. Saeji, "Parasitic or Symbiotic?: The Rise of the K-Pop Adjacent Industries," November 12, 2019, video, 24:49.

175 *BuzzFeed Celeb,* "EXID Plays 'Would You Rather,'" May 29, 2018, video, 5:48.

better now that I know EXID members would prefer to have a watermelon instead of a golf ball for their heads!

One of the channels that led this kind of YouTube trend was Buzzfeed, a digital media company focused on creating viral content. With Buzzfeed's addicting videos, polls, quizzes, and lists, I definitely spent a lot of time distracted in my school's library. Buzzfeed's celebrity interviews specifically focused on more of stars' personal lives. I caught up with former producer, Evan Ghang, who had actively advocated for Buzzfeed's expansion into the K-Pop scene after previously working at Mnet, a Korean music TV channel. Upon producing a successful video interview with K-Pop star Amber Liu, Ghang and the Buzzfeed team began to reach out to Korean entertainment companies. The companies were skeptical at first because they viewed Buzzfeed as just one of millions of YouTube channels.

However, after Buzzfeed's K-Pop content became very popular, companies eventually began to reach out to the channel first to have their idols star in their unique videos. After producing a number of viral Buzzfeed videos, Ghang has taken on a new role at KAI Media, the parent company of hello82, a YouTube channel devoted solely to K-Pop creative content. On this channel, you can watch as boy band VAV sings "Poison" in Portuguese, co-ed group KARD, who's especially popular in Latin America, guesses Spanish words, and an Argentinian fan tours Korea with her favorite star, Sunmi.[176] Ghang said excitedly:

---

176 "hello82," YouTube, last accessed March 15, 2020.

YouTube has grown so much as a platform [for creators], and online K-Pop content is definitely going to grow exponentially.

Podcast company DIVE Studios offers another source of K-Pop content for eager fans. I had the pleasure of speaking with CEO Brian Nam, who saw an opportunity to try something different with the K-Pop industry that was evolving so rapidly. As a huge fan of podcasts, Nam founded the company and became the first in the podcast industry to exclusively cover K-Pop content. When he began, there wasn't a single podcast for K-Pop fans or interested audiences. He capitalized on an awesome opportunity. Nam remembers:

We released a minimal sh*tty quality version which hit number 1 in 28 countries. We realized there was something here.

The intimate nature of podcasting generated massive interest from K-Pop fans worldwide. They could listen to well-known English-fluent stars like Eric Nam, Tablo, Jamie, and Jae of DAY6 host and share personal their opinions on topics such as K-Dramas and high school. In fact, as Nam recalled, "56 percent of the audience were first-time podcasters," meaning that their interest in K-Pop alone led them to discover a whole new form of media consumption. Nam emphasizes,

DIVE grew very organically, and one thing led to another.

DIVE also created a YouTube channel to showcase diverse content such as podcast previews and performances by Korean musicians while continuing to collaborate with K-Pop stars on new podcast episodes.

Taking DIVE into consideration, I wonder what industry has yet to be explored for K-Pop content. Maybe an alcohol brand? Whoever thinks of something great, please let me know. I'll handle the legal side. Just kidding. Kind of.

It's evident how important and useful online K-Pop creative content is, but by how much? I want to discuss the importance of "fancams"—K-Pop fans uploading their own live videos of their favorite stars' performances. Despite their amateur connotation, fancams have been instrumental to idols' success. While TV-produced performances of idol groups usually focus on the entire performance, fancams focus on one particular person. As an extension of fandom culture, fancams allow the viewers to not only get a better view but also a detailed, enhanced experience.[177] The aforementioned girl group EXID was on the verge of disbandment due to poor commercial performances, until October 2014,

---

177 Seoul Kyungjae Shinmoon, "[#복세편살] <14> '오늘의 떡밥은 뭘까?' 아이돌계의 큰손 '직캠' 문화" [[#Boksaepyunsal] <14> "What's Today's Gossip?" Idol Industry's Big Hand, 'Fancam' Culture, *Naver*, August 19, 2019.

when a fancam of the member Hani dancing to their song, "Up & Down" became a viral sensation.[178]

Not only did that video gain exposure, but the song itself also resurfaced and climbed back up the charts until it peaked at number one on both streaming and TV music show charts. Girl group GFriend also surged in popularity after a fancam showed them performing live and falling down during an unfortunate rainstorm.[179] The members slip and fall a total of eight times but continue to get back up and keep performing, which led *TIME* magazine to commend GFriend on their efforts.[180] After this incident, the track in question, "Me Gustas Tu," also proceeded to sweep major year-end awards.

If it weren't for the fancam videographers, K-Pop fans may not know about both groups in the capacity they do today. As a big fan of Hani myself, I am grateful. Bless you, stranger.

As if they foresaw all of this, Mnet actually began to upload professionally recorded fancams focusing on each member of an idol group in early 2014, some of which have very high view counts. In fact, an official Mnet fancam of BTS's Jimin performing "Fake Love" for the 2018 comeback stage garnered a massive 103 million YouTube views, whereas the

---

178 *pharkil*, "[직캠/Fancam] 141008 EXID(하니) 위아래 @ 파주 한마음 위문공연" [[Fancam] 141008 EXID (Hani) Up & Down @ Paju Hanmaeum Consolation Performance], October 9, 2014, video, 3:15.

179 *smile -wA-*, "150905 여자친구(GFRIEND) - 오늘부터 우리는 (Me gustas tu) @인제 SBS 라디오 공개방송 직캠/Fancam by -wA-" [150905 GFRIEND - Starting Today We (Me Gustas Tu) @ Inje SBS Radio Public Show Fancam by -wA-], September 5, 2015, video, 4:02.

180 Helen Regan, "This Video of a K-Pop Singer Falling 8 Times in 1 Song Will Inspire You to Keep Going No Matter What," *TIME*, September 7, 2015.

full performance featuring all seven members sits at only 11 million.[181] This example further illustrates the importance of fancam content for both promoting the artist and pleasing the fans. More importantly, this is an example of the industry directly catering to what the fans want. If thou hast asked for Jimin, thou shalt receive Jimin!

With all this hype over K-Pop content, there was bound to be more attempts to formally investigate and "explain" it.

As a part of its *Explained* series, Netflix produced a documentary synopsis of the K-Pop phenomenon that featured both singers and experts.[182] Hulu's documentary that VICE produced explores the scandals behind K-Pop's glamorous appeal.[183] BBC produced a number of video reports covering idol production, SM Entertainment's strategy, trainee life, and the industry's drug and sex crimes.[184]

I notice both pros and cons with some of the documentaries. Yes, they are easy to follow and comprehend for the average viewer. Yet, once again, we consider the "dark side of K-Pop"

181 *M2*, "[MPD직캠] 방탄소년단 지민 직캠 4K 'FAKE LOVE' (BTS JI MIN FanCam) | @MCOUNTDOWN_2018.5.31" [MPD Fancam] BTS Jimin Fancam 4K 'Fake Love' (BTS JI MIN FanCam) | @Mcountdown_2018.5.31], May 31, 2018, video, 4:07; *Mnet K-POP*, "[BTS - Fake Love] Comeback Stage | M Countdown 180531 EP.572," May 31, 2018, video, 4:02.

182 "Explained," Netflix, last accessed March 30, 2020.

183 "K-POP Machine," Hulu, last accessed March 30, 2020.

184 *BBC Radio 1*, "K-Pop: Korea's Secret Weapon?" January 18, 2018, video, 27:28; "K-Pop Idols: Inside the Hit Factory," BBC, October 25, 2019, video, 60:00; *Koreaboo*, "'9 Muses of Star Empire' BBC Documentary," September 20, 2014, video, 47:34; *BBC News*, "The Dark Side of K-Pop Clubs - BBC News," June 25, 2019, video, 8:31.

issue. If such narratives are the first K-Pop-related resources that someone encounters, they'll undoubtedly develop a negative view of K-Pop.

This is a consistent problem in Western journalism; the writers and producers tend to focus on one negative aspect of K-Pop, such as referring to the entertainment companies' idol production system as a "factory."[185] Rarely do the media dive deeper into a legitimate history of the Korean music industry or sociocultural factors to give equal weight to the positive side. This is largely a cherry-picking strategy to tell a stigmatized, sensationalized view of K-Pop. Why not provide a more comprehensive picture and suggest some well-researched solutions to the posed issues?

At the end of the day, there is more than enough third-party K-Pop content for everyone to further boost their engagement with the phenomenon. As K-Pop grows and diversifies, so will the different approaches to consumption and innovation. One day, I'll revive my YouTube channel for K-Pop content. Stay tuned.

185 David Bevan, "Seoul Trained: Inside Korea's Pop Factory," *SPIN*, March 26, 2012.

OUTRO

——

As an avid social media user myself, I cannot stress enough the importance of online technology in the future of global entertainment. Both the technology and K-Pop industries evolve rapidly, so by the time you read this book, there may be a completely new online trend that further enhances the K-Pop experience. Just when I thought Instagram and Twitter were indispensable to entertainment, visual media in apps like Tiktok suggested a new creative outlet for both the artists and the fans. If artists and companies don't know how to properly utilize online platforms for publicity in today's climate, they're in for a tough time in an already overcrowded market.

The challenge remains for entertainment companies to integrate the newest technology into business decisions. Fans will also need to keep up if they really want to be on top of the latest hot topic. But at the end of the day, technology is just a facilitator for fan support. More applications and platforms imply that we just have more tools at our disposal to engage with K-Pop. I don't need to be active on every single app, but I appreciate my range of options for an enhanced experience.

These are convenient times to become a fan, so why not go out and explore?

PART 4

THE IDOL SYSTEM

Is there any word in the world that's more enchanting than being someone's 'idol'?

- **G-DRAGON OF BIGBANG**

IN A 2008 ARENA INTERVIEW[186]

---

186 Hyeseon Chae, "'아이돌'에 대한 지드래곤의 생각" [G-Dragon's Thoughts on "Idol"], *Joongangilbo*, February 17, 2017.

INTRO

———

You're now going to learn what it's like to embark on the once-in-a-lifetime journey of becoming a K-Pop idol and all of what it entails. You'll have a legion of fans at your fingertips, sing and dance your heart out onstage, buy a fancy building in Gangnam, and be financially set for life. Exciting, right?

Actually, let's rewind a bit. How does one become a K-Pop idol? Better yet, how and where do companies find the talented youth who will carry on the global phenomenon?

After countless hours of teaching myself dance routines in front of my laptop, I wanted to take it to the next level. So, as a high school sophomore in Korea in 2008, I enrolled in a famous dance studio at the time called Winners Dance. I sought the most cost-friendly option with maximum instructor time and somehow ended up in a class called "Audition Prep Class," a precursor to today's "K-Pop Class." It was a nice break away from studying for the SAT, but the twenty-nine other kids in the class seemed a lot sterner and more vigorous than I was. One day, an instructor asked, "How many of you are planning on auditioning to be an idol?"

Everyone in the room raised their hand except for me and one other kid. Ten years later, I don't think I've seen any of those classmates on TV or YouTube. I reckon the oldest classmate in his early twenties at the time is probably married with kids now. Or, maybe not. Keep hustling, old man.

This is going to be an in-depth section—it's another one of those topics that could very well constitute its own book or dissertation. So, sit down (or walk around, if you read like that) and hang tight for the roller-coaster of a ride that is the journey to becoming an idol.

CHAPTER 15

THE TRAINEE

———

Idol production is the heart of the global K-Pop phenomenon. The idols you see in fancy music videos are the final polished culmination of years of systemized training and carefully planned production. Every idol starts as some form of "trainee" in the company, during which he or she is trained to become an idol for about three years.[187] The companies invest an average of 14.02 million Korean won (roughly $11,820 USD) per year on each trainee.[188] For the top K-Pop companies, this amount could reach up to 100 million won (roughly $84,390 USD).[189]

The trainee curriculum is highly structured thanks to decades of successful strategies from top companies. First,

---

187 Shinwoo Kang, "[썸_레터] 치열한 '연습생 입시' 세계…"14살은 늦었어요"" [[Some_Letter] The Fierce World of 'Trainee Entrance Exams'…'Age 14 Is Too Late'], *Seoul Gyeongjae*, June 3, 2019.

188 Korea Creative Content Agency (KOCCA), "2019 대중문화산업 실태조사보고서" [2019 Pop Culture/Art Industry Research Report], Naju, KOCCA: 2020.

189 Hayeon Kim, "'YG 보석함', 방예담 속한 데뷔조 1순위 연습생 TREASURE A팀… "1년에 최소 1억지원"" ['YG Treasure Box', #1 Priority Debut Group Treasure A Team Including Bang Yedam… 'Minimum 100 Million Won Support Yearly], *Topstarnews*, November 16, 2018.

the companies recruit trainees either through formal auditions or "street casting," as some companies like to do, in which casting directors scout venues like a concert hall, a school entrance, or literally the streets to recruit potential future idols. Minji Kim, former casting director of SM Entertainment, even decided to travel to China on a whim despite barely speaking Mandarin in the hope of scouting Chinese talent.[190] If such a journey leads to the company producing a global idol star, I suppose it's worth it.

You may be thinking, "Maybe it would be best for a prospective trainee to chill around hotspots like the company buildings hoping for a director to notice." No one should do this; it would be largely futile and also disturb the employees.

The formal audition processes depend on the company; for example, JYP Entertainment occasionally hosts special auditions for a specific team like a boy band, while SM Entertainment holds weekly Saturday auditions that attract roughly 500 people.[191] Today, some companies even host fifteen-second auditions on Tiktok.[192] Even if an auditionee passes and is accepted, the trainee pool is flooded; in 2019, the Korean Ministry of Culture, Sports, and Tourism (MCST) reported that there were a total of 1,204 singer trainees out of a 1,671

---

190 Yoonsun Huh, "아이돌을 만드는 사람들 <2>" [People That Create the Idols <2>]. *Allure*, May 15, 2016.

191 Sang-geun Yoon, "JYP, 차기 보이그룹 오디션 "2008년생까지 지원 가능"" [JYP, Next Boy Group Audition 'Allows up to 2008-Born Applicants'], *Starnews*, October 1, 2019; Haeseung Jeon, "SM엔터테인먼트 오디션, 매주 500명 넘는 지원자 몰린다" [SM Entertainment Audition, Attracts over 500 Applicants Weekly], *ChannelYes*, 2011.

192 Kang, "The Fierce World," 2019.

total (including actors, models, and comedians), a rise from 1,079 trainees in 2017.[193] These are all your competitors, or possibly, future groupmates. For now, you must outshine them all. Even if you're recruited as a trainee, there are no guarantees that you'll become a star.

Companies usually recruit trainees in their early teens, but ages can vary depending on the company's needs. Many auditions have a maximum age limit of nineteen. Trainee times can also vary; many current idols trained for more than five years.[194] Jung Eunji of Apink was a trainee for only two months before debuting at seventeen, whereas it took Jihyo of TWICE over ten years to debut at eighteen.[195] The trainee time largely depends on the group's image and dynamic, the company's strategy, and the trainee's unique talents. Unfortunately, a lengthy training period does not guarantee a debut either; the company may cut you from the team at the last minute.

So, what exactly is the company is looking for in a trainee? Well, according to my interview with Darren Won, former Section Chief of Artist Development at Source Music (which BigHit Entertainment since acquired), the relevant advice for all potential trainees is to be cognizant of what their strongest

---

193 KOCCA, "2019 Pop Culture," 2020.

194 Kang, "The Fierce World," 2019.

195 Jinhee Sung, "[HD인터뷰] 에이핑크 정은지, "보컬 트레이너? 이젠 가수로!"" [[HD Interview] Apink Jung Eunji, 'Vocal Trainer? Now I'm a Singer!], *Pickcon*, May 19, 2011; Yeojin Jung, "'뭉뜬' 트와이스 지효 "연습생 10년, 그만두려 회사 안 나가기도"" ['*Moongddeun*' TWICE Jihyo 'Trainee for 10 Years, Even Stopped Going in Order to Quit], *Joongangilbo*, October 25, 2017.

talents are and to have as much audition experience as possible. Usually, the company is looking for a particular position in a group, most importantly main vocals or image. It's important to be aware of recent idol trends and the company's known predilections; have there been recent girl groups with sharp-piercing power vocals or softer, mellow tones? If you're thinking about auditioning to become a K-Pop idol, make sure to not only practice but also do your research!

Once an aspiring trainee has passed the official audition, the company will likely present them with a binding trainee contract, as 81.9 percent of companies do.[196] The MCST officially enacted a standardized contract template in September 2019, and some of the main provisions address a three-year fixed date, trainees' privacy and human rights, company's right to terminate should the trainee not progress, trainee's right to terminate for sexual assault, as well as a confidentiality provision. Of course, they can amend the contract as needed.[197]

Some of the contract provisions are obvious common sense; the trainees should try their best to learn and improve, and the companies should ensure they get their investments' worth. However, you may be wondering why human rights and protection against sexual assault are literally written into the contract.

Unfortunately, the fact that the government incorporated them into the contract template implies that trainee abuse and labor violations have occurred. Despite the contract

196 KOCCA, "2019 Pop Culture," 2020.

197 Ministry of Culture, Sports, and Tourism (MCST), "대중문화 연습생 표준 계약서" [Pop Culture/Arts Trainee Standard Contract], MCST: September 9, 2019.

reform, trainee protections are ultimately just a standard and not word-for-word requirements. I sincerely hope that the trainee teens—who are very young and still developing—will not experience abuse while pursuing their dreams.

Once the trainee agrees to and signs the contract, they're now officially en route to becoming an idol. They've impressed the audition judges, talked at length with management—and probably their parents and an attorney—over the contract, and are excited to begin their new life as an idol trainee.

What's next?

Let's break this down a bit. As Won explained to me, the artist development team oversees all trainee activity, from recruiting and management to training schedules and evaluations. The specifics include things like teaching trainee etiquette, coordinating stylists for possible TV filming, and conducting monthly evaluations.[198] Directors and managers like Won would plan your daily routine in conjunction with the relevant coaches. Won says:

The importance of training the future idol star lies in serving as an educator role for the youth. Transparent communication and emotions are key and serve as a challenge for both sides.

198 Bosun Hwang, "아이돌을 만드는 사람들 ② 류재아" [People That Create the Idols 2) Ryu Jeah], *Singles*, February 15, 2018.

For trainees at most companies, their schedule generally consists of dance, acting, vocal, and foreign language lessons as well as physical training. These lessons start early in the morning and can possibly last past midnight. If the trainees are currently attending middle or high school, they'll start their lessons right after class ends in the afternoon. Any time without scheduled classes are for individual or group practice to prepare for the monthly evaluations. Social media use and dating are absolutely prohibited, and trainees must not only exercise but also manage their food intake as the company will periodically check in regarding their physical appearance.[199] Since I need my daily dosage of Instagram, if I were a trainee, I'd be making a huge sacrifice on top of the already rigorous training sessions!

If you're an older reader, think about how you were as a teenager. You probably weren't particularly stable and were very curious about the world. The idols who make it to the top must endure their difficult teenage years in addition to their training programs.

I caught up with Nayoon Kim, a Top 9 finalist on the first season of *K-POP Star*, former idol trainee, and current social media influencer. According to Kim, not much has changed in the ten years since she was a trainee:

---

199 Seulbi Lee, Yoojin Sung, and Soojung Yoon. "하루 17시간 춤, 노래 연습…'마음의 병' 돌볼 시간도 없다" [Daily 17-Hour Dance, Vocal Practice... No Time to Attend to the 'Heart's Disease'], *Chosunilbo*, December 20, 2017.

You're at the bottom of the pack. You have to prove your skills to gain both the company's and the fellow trainees' respect to make your way to the debut group.

Imagine all of the petty high school drama plus the internal politics of a strict job atmosphere. Trainees must work hard and hustle while handling the social, mental, and physical stress that comes with the trainee environment. Being a trainee really is like working for the company, as the trainees may transfer between companies should their current one have no plans for them. But, if you're lucky, management will favor you; Kim elaborates,

Sometimes, trainees who were closer to the management and teachers would be favored. Of course, there's favoritism within most companies.[200]

With ample skills and some luck involved, a trainee may finally debut and become an idol. However, even if they don't make it, plenty of former idol trainees succeed as TV personalities, solo artists, and YouTubers while others leave the entertainment industry.

---

200 "Kpopalypse Interview - Kim Nayoon," *KPOPALYPSE* (blog), April 8, 2020. Accessed April 23, 2020.

In recent years, company executives and TV producers decided it would be a fantastic idea to shed light on the trainee life. TV stations like Mnet started to produce reality shows featuring the trainees competing, and the whole world will be watching who makes it to the debuting group. The stakes are very high; they must beat out the other contestants and also capture the audience's support in the process. Even if you don't make it, decent public exposure can always work to your benefit in the industry.

Korean TV shows such as *WIN* (2013), *SIXTEEN* (2015), and *Finding Momoland* (2016) depicted trainees competing to debut with their specific companies. From the company's perspective, this is a great opportunity to promote the group even before it's actually finalized because they can gradually build a fandom and gain exposure to a large audience. For more recent shows like *I-LAND* (2020), either the Korean and sometimes even international audience would vote for their preferred member(s) to debut, or the judge(s) would have the final say in selecting the debuting trainees.

In contrast, the *Produce 101* series (2016-2019) invited 100 trainees from various Korean companies (later including Japanese and Chinese). Each trainee contestant would be ranked from 1 to 100. The goal for the contestant was to make it into the top 11 or 12 (depending on the season) to form a project supergroup. They would return to their respective companies after promotional activities. The series ended in 2019, as the producers were guilty of vote-rigging and fraudulent tactics to give unfair advantages to certain contestants over others.[201] *Produce 101* allowed many trainees to shine and progress a step closer to stardom but ultimately left a bitter taste in the audience's mouths, including mine. If I were ranked number 12 and missed out on the top 11 set to debut, I would be not only be devastated but furious upon news of fraud.

Nonetheless, an important byproduct of the *Produce 101* series is the strengthening of the audience's and fandoms' participatory culture. Not only do the fans cheer, but they can actually participate in the process of creating the project group as the "nation's producers." In the *Produce 101* context, this strengthens the fans' emotional bond to particular trainees and leads fans to urge their friends, family, and even strangers to vote for their specific favorite trainees.

TV reality shows have started to allow international auditionees; over 3,000 people from fifty different countries applied to take part in Mnet's 2019 reality show *UHSN: Ticket to K-POP*.[202] Now, trainees have to compete not only with Koreans but with everyone from around the world who's set on becoming a K-Pop idol. Things are getting even more competitive.

Despite changes such as this, as Kim mentioned, the idol trainee system has largely remained the same in recent history. A lot of financial and human resources are invested in creating

201 Donggun Kwak, "검찰, '프로듀스 101 순위조작' 안준영 PD에 징역 3년 구형" [Prosecution, 'Produce 101 Ranking Fraud' Demands 3-Year Sentence for Producer Ahn Joonyoung], *MBCNews*, May 12, 2020.

202 Sookyung Kim, "BTS 같은 스타 되고 싶어 'K팝 유학' 옵니다" ['K-Pop Abroad Education' to Become a Star like BTS], *Chosunilbo*, August 1, 2019.

the future idol stars. Business strategies have changed to cater to a more global K-Pop audience, but they all still begin with scouting the right talent and vigorously training them to possibly spearhead a group one day. Beneath the glamorous K-Pop performances and videos, thousands of trainees and countless aspiring trainees struggle every day to reach their dreams. For the few who are chosen to debut, their years of trainee life may pay off. Let's find out how.

CHAPTER 16

THE DEBUT

———

200 DAYS UNTIL DEBUT

After months and possibly years of consistent practicing, a trainee has finally received the green light to join the upcoming debuting idol group. They'll debut along with several others in the company's newest project on a designated date.

So, what's next? When will the group record a banger of a hit debut single? Will they have fans waiting for them outside all the time? Most importantly, when's the first paycheck coming in?

Let's hang on for a second and get to the formalities first. The trainee-turned-idol needs to sign a new exclusive, full-time contract with their company.[203] This is where things get real.

Until recently, there was no uniform standard for required provisions in or the duration of an artist's contract. Artists

———

203 Korea Creative Content Agency (KOCCA), "대중문화 예술인 표준 전속 계약서" [Pop Culture Artist Standard Exclusive Contract], last accessed May 9, 2020.

were bound to their contracts and held financially accountable when they generated insufficient returns on their company's investments. Idol group JYJ's lawsuit against SM Entertainment was a pivotal incident that led to contract reform. In 2009, JYJ—then known as TVXQ—filed for an injunction against the exclusive contract that bound artists for an astounding thirteen years to SM Entertainment. As a result, the Korean Fair Trade Commission enacted a standard contract for the artist-company relationship, limiting the suggested duration to seven years.[204] Hence, most idol groups today are contractually obligated until the seven-year mark, upon which negotiations, contract renewals, or disbandment are possible.

As an aside, the seven-year hurdle is a major challenge, if an idol group doesn't re-sign, many disband or have members leave. Girl groups like Apink re-sign and continue while others like SISTAR disband.

For male idol groups that are comprised of most if not all Korean members, the South Korean mandatory military service is an added hurdle. Because the service lasts around a year and a half, trainees can freeze their contract until their discharge, upon which the duration would resume. However, the interpretation of what activities fall under the seven-year obligation differs among companies, leading to lawsuits from unhappy artists.[205]

---

204 Jungyeon Lee, "억울한 JYJ...아직 끝나지 않은 전쟁" [Unfair for JYJ... the War Continues], *DongA*, July 3, 2014.

205 Wooyoung Cho, "[연예기자24시] 제2의 노예계약 분쟁, 터질 게 터졌다" [[24hour Celebrity Reporter] the 2nd Slave Contract Dispute, Finally Breaks Out], *StarToday*, November 29, 2014.

Trainees must be cognizant of their rights and obligations as a legitimate artist of the company before signing a contract. Once they do, it's officially en route now. It's happening—they have a fair and beneficial contract in one hand and microphone in the other!

100 DAYS UNTIL DEBUT

As a trainee approaches their official debut date as a K-Pop idol, the company will spend a lot of effort into hyping up the crowd. The trainee will take part in endless videos and photoshoots for marketing material and teasers that introduce the group, the members, and the album concept to the world. Through the teasers, the audience can get a better sense of the group members' distinct appearances and personalities. If a particular individual member attracts attention, the company can use the data to implement in future promotional strategies. Word spreads fast on social media thanks to the potential or existing fandom, so companies always monitor public opinion.

In 2012, SM Entertainment spent approximately 100 days promoting idol group EXO before their official debut through individual video teasers showcasing each member's talent. They even assigned each member a "superpower," like time travel or water bending. In the process, SM Entertainment created EXO's own universe—as well as intellectual property— to alert the world of the group's unique concept and theme before their official debut.[206] Some companies utilize social

---

206 Myungseok Kang, "아이돌 그룹, 이렇게 탄생한다" [Idol Group, This Is How They're Born], *Hankookilbo*, May 27, 2015.

media platforms to have their upcoming idols star in diverse content such as busking (street performances), pre-debut documentaries, and dance covers.

Prior to the official debut in May 2018, girl group (G)I-DLE partnered with social media channel Dingo to launch a series of YouTube videos featuring members bungee jumping and dancing in cities around the world.[207] Upon the group's debut, I could already identify each member and supported them even more.

Perhaps the term "debut" is flexible because upcoming idols technically introduce themselves before their official debut single. However, nothing is set in stone yet, so they must keep on guard and hustle. Their collaborations with the photographer, fashion stylist, and visual director are critical because they essentially craft how they're presented to the world.[208] It's best to flaunt their biggest strengths and most charming facial expressions in these previews—they dance, smile, and pose their heart out. One day, their life-sized decals may be all over the streets and posters while their faces will be on the walls in restaurants or even on tall buildings for large-scale brand endorsements.

On that note, consider how many professional human resources the idol production has required thus far.

207 *Dingo*, "걸그룹 데뷔를 앞둔 한 소녀에게 어마무시한 일이 일어났다?! 데뷔 전부터 살벌한(?) 신인 걸그룹 '아이들'!" [Something Scary Happened to a Girl Nearing a Girl Group Debut?! Fierce(?) before Debut, Rookie Girl Group 'Idle!'], April 26, 2018, video, 6:37; *dingo music,* "2018 Idol Dance Medley (G)I-DLE," April 20, 2018, video, 1:58.

208 Yoonsun Huh, "아이돌을 만드는 사람들 <1>" [People That Create the Idols <1>], *Allure*, May 14, 2016.

In addition to gearing up for their debut, trainees also need to record their music. The directors and executives have already discussed the plans for the group's music in numerous meetings, so they head to the studio. The duration of the recording session will depend on their skills and position in the group; for example, if they're the main or lead vocalist, they'll likely sing a bigger portion of the song.

Here's a rundown of key music-related positions for your reference:

- **Main Vocalist**: Sings the main chorus and/or the important highlight parts.

- **Lead or Sub Vocalist**: Sings important highlights, distinct ad-libs, etc. Main and Lead used to be interchangeable but are now usually separate due to a higher general skill level for all group members.

- **Main Dancer**: Takes the lead in formation for the dance choreography. May have a dance solo and is often center stage. May either be a vocalist or a rapper.

- **Rapper**: K-Pop idol music generally includes a rap part. An English-speaking or dance-focused member usually has this role. A few embark on solo rap careers.

- **Music Producer**: There's been an increase in talented self-producing idols who do so from the onset. Many idols have successfully produced and led their groups' musical direction to mainstream success, like G-Dragon, Zico, RM, Jeon Soyeon, and Woozi.

So, do the idols get to choose their roles? What if someone wants to be the main vocalist and the main dancer so they can have the most stage time?

During the training sessions and monthly evaluations, the artist development team, coaches, and upper management all chime in on the composition and dynamic of a group based on the trainees' skills. They decide what kind of music genres the idol group will draw from and whether the group will be vocals-focused and skilled in a capella or if the members will instead concentrate on intricate dance choreography and performance. These conversations are at the intersection of business strategy and musical direction. The company will decide, and the trainees shall follow.

Of course, K-Pop cannot be complete without the dance choreography. Companies frequently contact well-known global choreographers like Kyle Hanagami, Parris Goebel, and Keone Madrid, as well as Korean choreographers including Lia Kim, Bae Yoonjung, and Choi Young-jun for collaboration. The ideal choreography would not only capture the artist and songs' image and themes but also have a catchy aspect—a movement, formation, or repeated signals—that perfects K-Pop's audiovisual experience.

After rigorous recording and dance sessions involving both harsh and encouraging words from the management, it's time to film the corresponding music video. Once the music video is uploaded to YouTube, everyone around the world can see the result of the group's hard work.

The music video not only presents the music and performance but also the idol's image and album's theme. GFriend's debut single "Glass Bead" showcased six schoolgirls dancing in a gymnasium and attending class to present an approachable, "girlfriend-like" image. In contrast, BLACKPINK's "Boombayah" portrays four girls on motorbikes who later dance in a classroom with scattered, upside-down desks for a more rebellious persona.[209]

The video may release before or with the single release, depending on the marketing strategy; do they want to tease the audience even further by releasing the video before the song or give them what they want simultaneously?

It doesn't really matter. Either way, the group's Debut Day is coming.

DEBUT DAY

It's time! The group's debut album containing the lead single just dropped today. You should wish them congratulations on the hard work. Fortunately, this is just the beginning. Where are they headed next?

Depending on the company, the idol will perform at the group's official debut showcase, usually hosted at a concert hall with journalists and fans. They'll also perform on music programs on Korean TV networks, either live or pre-recorded. There are currently six different TV shows—each on a different channel and day of the week. Whether they'll perform for six consecutive days or not depends on your company's

---

209 1theK, "[MV] GFRIEND _ Glass Bead," November 2, 2017, video, 3:43; BLACKPINK, "BLACKPINK - Boombayah M/V," August 8, 2016, video, 4:03.

influence in the industry and business strategy. Either way, they're hyped! And slightly nervous.

On TV music programs, major companies like YG Entertainment or SM Entertainment can negotiate for a rookie idol group to perform their entire single, pre-record the performance for better quality, or even perform more than one song. Smaller, newer companies lacking a position in the market do not enjoy this privilege. If such a small company succeeds in booking their group a slot on the show, the program may even ask the group to trim a verse from the single and corresponding performance.[210] Differences like this serve as a reminder that the K-Pop industry is tightly-knit and large companies and broadcast networks dominate. Rookie idols don't have a lot of power, either, unless they've built a solid following prior to debut. Their most pertinent goal, nonetheless, is to perform to their fullest onstage. With the K-Pop talent pool increasing every year, success is contingent upon fulfilling both their own and the company's obligations to the fullest.

Nowadays, the company even communicates directly to a group's fandom by establishing the official color, merchandise, and upcoming schedule. The more unified the fandom, the more buzz the group will have going forward in promotions and sales.

For a sophomore single or album, the process is largely similar to the timeline outlined above. When the company establishes the album theme and musical direction, the idols and the supporting team get to work immediately on another round

---

210 Kang, *"Idol Group,"* 2015.

of song producing and recording, teaser video filming and photoshoots, album and art design, dance choreography, and rigorous marketing on social media and TV, all according to the business strategy. The idols will be constantly traveling—likely all over the world—to get the group's name out there.

With the right talent, efforts, and luck, an idol will get to live their dream—the adoration of fans around the world, financial wealth, and an industry legacy for the upcoming generations.

Right after their debut, however, they'll need to dedicate 120 percent every time they're on stage—you never know who will be watching. The ideal scenario would be that the idols' exposure and popularity grow bigger with each album, gradually solidifying both the idols' and the company's position in the domestic market. The debut marks the beginning of this process, but there's no telling how long the process will take. There are so many factors and paths that account for a K-Pop idol's success. In my opinion, an idol's career should be a marathon, not a sprint. So many idols have come and gone with hit songs and unmatched talents, but only a handful stay active and relevant in the industry.

CHAPTER 17

THE BREAKTHROUGH

————

Alright, the group is going to make it! The company will build and elevate the idol's career to the top. But how will they do this?

First, they need a breakthrough where things get big for the artist, the company, and the fans. Every rookie idol's dream is the breakthrough moment, whether it's reaching number one on online streaming charts, winning the number one song of the week on TV music programs, or even just gaining positive recognition on social media. Given the over-saturation of idols in the Korean music industry today, the barrier to commercial and mainstream breakthrough has been getting harder to overcome. Despite its difficulty, there are still several strategies that can help artists achieve their breakthrough moment:

- **A strong company/label:** A rookie group from a major company, especially SM, YG, JYP, and BigHit Enter-tainment, is bound to generate attention long before the official debut. The fans get excited for each group announcement because they know those companies do a great job of guaranteeing skills and performance from the talent, as fans have seen with their successful past and present artists in the industry. The time it takes to achieve a breakthrough may be a bit shorter for these rookies, though it's not guaranteed. WINNER and BLACKPINK from YG Entertainment hold the records for the shortest time from debut date to reaching number one on a Korean TV music program with six and seven days, respectively.[211]

- **A hit single:** The JYP-produced Wonder Girls' single "Tell Me" (2007) phenomenon swept the entire nation of Korea and spawned an array of cover dance videos and performances. The retro-inspired melody, catchy chorus, and an easy-to-follow dance routine appealed to the entire nation; basically, everyone could do the simple but trendy finger points, waves, and chest pops. For a K-Pop song to be a massive hit, especially for a rookie artist, there must be mainstream appeal.[212]

- **Viral/Meme Content:** Girl group Crayon Pop released "Bar Bar Bar" in 2013, which catapulted the relatively unknown group to international fame. The song's unique and catchy chorus in conjunction with the group's comedic appeal and jumping dance even

211 MASHIHO, "아이돌 그룹이 공중파 음악방송 1위까지 걸린기간 2018 최신본" [The Amount of Time It Took for Idol Groups to Reach #1 on Terrestrial Music TV Programs 2018 New Edition], T-Story, last modified 2018, last accessed May 2, 2020.

212 Hyeonmok Jung, "전국에 '텔미' 열풍" ['Tell Me' Syndrome All over Nation], *Joongangilbo*, November 6, 2007.

earned Lady Gaga's support.[213] However, unless a song is incredibly catchy to a wide mainstream audience like "Bar Bar Bar" or "Gangnam Style," it's difficult to rely solely on the music and performance for the breakthrough.

- **One-member Strategy**: Companies often designate a certain member to star in variety TV shows, during which they would participate in comedy, singing, MCing, or take the lead in musical direction for mainstream exposure. Although the desired effect is to boost the entire group's popularity, constantly promoting that one member may unintentionally deflect the attention away from the group and draw it to the individual for a solo career. Hyuna of group 4minute was the main figurehead of the group, so journalists frequently heralded 4minute as "Hyuna and girls" until disbandment. As you can see, this particular strategy has its drawbacks.[214]

- **A Korean fandom**: A tightly knit Korean fandom can help generate the initial traction needed for a group to hit the ground running. When loyal fans mass stream the single and purchase physical albums in bulk, the song will gradually rise up in both online charts and TV music program charts.

---

213 Sejung Lee, "크레용팝 활동 재개? 엘린 "다시 태어나도 크레용팝"" [Crayon Pop to Resume Activity? Elin 'Crayon Pop Even after I'm Reborn'], *BizTribune*, December 23, 2019.

214 Yeonji Kim, "'배우 선언' 포미닛 전 멤버들, '현아와 아이들' 이미지 벗을까" ['Actress Declaration' 4Minute's Former Members, Can They Leave 'Hyuna and Girls' Image Behind], *JTBC News*, March 7, 2017.

Naturally, the Korean media will report on it. With more buzz about them, the idols will get invited to TV variety programming that appeals to wider national audiences. More exposure to the public will further strengthen commercial performance.

- **An international fandom**: Since K-Pop now has a strong global presence, having an international fandom is just as crucial as a domestic one. Newer K-Pop groups have even gained greater attention overseas first and then won over the Korean audience later. More on this in the section, "The Fandom Culture."

- **Social Media**: As we discussed in Part 3 of this book, there are myriad social media strategies for K-Pop groups, and it would be foolish for a company not to utilize social media marketing to promote a rookie artist today.

All of these strategies are just guidelines and formulas that the companies have implemented in some form during the past few decades. Of course, the standard for what constitutes a breakthrough varies according to the company's goals. Depending on the group and their talents, the company may want a specific path for the idols. They may push for their idols to become Korea's top K-Pop group and even make it to Oricon, Billboard, and the Grammys. Other times, companies are less hopeful and will be satisfied if their idols are even recognized when walking down the street. It all depends on a variety of mitigating factors.

So, what happens after an idol makes it? We have quite a few feel-good anecdotes throughout K-Pop's history as idols achieve commercial success for the first time despite obstacles such as disbandment or financial hardship. For example, idol stars like Sunmi and Sejeong, who both lived in impoverished settings before becoming idols, could finally support their families as they became big stars after their respective breakthrough years.[215] In 2019, boy band NU'EST finally achieved number one on domestic TV music programs seven long years after debuting in 2012.[216]

We'll later take a further look at the three elements required for a successful commercial breakthrough in the next three parts: the music, business strategy, and fandoms. There will be a lot more info to digest regarding how they all come together, but the big picture is straightforward: there are a lot of fish in a small pond. Becoming the largest fish may be the first goal, but maintaining a solid position in the K-Pop pond for an extended period is much more worthwhile. But up next, we'll be diving into some deeper discussions on the downsides of the idol system. Get ready.

215 Yoonsun Cho, "'토크몬' 선미, 가슴 아픈 가족사 "父 돌아가신 후 이선미로 개명"" ['Talkmon' Sunmi, Heart-Wrenching Family Story 'Changed Name to Lee Sunmi after Father's Passing'], *Chosunilbo*, February 6, 2018; "세정, 가슴아픈 가족사고백 "형편 어려워 결식아동 급식카드로 끼니 해결"" [Sejung, Heart-Wrenching Family Story Confession 'Had to Eat with Meal Vouchers for Low-Income Youth'], *Joongdoilbo*, March 2, 2018.

216 Hyojin Im, "뉴이스트 'BET BET' 공중파 첫 1위 "러브에게 감사"" [NU'EST 'Bet Bet' First #1 Win on Terrestrial TV 'Thanks to the Loves'], *SeoulEN*, May 11, 2019.

CHAPTER 18

K-POP'S SOCIAL ISSUES AND NEED FOR REFORM

—

As most of you are aware, the entertainment industry, in general, is far from a utopia. This section won't be particularly uplifting, but it's still important. In this chapter, I will present several underlying issues in South Korea and the need for further industry-wide—and possibly nation-wide—reform. However, please keep in mind that all of the issues I discuss here are not exclusive to K-Pop. Negatively viewing K-Pop exclusively because of the downsides would be unfair and stigmatizing because entertainment industries everywhere have their own similar pitfalls.

CONTRACT DISPUTES—DURATION

It costs roughly 500 million Korean won (roughly $451,009 USD) to fund six weeks of an idol group's debut promotional activities, with a bulk for the music video (~$135,302 USD) and viral marketing costs (~$94,711 USD).[217] Unsurprisingly, companies want to legally protect themselves when making such a large investment. Let's head back to the discussion regarding an idol's contract.

Prior to the standard contract, a 2010 FTC survey reported forty-seven out of ninety (52.2 percent) underage celebrities had contracted with an entertainment company for over ten years.[218] Thankfully, the standard contract that the government implemented in 2009 and that the FTC and MCST have since amended reduced that length to seven years. Today, most industry companies use this amended contract; however, even after the enactment, what happens during the standard seven years and how to interpret the contract is still up for debate. Why do contract disputes occur, and are they the end-all-be-all for both parties? Case-specific scenarios continue to challenge whether a government-enacted standard is, in fact, effective in balancing the power dynamic between the company and artists. Let's dive in.

The 2014 lawsuit from boy band B.A.P. against their company, TS Entertainment, challenged the unfairness of the seven-year requirement. B.A.P. argued that unbeknownst to them, TS wrote their contract to expire seven years *after* B.A.P released their first album instead of a seven-year expiration from the signed date. So, the time spent on producing

217 Gunwoo Kim, "아이돌 한명 키우는데 얼마? 데뷔활동만 5억원" [How Much to Raise One Idol? Debut Promotions Cost 500 Million Won], *Joongangilbo*, October 2, 2015.

218 Wooyoung Cho, "제2의 노예계약 분쟁, 터질 게 터졌다" [The 2nd Slave Contract Dispute, about Time It Happened], *StarToday*, November 29, 2014.

an album—which could last several years—would not be included in the contractual seven years.

B.A.P. and TS eventually reached a mutual agreement and the group made a comeback the next year. Unfortunately, they later disbanded after failed negotiations.[219] I think B.A.P. could have been even more popular had company disputes not hindered their momentum.

As a counterexample, boy band EXO and SM Entertainment's contract will last a total of ten years, from 2012 to 2022, because an addendum provision extends the duration another three years after the standard seven. Both parties likely reached a mutual agreement pertaining to the addendum provision, leaving flexible wiggle room for global activities that may not be included in the standard seven years.[220] Flexible communication between both parties is required for a healthy mutual relationship, especially during contract negotiations and renewals. The companies should secure their financial investments while treating and managing the artists fairly.

CONTRACT DISPUTES—PHYSICAL ABUSE

On a different note regarding contracts, in 2018, when idol band The Eastlight sued producers for physical abuse, the effectiveness of the standard contract came under public

---

219 Soyoung Park, "B.A.P, 월드투어에 소송과 복귀까지..7년 징크스 끝 결국 해체" [B.A.P, from World Tour to Lawsuit to Comeback... Eventual Disbandment after 7 Year Jinx], *OSEN*, February 18, 2019.

220 Jiyoung Hwang, "엑소에겐 없는 '마의 7년'" [No 7-Year Tribulation for EXO], *Joongangilbo*, February 11, 2019.

scrutiny once again. To make matters even worse, all of the members were minors. Fortunately, the accused producers received jail sentences in 2020.[221] This case led to questions about whether the contract sufficiently protected the necessary human rights for K-Pop idols; despite an explicit provision meant to protect minors' physical and mental health, that clearly didn't happen in this situation. According to an anonymous entertainment executive in a news report, there are technically no repercussions for not complying with the standard contract.[222] Ugh!

CONTRACT DISPUTES—TRADEMARKS

The last example we'll look at has to do with trademarks, which are often a topic of contention, either when an artist sues for termination or nullification of a contract or the duration has expired.

In 2016, five members of the boy band BEAST, produced by Cube Entertainment, were not allowed to retain the group name when they decided to sign with a new company after their contract with Cube expired. Cube had legal rights to all of BEAST's trademarks, and the two parties did not reach a negotiation settlement to use the trademarks. The members decided to start anew under the group name HIGHLIGHT, leaving all BEAST-related terms, logos, and memories

---

221 Soojung Im, "보이밴드 '더이스트라이트' 폭행 묵인 기획사 회장 집유 확정" [Agency CEO Silent over Boy Band 'The Eastlight' Assault Is Confirmed House Arrest], *Yonhap News*, March 26, 2020.

222 Yoojin Lee, ""안 지켜도 그만"…허울뿐인 표준계약서에 멍드는 '연예인 인권'" ['No Worries for Noncompliance' … 'Celebrity Human Rights' Damaged over a Silhouette of a Standard Contract], *Kyunghyang*, October 23, 2018.

behind. After Cube had announced the creation of an entirely new three-member BEAST—later confirmed a rumor—the role of trademarks in the K-Pop industry resurfaced.[223]

Legal conflicts like trademark disputes remind us that at the end of the day, the artists and company have a business relationship—quite often nothing more and nothing less. It's imprudent to bash the companies for all aspects one may deem subjectively unfair for the artists—don't forget K-Pop is a business. However, when concerned voices are speaking out consistently over a particular legal issue, it's not a stretch to call for social reforms. I do believe that a family-type relationship between artist and company would definitely be possible for everyone given the right reforms.

ONLINE BULLYING AND MENTAL ILLNESS
Trigger warning re: suicide in this section.

Being an idol is a challenging job not only for the physical toil but also for the mental stress that accompanies it. Think about it—the entire world watches what you do and will either cheer or criticize you when they feel like it. Korean online forums and portals have long been the subject of scholarly curiosity due to their history of malicious commenting. In Korea particularly, celebrities are held to a higher standard of behavior, and even slight mistakes can result in a barrage of hostile online comments. Especially when the nation is on edge about a major issue, such as the coronavirus or

223 Seungjoon Yang, "'비스트'를 비스트라 부르지 못하고… K팝의 그늘" [Can't Call BEAST 'BEAST'… K-Pop's Shadow], *Hankookilbo*, February 26, 2017.

heightened South Korea-Japan tensions, online citizens, or "netizens," don't hesitate to engage in outright criticism of what they deem unacceptable behavior.

The root of the issue is the anonymous commenting culture on Korean forums, social media platforms, and search engines like Naver and Daum. Since netizens are free to comment without hesitation because their real identities are hidden, pretty nasty and critical comments are plentiful. Korea is well-known for having enacted an official cyber defamation law that has held malicious commenters both civilly and criminally liable, yet debates surrounding reform have ensued.[224] This isn't just a K-Pop problem; anyone can become the target of online bullying or doxing—celebrities, politicians, and even civilians.

Idols Sulli and Goo Hara, close friends who the online community viciously criticized for their respective personal beliefs and scandals, both died by suicide just one month apart in 2019. Online commenters and journalists alike had criticized Sulli over the years for her nonconformist views and activities regarding women's societal standards as well as for her relationship with rapper Choiza who was fourteen years her senior.[225] Goo had been involved in a blackmail scandal and legal battle against an assaultive ex-boyfriend, during which an alleged "Goo Hara video" surfaced as a trending search term, which was likely sexual in nature.[226] Both of these idols

---

224 Hyonhee Shin and Hyun Young Yi, "K-Pop Singer Decries Cyber Bullying after Death of 'Activist' Star Sulli," *Reuters*, October 16, 2019.

225 Ibid.

226 Se Eun Gong, "'Stars Have Feelings. We Are Not Dolls': South Korea Mourns K-Pop Star Goo Hara," *NPR*, November 25, 2019.

had also suffered from depression. Prior to the incident, Goo addressed malicious commenters on social media:

> You have the freedom of expression. But can you think about what kind of person I am before making malicious comments?[227]

As Nayoon Kim, former idol trainee, reiterated to me, mental health is still very stigmatized in Korea. Despite the trainees' and artists' contracts guaranteeing mental health treatment in times of need, Korean society has only slowly started to recognize celebrities' mental struggles. Many idol stars have stated their concerns either publicly or through self-written music, most notably Jonghyun of SHINee who died by suicide in 2016. His will alerted the public, from SHINee fans to psychiatrists, about a growing problem:

> I am in pain because of me, because of my imperfections. Doctor, is this what you wanted to hear? No, I didn't do anything wrong. I used to think it's so easy to become a doctor, as [they] blamed my personality in a calm voice.[228]

---

227 "악플에 아팠던 구하라…"연예인, 말못할 고통 앓아" 호소하기도" [Goo Hara Hurt from Malicious Comments… Appealed 'Celebrities Suffer from Indescribable Pain'], *DongA*, November 24, 2019.

228 Hyeseon Chae, "종현 유서 공개 "이만하면 잘했다고 고생했다고 해줘"" [Jonghyun's Will Revealed 'Tell Me I Did Well and That I Tried Hard

As of 2020, the industry has become slightly more accommodating of idols who wish to take time off for mental health recovery. Idol band DAY6 in 2020 suspended all promotional activities one day before their album release due to several members' mental health concerns. Companies allowed members of groups TWICE and Monsta X to go on hiatus for mental health recovery, missing the group's promotional activities. While it's good to see a few efforts from the companies, there is still no uniform requirement to do so.

I feel like more progress should be made, but ultimately, improvement of idols' mental health hinges on Korean society's willingness to become more aware of the gravity of these stigmatized issues and the need for adequate resources. I really hope Korean young adults, in general, will be able to seek mental help without the added social stigma.

While it's clear that idols are held to a higher societal standard than anyone else, it's still ambiguous as to who should determine this standard and to what extent criticism should be allowed. South Korean citizens have the freedom to voice their opinions, yet a barrage of targeted criticism may become a modern-day witch hunt resulting in tragedies like the aforementioned suicides. Global fans have voiced their concerns for what they deem as Korean netizens' overreactions; however, an understanding of Korean cultural norms and viewpoints as well as their discrepancies with the rest of the world's is crucial for effectively mitigating unfounded criticism.

Now'], *Joongangilbo*, December 19, 2017.

At the same time, I call for more reforms to online commenting and cyberbullying. In October 2019, search engine Daum no longer allowed online users to comment on its celebrity news articles, and its competitor Naver did so as well the following March.[229] Naver also decided to publicize all users' commenting history, which caused a massive 83.4 percent decline in malicious comments in May 2020.[230] Yet, this is just a temporary solution; social media platforms are an outlet for voicing opinions, and there's no rule preventing an anonymous user from criticizing or ridiculing celebrities on their own pages. Perhaps it's not just a matter of fortifying domestic laws, but a need for an undivided public cognizance of this social issue.

A GENDERED PHENOMENON AND SEXUALIZATION

The K-Pop industry has long been the source of debate for reinforcing gender stereotypes and specific beauty standards. Undoubtedly, the industry produces idols, commercializes them, and therefore objectifies them. This process, coupled with existing Korean societal views, just increases the number of issues.

If you recall, from a young age, trainees must maintain and care for their appearances. Female trainees, in particular, are

---

229 Jihye Yoo, "네이버 연예뉴스 댓글 서비스 폐지·댓글 이력 공개 한달, 어떤 변화 있었나?" [One Month since Banning Naver Celebrity News Commenting and Displaying past History, What Changes Have There Been?], *DongA*, April 7, 2020.

230 Sanghyun Lee, "작성 이력 공개에 네이버 악플 급감...유튜브서도 가능할까?" [Naver's Malicious Comments Rapidly Decline upon Displaying User's past Comments... Will It Be Possible at YouTube Too?], *MK*, May 22, 2020.

to be cautious of their dietary habits and maintain a certain weight determined by the company. Solo artist Maydoni was formerly an idol trainee at YG and JYP Entertainment for eight years, starting from age eleven. She reported:

> I was told to reduce my weight to below 38kg (84 lbs) before debuting. This was very stressful especially during an age when kids eat a lot.[231]

Girl group Nine Muses' company specifically recruited models and stated the member candidates needed to be "pretty, slim, and tall" as "basic requirements."[232] Again, remember that K-Pop is showbiz. How idols look is very important, and these visual standards are the core of idol presentation.

Korean society in general enforces strict beauty standards, which have shaped the direction of female idol production throughout K-Pop history. For most of the past two decades, female idol album themes generally relied on either overt sexual appeal or cute schoolgirl characterizations. For the former, an idol's stage attire would often include intentionally exposing clothing while promotion and journalism would probably focus on the idols' bodies. In 2009, the

231 Gayoung Lee, ""YG·JYP 연습생 8년⋯38kg로 살빼고 男과 택시 탑승금지"" [YG, JYP Trainee for 8 Years... Reduce Weight to 38kg and No Riding in Taxis with Men], *Joongangilbo*, April 8, 2019.

232 "'9 Muses of Star Empire' BBC Documentary," *Koreaboo*, September 20, 2014, video, 47:34.

term "honey thigh" was a trending term that described female idols' emphasis on revealed thighs, which ushered in a debate over the appropriateness of mainstream objectification.[233] TV shows and live showcases have most—if not all—female idols perform the very Korean concept of *aegyo*, "The complex performance of lovability and cuteness," which frequently involves high-pitched voices, nagging or childish facial and bodily expressions, or confused behavior.[234]

Interestingly enough, idol girl groups that debut with a wholesome, schoolgirl image may later make a 180-degree turn and embrace an image emphasizing sexiness and bodily features.

To understand why, let's look at Korean societal ideals. For starters, South Korea already has pervasive gender inequality in terms of pay gaps, women's working environments, and Confucian patriarchal perspectives. Unsurprisingly, a Korea University study discovered that K-Pop consumption actually reinforces gender norms amongst fans, especially in countries with high gender inequality like Korea.[235]

Despite their constant sexualization and objectification, girl group members still must be "kind, submissive, and

---

233 Jinhee Kim, "'꿀벅지'가 무슨뜻? '신조어' Vs '불쾌' 논란" [What Does 'Kkulbeokji' Mean? Controversy over 'New Word' vs. 'Discomfort'], *Joongangilbo*, September 23, 2009.

234 Aljosa Puzar, "Asian Dolls and the Westernized Gaze: Notes on the Female Dollification in South Korea," *Asian Women* 27, no. 2 (2011): 99.

235 Xi Lin and Robert Rudolf, "Does K-Pop Reinforce Gender Inequalities? Empirical Evidence from a New Data Set," *Asian Women* 33, no. 4 (December 2017): 27-54.

mature."[236] Also, society generally holds female idols to an even higher standard of expectations than their male counterparts; girl group AOA received backlash for failing to identify patriotic Korean activist *Ahn Joong-Geun*, yet both the media and public were less interested when male idol P.O. misidentified the ancient Korean kingdom of *Shilla* as China.[237] Female idols' feminist viewpoints receive widespread backlash as well, whether it be for just sharing a "girls can do anything" quote or commending a fiction novel on sexism.[238] However, when male celebrities, including number one TV personality Yoo Jae-Suk or RM of BTS have commended the same novel in question, there was no such reaction.[239]

Further, sponsor-culture, in which executives ask female celebrities or trainees to perform sexual favors in exchange for financial or social support, is rampant in the entertainment industry as a whole, not just in K-Pop.[240] So, not only do female idols and trainees have to survive all of the toils I outlined earlier, but there is also an added complex layer of challenges that they must endure.

---

236 Chaewon Chung, "How Female K-Pop Idols Suffer Gender Inequality and Are Held to Different Standards: 'It's Totally Unfair'," *South China Morning Post*, February 22, 2020.

237 Ibid.

238 Tamar Herman, "Female K-Pop Stars Face Criticism for Seemingly Feminist Behavior," *Billboard*, March 26, 2018.

239 Online Issue Team, ""유재석·방탄소년단 RM'도 읽었다...'82년생 김지영' 페미니스트 논란" ['Yoo Jaesuk, BTS RM' Also Read It... 'Kim Ji Young, Born in 1982' Feminist Controversy], *AsiaKyungjae*, March 20, 2018.

240 Woori No, "또 '연예인 스폰서' 폭로...달샤벳 백다은, '장기 스폰서 제안' 에 "보내지 마"" ['Celebrity Sponsor' Exposed Again... Dalshabet Paik Daeun Sends 'Don't Send Me This' to 'Long-Term Sponsor Offer'], *Chosun*, September 11, 2018.

Despite the challenges and double standards, more female idols are breaking the paradigm by introducing newer musical themes and personas instead of the expected norm. I commend Mnet's recent TV show *Queendom*, a competition between popular female idols that lets them pursue the themes and musical direction they desire. AOA performed in black suits instead of exposed outfits. Girl groups Ohmygirl and Lovelyz rocked *girl crush* performances with a fierce stage presence instead of their usual "fairy" themes.[241]

Korean netizens had criticized Hwasa of Mamamoo for her appearance that didn't comply with the existing idol beauty standards. Some even circulated a petition requesting her to leave, as they thought "Mamamoo would be a pretty group without her." As years went by, however, Hwasa rose to stardom after the public became receptive toward her open, down-to-earth personality and flashy performances reminiscent of Beyoncé.[242] If female idols are capable of perfectly executing diverse personas and talents, it seems unfair to confine them to one single public image that someone else decided for them.

We should also be able to interpret "sexiness" in different ways, without relying on outdated societal notions that sexiness equals having a nice body. However, industry reform hinges

241 Youngwoon Kang, ""섹시 강요당하는 여자 아이돌, 진짜 `아티스트` 라는 걸 증명한게 가장 기뻐요"" ['I'm the Happiest about Proving That Female Idols Who Are Confined to Sexy Concepts Are Real 'Artists''], *MK*, November 7, 2019.

242 Hyeseon Chae, "'너만 없었다면 예쁜 그룹이었을 텐데...' 악플로 상처받은 걸그룹 멤버" ['It Would've Been a Pretty Group If Not for You...' Girl Group Member Who Was Hurt by Malicious Comments], *Joongangilbo*, April 8, 2017.

upon greater public awareness and collective pressure on the Korean government to take more direct action.

Of course, male idols are not free from sexualization and beauty standards either. During the time "honey thighs" was trending, the male counterpart was "chocolate abs."[243] There's also a separate topic of defining and redefining masculinity as K-Pop expands outside of Korea. The "flower boy" aesthetic has been prevalent throughout Korean pop culture, with both the industry and public tending to prefer a hybrid masculinity consisting of soft, gentle faces as well as certain bodily features like tallness and chiseled abs.[244]

Although extreme reliance on this standard has declined in recent years due to a diversity of male idol talent, discussions persist as the Korean concept and normalization of masculinity challenges its Western counterpart. Western society still judges a straight male for wearing makeup, which is a critical part of the K-Pop visual presentation.[245] Male K-Pop idols with heavy makeup may be called "feminine" or "gay" in the West, despite such visual standards having been in place for decades in South Korean entertainment.

Outside of the entertainment industry, Koreans heavily emphasize appearances and live within a thriving cosmetics

---

243 "Flowerboys and the Appeal of 'Soft Masculinity' in South Korea," *BBC,* September 5, 2018.

244 Ibid.

245 Ibid.

and plastic surgery industry.[246] Undoubtedly, cultural perspectives around how male idols look will differ, but I don't think it's a matter of attempting to resolve conflicting perspectives. If K-Pop artists continue to succeed and their audiences can appreciate the artists for who they are, there's no need to convince others whether a male K-Pop idol should adhere to already established notions of masculinity. Here's to hoping for more diversity and acceptance!

With K-Pop's globalization, we may see a greater variety of idol themes unrestricted by pre-existing gender norms and beauty standards. A bigger global audience implies a wider variety of opinions, and thus industry executives and producers will need to be further cognizant of such social issues that have unfortunately plagued the industry for the past decades.

Unfortunately, we cannot eradicate the dangers perpetuated by broader Korean society like plastic surgery addiction, unhealthy dieting, and other gender inequalities overnight. We need a culmination of factors, including the general Korean audience's wider acceptance of idol diversity, the global audience's greater awareness of these issues, and more amplified voices that speak out for the idols, to propel both the K-Pop industry and Korean government to take direct and impactful action.

---

246 Hyun-su Yim, "K-Pop Boy Bands Defy Traditional Idea of Masculinity," *The Korea Herald*, September 3, 2018.

OUTRO

———

Becoming an idol is quite a ride, huh? Over 400 idol groups debuted in a decade, but as little as one or two survive after a year.[247] To say it's not easy would be a huge understatement.

In all seriousness, there's obviously a lot more that goes on behind the scenes of the seemingly glamorous life. The industry produces and trains idols, and the building and hustling process continues for years. At the end of the day, it's the fans who provide the livelihood and financial support for an idol to carry on with this career. It's not only a question of how bad someone wants it but also of whether it's feasible to make it.

Being an idol is not just about singing and dancing; they are a part of the collective phenomenon, which is full of breakthroughs and downsides. Since we now have a more holistic understanding of the idols who comprise the core of the K-Pop movement, we'll be taking a detailed

———

247 Digital Issue Team, "10년간 데뷔 아이돌 436팀…1년에 한두팀만 남기도" [436 Idol Teams Debut within 10 Years… Even Only One or Two Left during One Year], *Chosun*, July 22, 2017.

look at the specific strategies that help the idols become famous in the first place. For now, though, go enjoy a K-Pop music video.

PART 5

THE MUSIC

Since I was born as BoA the artist, I might as well do all that I can before I die. The music, performances, dancing... until I can't anymore.

- BOA

AT HER 20TH ANNIVERSARY V LIVE BROADCAST[248]

---

248 Seunghyun Choo, "[이주의 가수] 보아의 20년, '아시아의 별'은 여전히 찬란하다" [[This Week's Artist] BoA's 20 Years, the 'Star of Asia' Still Shines Bright], *SeoulKyungjae*, August 29, 2020.

INTRO

———

If you listen to K-Pop, your experiences will vary largely depending on the artist. This part of the book will explore how a company writes, produces, and distributes K-Pop music. We'll also engage with how K-Pop music influences have shifted in light of broader pop music trends, as well as differences across various artists, producers, and companies. Furthermore, I'll be providing an overview of the general Korean music business and its relevance as K-Pop acts branch out to the global scene.

The music is a core piece of the K-Pop phenomenon; we need to understand both the sounds and the production. Enhanced technology and new platforms imply that there are more relevant players in the music market today than ever before. I hope to instill in you the same fascination I have for the musical components that have propelled K-Pop to worldwide recognition.

CHAPTER 19

MUSICAL INFLUENCES

———

In this chapter, I will be discussing the shifts in K-Pop's musical trends. I'll discuss where modern K-Pop and the idol-company synergy stands in the broader scope of Korean pop music; an analysis of the latter is a lengthy discussion dating back to the 1950s that I won't be covering here.

Starting from the mid-1990s, genres from primarily Black artists such as hip-hop and R&B heavily influenced K-Pop. These influences marked a shift away from the industry's prior reliance on the standard Korean ballad or hybrid dance-pop drawing from Eurodance, techno, and J-Pop in the early 1990s. After the introduction of rap verses, adlibs, and English lyrics, the industry started seeing more foreigners and Korean-Americans active in the K-Pop industry.[249] The 1990s was the golden age of Korean pop music, and the industry was very diversified with a variety of solo artists and groups.

———

249 Gyu Tag Lee, 케이팝의 시대 [The K-Pop Age], (Seoul: Hanwool Academy, 2016), 96.

Often considered as the pioneers of K-Pop, '90s boy band Seo Taiji & Boys released a debut single "I Know," which drew influence from the new jack swing rhythm that all-time greats such as Michael Jackson and Madonna made popular.[250] As a self-produced act, Seo Taiji & Boys became trendsetters and a voice for the younger generation tired of the same old music.[251]

Seo Taiji & Boys further experimented with a diversity of genres, including gangster rap in "Come Back Home," heavy metal in "Classroom Idea," as well as *gookak* (Korean classical music) in "*Hayeoga*." Their lyrics invited discourse on prevalent social issues of that time. In "Come Back Home," they urged runaway teenagers to return home. "Classroom Idea" spoke out against the strict Korean educational system and "Regret of the Times" expressed lament for their generation.

After Seo Taiji & Boys disbanded in 1996, entertainment companies began to systematically produce idol groups. Early idol groups like H.O.T, Sechs Kies, and Shinhwa implemented gangster rap and heavy metal guitar riffs, whereas *god* frequently utilized funk and R&B-inspired dance tracks.

K-Pop producers have always kept current global trends in mind, and legal sampling and remakes gradually replaced blatant plagiarism.[252] JYP-produced artist Rain's 2003 hit

250 Blanca Mendez, "Seo Taiji & Boys Pioneered Socially Conscious K-Pop for Groups Like BTS," *VICE*, August 1, 2017.

251 Chung-un Cho, "K-Pop Still Feels Impact of Seo Taiji & Boys," *The Korea Herald*, March 23, 2012.

252 Sungmin Kim, 케이팝의 작은 역사 [K-Pop's Small History], (Seoul: Geulhangari Publishers, 2018), 73.

"How to Avoid the Sun" legally sampled Sting's "Shape of My Heart" and became a massive hit. In the '90s, many K-Pop songs had illegally sampled other songs and later settled upon a copyright claim. After contacting foreign songwriters became easier during the 2000s, illegal sampling became much less common. Of course, this isn't to say that plagiarism didn't exist in the 2000s—Lee Hyori's "Get Ya" directly plagiarized Britney Spears's "Do Something" in 2006—but the means and modes of production have notably diversified.[253]

In the early-mid 2000s, the Korean music industry welcomed a diversity of popular genres in which idol groups were a minority. Popular dance hits from solo artists like Lee Hyori's "10 Minutes" (2003) and Se7en's "Passion" (2004) showcased influences from American R&B and hip-hop as well as Europop. Ballad and R&B singers thrived and swept the end-of-year awards while rappers gained greater mainstream prominence. During this era, SM Entertainment would continue to produce idol groups that performed both bubblegum pop and SM Music Performance (SMP), SM's distinct sound combining rock, techno, and dance-pop combined with socio-critical lyrics.[254] Long story short, Koreans fondly remember the diverse music from this period, and the popular singers of this generation continue to perform well commercially.[255]

---

253 Kiwon Shin, "표절 시비로 저작수익 넘어간 노래 수두룩" [Many Songs' Royalties Lost Due to Plagiarism Scandals], *Hankyung*, March 29, 2006.

254 Daehwa Lee, "SMP에 대하여" [About SMP]. *IZM*, August 2008.

255 Hyejung Jung, "가요계는 '2000년대 가수 앓이'중...박효신, 임창정, 젝키에 열광" [Korean Pop Industry 'Longing for Singers of 2000s'... Hype over Park Hyo Shin, Lim Changjung, Sechs Kies], *KBS News*, October 24, 2016.

It wouldn't be until the late 2000s when the "hook-song" became a popular musical trope. Especially with the success of previously mentioned Wonder Girls' "Tell Me" (2007) and BIGBANG's "Lies" (2007), many idol acts began to incorporate a catchphrase, syllable, or "hook" in the chorus.[256] A song that continuously blasts the same catchy phrase in your ears gets stuck in your head. Consequently, everyone would be humming the same melody and simple lyrics everywhere you went, which resulted in huge exposure and success for an artist. The popularity of the hook song would mark the beginning of a new musical era that opened up many doors for K-Pop so it could reach global fans who still remember Girls' Generation's "Gee" (2009), Super Junior's "Sorry, Sorry" (2009), and T-ARA's "Roly-Poly" (2011).

Yes, all three of those titles are the very hooks repeated throughout. The hook-song idea is still relevant in the industry because it works well; 2NE1's "I Am the Best" (2011), Psy's "Gangnam Style" (2012) and EXID's "Up & Down"(2014) in the early-mid 2010s all went viral and gained commercial success. Throughout the 2010s, newer idol groups continued to release modified hook-songs like EXO's "Growl" (2013), TWICE's "TT" (2016), and I.O.I's "Very Very Very"(2016). I advise you not to listen to hook-songs right before an important exam; many Korean students have unfortunately fallen victim to these catchy hooks and consequently underperformed on exams because they couldn't remember what they studied.[257] I know I've definitely done that.

256 Hyunmok Jung, "멜로디·가사 반복 '후크송' 바람몰이" [Trendsetting 'Hooksong' with Repetitive Melody/Lyrics], *Joongangilbo*, October 21, 2008.

257 "수능 금지곡: 헤어나올 수 없는 '수능금지곡' 탈출구 찾기" [Forbidden exam songs: Finding escape route for 'forbidden exam songs' you can't escape from], *BBC News Korea*, November 14, 2018.

Particularly in the 2010s when the global K-Pop phenomenon began to spread, both the domestic and international markets welcomed a variety of genres. For example, many international DJs collaborated on many K-Pop hits in the early 2010s because Electronic Dance Music (EDM) was highly influential at the time. With the mainstream success of Mnet's hip-hop competition TV program *Show Me the Money* and trap-based hip-hop worldwide, Korean rappers became co-songwriters and lyricists for idol groups. Previously niche genres such as lo-fi, alternative R&B, and emo rap resurfaced and influenced the K-Pop realm. Whether it be songs like house-driven f(x)'s "4 Walls" (2015), trap-based BIGBANG's "Bae Bae" (2015), the Skrillex-produced dubstep in 4minute's "Hate" (2016), pop-rock in DAY6's "Shoot Me" (2018), or city-pop in Sunmi's "Pporappippam (보라빛 밤)" (2020), seek and you shall find.

Still, some make the relatively common yet bold assumption, "All K-Pop songs sound the same." This opinion isn't unwarranted because K-Pop draws influences from worldwide music trends while still maintaining the unique flavor that distinguishes it. Yet, I find this an unfair statement because I guarantee there's at least one K-Pop artist who touches upon each sound or genre someone is looking for. Equating K-Pop to a single genre without having researched is problematic.

K-Pop sounds and musical direction not only depend on the artist but also on the particular album's theme. For example, Girls' Generation's 2013 album and single "I Got a Boy" received much musical scrutiny at the time for blending three separate songs into one. After a hip-hop beat-driven intro rap, the succeeding Part A has an EDM rhythm before switching to a dubstep-driven Part B with faster beats per minute. The song also reverts between the two beats throughout. The critical reception was mixed; some critics commended this fresh experiment while others were confused. Girls' Generation had been building up a specific girl group image with hook-songs and approachable themes, which the fierce femme concept of their previous 2011 album *The Boys* subsequently replaced. Roughly a year after their 2011 release, they worked with completely new songwriters and took a different musical direction.[258]

Let's look at the specific changes in Girls' Generation's musical direction and image according to their song's main themes:

- *Gee* (2009): Shyness, trembling hearts

- *Oh!* (2010): Shyness, fondness for *oppa* (an older male figure)

- *The Boys* (2011): Confidence, girl power

- *I Got a Boy* (2013): Gossip

- *Lion Heart* (2015): Heart-taming

Girls' Generation changed from shy girls who avoided eye contact to women striding in confidence to finally taming a fictitious "boy." The discrepancy and diversity in their songs illustrates that a K-Pop act may adopt completely different personas with each new album. Changing personas often

---

258 Jinsub Lee, "진지하게 '소녀시대' [I Got A Boy] 를 듣다" [Seriously Listening to Girls' Generation's [I Got a Boy]], Korea Creative Content Agency, last modified January 14, 2013.

implies a new musical direction comprised of different genres or collaborations with different songwriters. After the producers decide the direction, the A&R (Artists and Repertoire) team, the artists, and company executives embark on the quest to create and record the perfect new song.

These songs are often catered toward audience demographics; recall the localization strategy of TVXQ becoming "*Tohoshinki*" for Japanese promotions. Today, companies release and distribute K-Pop songs to multiple regions simultaneously in the corresponding language versions that cater to the specific regional fans.

In 2012, SM Entertainment decided to take the existing localization strategy further by debuting two groups at the same time: EXO-K for the Korean market, and EXO-M for the Chinese. In the latter, four of the six members were Chinese, so the group promoted the same music as EXO-K but in Mandarin. After a debut year of separate activities, in 2013 EXO-K and EXO-M joined for a twelve-man group EXO. Their first LP *XOXO*, released in both Korean and Chinese versions with the commercial success of over one million physical copies sold that year (including the original and repackage).[259]

The tracklist was identical across the two versions, but the lyric line distribution was different; the Korean version would emphasize EXO-K members while the Chinese version emphasized EXO-M members. It appeared as though EXO would continue with this two-country strategy until 2014 when three

---

259 Jaehoon Lee, "엑소 'XOXO' 100만장↑ 대기록, 12년만의 밀리언셀러" [EXO's 'XOXO' Sets Huge Record of 1 Million+ Copies, Million-Seller after 12 Years], *Joongangilbo*, December 27, 2013.

of the Chinese members left the group and SM Entertainment retired the EXO-K/EXO-M distinction. The company also phased out EXO's initial Chinese promotional strategies as well.

Co-ed idol group KARD's music reflects their massive popularity in Latin American countries. KARD's songs such as "Hola Hola" and "Oh Nana" draw heavy influence from Latin rhythms, dancehall, and reggaetón that appeal to a particular demographic.[260] SM Entertainment's veteran idol boy band Super Junior also recently experimented with Latin influence in "Lo Siento" (2018), a collaboration with Dominican-American singer, Leslie Grace.

Considering SM Entertainment's earlier concert touring successes in South American countries in the early 2010s, this was a fresh take into a specific market. "Lo Siento" ranked favorably on Billboard's Latin Charts at number 13 and won the "Feat Favorita" award at Kid's Choice Awards Mexico.[261] The integration of English, Spanish, and Korean lyrics with Latin music influences with the traditional K-Pop flair resulted in a unique sound that appeals to both the specific demographic of fans and the general audience.

I hope after reading this chapter that you don't think all K-Pop music sounds the same; how could it when both the musical influences and direction vary per artist?

---

260 Diyana Noory, "K-Pop Is Worldwide, but K.A.R.D Are the Idols Who've Already Started There," *VICE*, April 26, 2017.

261 Jeff Benjamin, "Super Junior Debut on the Latin Charts with Leslie Grace & Play-N-Skillz on 'Lo Siento'," *Billboard*, April 24, 2018; "Super Junior Wins Best Featuring Award at Kids' Choice Awards Mexico 2018," *KBS World*, August 22, 2018.

CHAPTER 20

HOW ARE HIT K-POP SONGS AND ALBUMS MADE?

———

Before I discuss exactly how songs are made, let's go to the meeting room. The A&R team—the pros who bring in certain professionals for music production and who coordinate the collaboration process—has become crucial to K-Pop today. According to Jaden Jeong, A&R veteran who collaborated with successful acts like 2PM, Infinite, and Heize, A&R's role in K-Pop has only recently come to light, mostly due to the rise of social media and online fandoms.[262]

If you haven't noticed by now, producing a K-Pop album involves not just the music but also a lot of other factors such as the choreography, visual styling, fashion, and art direction. All of these factors comprise the act's public image, which is

262 Mikyung Sun, "헤이즈 만든 제이든 정이 말하는 A&R의 모든 것" [All of A&R Explained by Jaden Jeong Who Launched Heize], *Chosunilbo*, June 15, 2018.

critical to how an audience receives them. Gone are the days when merely receiving an amazing song from a star producer would be the ticket to stardom. Of course, good music still appeals to everyone. But audiences probably won't even bother to pay attention to a particular song in the first place if they've never heard of the artist. Also, if a particular song doesn't match the artist's public image—such as Eminem singing a love ballad or Adele rapping—it probably won't be received favorably. That's what the A&R team is for.

The A&R team coordinates the artist's public image and musical direction by consulting both relevant experts and the artist. Today, the K-Pop industry depends a lot on audience reception; for idol acts, fandoms are critical, whereas non-idols often depend on the general public. Either way, the artist needs a public image that stands out and meshes well with their musical direction. The shaping of the public image depends on the artist's strengths and unique traits, whether it be flawless dance choreography, songwriting skills, or just a young age.[263]

Album production focuses on amplifying the artist's image with songs that fit the musical direction. In JYP Entertainment, the *producer*, Park Jin-Young, would often serve as the main executive overseeing newer artists, doing everything from composing their debut tracks to developing their image. However, the *artist* Park is a different persona; for his new solo album, Park openly collaborated with the A&R team to discuss what would be best for his own public image and direction. Jaden Jeong actually picks Park as his most

---

263 Ibid.

memorable artist to work with, commending his humility and eagerness to listen.[264]

A&R must effectively coordinate and collaborate with the appropriate producers, choreographers, art directors, and many other experts, since identifying and defining what the audience actually wants is a challenge. For the music, A&R must analyze which songwriters and lyricists would be appropriate for a K-Pop artist's new album. Should boy band Monsta X work with European EDM producers for a "party people" image in the summer? Or should we ask star Korean producers who have a proven track record of domestic commercial success? These are questions that need to be answered before and during the production process.

What I find most interesting about music production is the varying strategies across companies.

Ever since the 1990s, SM Entertainment has increasingly collaborated with foreign producers instead of producing exclusively in-house and does so even more today. After soliciting and licensing demo tapes from global producers, in-house producers such as Yoo Young-jin or Kenzie modify them to add the K-Pop flair.[265] In 2016, SM started the "SM Station" project, in which every week it would release a collaboration track with various artists, producers, and songwriters from

---

264 Eungoo Kim, "K팝의 세계관 누가 만들까? A&R 주역 정병기(인터뷰)" [Who Creates K-Pop's Universe? A&R Lead Jeong Byung-Gi (Interview], *Edaily*, March 8, 2019.

265 Eunwoo Kim, "[미국음악일기] 케이팝 원조 SM을 이끈 '송캠프' 시스템" [[US Music Diary] 'Songcamp' System That Led K-Pop's Origins in SM Ent.], *Bizhankook*, March 13, 2017.

around the world.[266] A&R would identify relevant collaborators for this project, which treated audiences to never before seen collaborations ranging from Wendy (of Red Velvet) and John Legend, EXO and Yoo Jae-suk (Korea's number one TV personality), and BoA and Beenzino (popular Korean rapper).

In contrast, YG Entertainment has largely relied on in-house producers for both new and existing artists, most notably Teddy, who's responsible for the successful hits and albums behind top idol groups like BIGBANG, 2NE1, and BLACK-PINK. The in-house production system allows more room for creative control and a proven synergy with teammates. It's easy to wonder, though, if this system possibly hinders musical experimentation. If you consider this decision from a business perspective, however, why revamp a process that's known to be successful?

For JYP Entertainment, founder Park used to oversee almost all aspects of the company from handpicking trainees to songwriting to choreographing dance routines. However, recently, there's been an increasing emphasis on external collaboration. No matter how talented some producers are, it's a challenge to stay on top of every music trend.[267] In newer JYP-produced groups like rock band DAY6, which relies on self-production under a sub-label, and girl group TWICE, whose debut single they outsourced, we see that JYP is headed toward newer, more innovative approaches to music production.

---

266 Hyosook Kim, "이수만 "SM만의 새로운 음악 공개 채널 'STATION' 공개... 태연이 첫 주자"" [Lee Soo-Man "Presenting "SM's Newest Music Channel 'Station'... Taeyeon as Starter"], *Seoul Kyungjae*, January 27, 2016.

267 Kim, "'Songcamp' system", 2017.

Additionally, I want to introduce a notable K-Pop production method called the songcamp, which refers to a group of diverse musicians gathering together to produce, collaborate, and discuss new musical forms in a large rented house or studio. When you're surrounded by like-minded talent, you're bound to create something fresh. Nowadays one particular song may have more than ten different people who worked on different parts during and after the songcamp.[268]

In Korea, SM Entertainment hosted a series of songcamps and invited songwriters such as Bruno Mars, Teddy Riley, and Lady Gaga, which resulted in new K-Pop collaborations.[269] According to songwriter Priscilla Renea who co-wrote Girls' Generation's "I'm a Diamond," the diversity of melodies in a K-Pop song keep the songcamp sessions more innovative than the American counterpart.[270] New stimuli fosters creativity; if global songwriters experiment with new melodies and rhythms in K-Pop that they couldn't find before, the end product is bound to be fresh.

Let's observe how a team writes a song from start to finish, with two very different examples. These particular stories are quite intriguing, as they involve some top K-Pop acts of the past decade.

---

268 Seungjoon Yang, "가요시장 콤비시대 지나고… 이젠 12명 '집단 창작' 시대" [Korean Pop Market past the Duo-Era… Now an Era of 12-Person 'Group Creation']. *Hankookilbo*, June 14, 2019.

269 Kim, "'Songcamp' system", 2017.

270 Elias Leight, "How American R&B Songwriters Found a New Home in K-Pop," *Rolling Stone*, May 2, 2018.

WORDS FROM A MULTI-PLATINUM VETERAN

If I had to choose one keyword to describe the K-Pop music scene today, it would be "diversity," since the scene has come to be full of so many talented people and creative minds. But why did this happen?

For one thing, more simplified music production processes allow more talent to rise above the surface. There are also social media platforms along with Spotify and Soundcloud that openly support indie artists. In addition, the role of the executive producer is critical. "Producer" can suggest a lot of different roles, but here I mean the professional who not only discovers rookie talent but also helps shape their musical direction and public image.

I connected with multi-platinum record producer Hyuk Shin, founder of 153/Joombas Music Group and industry veteran. Shin was also the first Korean producer to rank in the Billboard Hot 100 chart with Justin Bieber's "One Less Lonely Girl" (2009). Shin discovered a rookie singer-songwriter known today as DEAN; even after only hearing a rough demo cover of Chris Brown's "Forever," Shin knew DEAN was special. There was no one else in the scene who pulled off the contemporary R&B sound like DEAN could, and he also had the suave style that would appeal to a wide audience.

By producing and launching DEAN, Shin wanted to further diversify the scene. There was bound to be a demographic of fans who loved Korean R&B styles that recognized DEAN's talent. After successfully co-producing DEAN's debut album in 2016, 153/Joombas Music Group currently works with singer-songwriter NIve, whom Shin believes captures youthful colors through falsetto-style singing. Shin posits that soon the general public will come to recognize that K-Pop is so much more than just perceived notions of idol pop—it's full of diverse colors and talents.

After producing and collaborating with talent such as DEAN and NIve, Shin is adamant about the importance of collaboration. Gen Z, Millennials, and Gen X all have different sources for musical inspiration, but through collaborations, veterans like Shin can not only produce and mentor upcoming talent but can also create music together that appeals to a wide audience.

I also want to highlight Shin's story about his musical legacy. Shin is the mastermind songwriter behind many monumental K-Pop hits, including "Growl" (2013), which propelled boy band EXO to stardom and the "million-seller" title. When I first heard this song, I knew everything about the beat, melodies, and choreography was legendary. Seven years later, I would be asking the writer how he wrote and produced this song.

As a huge fan of The Neptunes and Pharrell Williams, Shin wanted to create an inspired K-Pop song. So, he whipped up a melody ("top-line") with a collaborator. Interestingly, even as an experienced songwriter, Shin didn't intend on sending this song to the companies; he'd just made it for fun. Shin's brother had different ideas, however; after listening to it, he suggested Shin pitch it to companies, which Shin declined. However, SM Entertainment later contacted him out of the blue. Apparently, Shin's brother sent it to them without telling him!

After this serendipitous incident, the rest is history. Shin, as the executive producer of what later became "Growl" (*Eu-reu-rung*/으르렁), hosted songwriting sessions with collaborators to polish the top-line melodies. Lyricist Seo Ji-Eum pitched a catchy theme to replace the demo's hook "Put it on" with "*Eu-reu-rung*," which provided the song with a fresh new concept.

About the songwriting process and creativity, Shin suggests:

> Sometimes as a songwriter, I really feel it's better to create from the heart rather than to follow trends. Labels love it too, since it's fresh and genuine. I try to recommend this to aspiring and rookie songwriters: have that inspiration and passion drive your work.

If you're a professional musician or even a hobbyist aspiring for a breakthrough, take note. Who knows—there may be a serendipitous moment coming your way.

THE STORY OF "BLACK SWAN"

In early 2020, boy band BTS announced their upcoming full-length album *Map of the Soul: 7*. Rather than release the album all at once as Korean artists usually do, BTS and BigHit Entertainment followed the global formula: promote the first single then subsequently release the album. This strategy prolongs audience engagement and boosts the album's longevity, especially in the U.S. market. Who doesn't like a well-crafted appetizer before the main dish?

The appetizer here—or the first single—was "Black Swan," which featured strings with emo rap and trap-influenced beats to create a dreamy mood. We can break this track down into multiple sections: Intro, Verse 1, Pre-chorus, Chorus, Verse 2, Pre-Chorus, Chorus, and Outro. Unlike this one, a lot of K-Pop songs actually include a bridge or climax, during which the main vocalist belts a high note, or a flashy dance break takes place.

As an aside, I want to tell you a quick story about one of the "Black Swan" co-songwriters to illustrate how some K-Pop songs come to be. But first, let's lay the groundwork.

In contrast to the old days and to what most people may think, many current pop songs involve multiple songwriters instead of just one person. Different songwriters may work on different sections and melodies while an executive producer weaves the material together as one track. It's very important to ensure the end product is coherent, otherwise, we'd have random, disharmonious melodies within the same song. Thus, communication and feedback are critical. K-Pop is no exception; in fact, globalization allows for producers and artists to collaborate with and give feedback to others all around the world rather than only to those in Korea.

If you were an album's executive producer, where would you find a song to use if you didn't compose it yourself? You may already have your songwriting squad or homies that you've worked with before, but suppose the management told you, "We want something we haven't heard before." While you're trying to figure out the problem and trying to squeeze out some creative juices, there's also a job for A&R. These pros need to consider if a particular songwriter would be a right fit for the artist and album concept, as well as negotiate if need be. Sometimes this isn't easy, since musicians may have adamant beliefs about their creative process. If there's no wiggle room for feedback, ultimately, they may not be a great fit for the album. The search for the right songwriter should be a well-planned one.

So how was "Black Swan" created? On the other side of the world in Los Angeles, Clyde Kelly works somewhat like Batman—a corporate consultant by day, a singer-songwriter by night. Thanks to advances in music technology and streaming platforms, he was able to skillfully produce his own music and distribute it all by himself. A decade ago, it would've been a lot more difficult to get his name out there; he'd have to make demos, send them to labels, wait, and perform at local venues, hoping that someone saw the show or watched his YouTube videos. Today, there's no need to go down that arduous, traditional route. With the right resources, songwriters can self-publish music on streaming platforms while retaining all copyright and royalties. If they're lucky, as Post Malone was with the track "White Iverson," the songs may trend virally on SoundCloud, which could possibly lead to record deals at a major label. Since Kelly still had a daytime job to attend to, this method allowed him to capture the best of both worlds.

Then one day, he received an email from BigHit Entertainment's A&R team saying that BTS would love to collaborate for their upcoming single. How on earth did they find him?

When I asked him this very question, Kelly shrugged and said:

I still don't know how they found me.

If I were to guess, BigHit's A&R must have been researching and working diligently to find just the right fit for the single. Upon finding Kelly, they sent him a couple of beats and Kelly cooked up three or four different demos of "Black Swan." Since a demo doesn't require coherent lyrics at that stage, there was no need for Kelly to worry about that aspect. After a bit of back and forth feedback with A&R, Kelly's demo ended up forming the melody for Verse 2 while BTS and other songwriters worked to fill in the other parts. The end result was "Black Swan"—something we hadn't heard before from BTS.

"Black Swan" ranked number fifty-seven on the Billboard Hot 100 while charting number one on iTunes in ninety-three countries.[271] This success could not have been achieved without the meticulous songwriting and conceptualizing that a K-Pop act's major comeback involves. A few weeks later, BTS released their full-length album, which global charts received very well and dominated album sales. In July 2020, "Black Swan" topped number one on iTunes in 103 different

---

271 Soyoung Hwang, "방탄소년단, 'Black Swan' 전세계 93개국·지역 아이튠즈 톱송 1위," *Ilgan Sports*, January 18, 2020.

countries, shattering Adele's previous record.[272] Best of all, BigHit wanted to work with him again; Clyde Kelly's major breakthrough into the K-Pop industry had just begun.

Although companies still differ in their music production philosophies, they all recognize the importance of catering to a global K-Pop audience. Even though most artists promote generally in Korea, fans all around the world will be watching, listening, and supporting. For a successful song release, companies must be wary of global music trends, consider musical experimentation, and coordinate with business strategy.

272 Bryce Rolli, "BTS Just Shattered a Major iTunes Record Formerly Held By Adele," *Billboard*, July 6, 2020.

CHAPTER 21

LYRICS: I DON'T KNOW WHAT THEY'RE SAYING, BUT I LOVE IT

———

I have no idea what "Despacito" and "Macarena" mean in Spanish, but that doesn't stop me from busting out my moves on the dance floor when these songs come on. Sometimes I wonder if this is how foreign K-Pop fans feel, especially since the Korean lyrics barely have any linguistic similarities to Latin-root languages. Is the language barrier a detriment to K-Pop consumption?

During the attempts to break into the Western market in the late 2000s, K-Pop acts intentionally promoted English-only singles, which did set Billboard records. Yet, if the worldwide commercial success of "Gangnam Style" and today's popular idol groups have taught us anything, it's that music ultimately has no language barriers. However, since Korean is a difficult foreign language, it would be challenging for a K-Pop song to rely exclusively on Korean lyrics without either a catchy point or some other English component.

I discussed previously how the mid-late 1990s saw a greater emphasis on Black musical influences as well as on English lyrics. We see examples of such lyricism in works from Shinhwa's "T.O.P. (Twinkling of Paradise)" (1999), god's "Friday Night" (1999), and BoA's "No.1" (2002). Continuing in the 2000s, K-Pop increasingly included English in verses and choruses as a catchy distinguisher. BIGBANG's "Lies" (2007) kicked off with a catchy English chorus that propelled the group to mainstream stardom, as did Wonder Girls' "Tell Me" that same year. Other examples from this period include Rain's "Rainism" (2008) and TVXQ's "Mirotic" (2008). What do words like "Rainism" and "Mirotic" even mean, and why a heightened emphasis on English words?

Some music critics have posited that the Korean language's intonation doesn't mesh well with Western-influenced sounds. Further, they argued that English lyrics allow easier rhyming and may elevate either the sophistication or catchiness of a song.[273] At the end of the day, in entertainment, generating exposure and attention are critical. If a K-Pop song fails to elicit some sort of attention quickly, the audience will likely just move on to another song unless it resurfaces much later.

We cannot ignore the importance of catering to global fans, especially given that social media facilitates K-Pop's global dissemination. If a K-Pop song was entirely in Korean without any English lyrics whatsoever, the barrier to entry for foreign listeners would likely be very high, especially since learning and pronouncing the Romanization of Korean lyrics requires

---

273 Eunah Song, "요즘 가요 왜 영어가사 일색일까?" [Why Is *Gayo* Nowadays Full of English Lyrics?], *Segye*, July 31, 2013.

patience and effort. The hook-song model responded to this potential issue by integrating an easy catchphrase or two, as in songs like "Growl" (2013).

Despite "Growl" not containing many English lyrics, the Romanization for the Korean title and hook "으르렁" is "*Eu-reu-rung*," (often pronounced "*Uh-ru-rung*") which is easy to sing along to. No one really had an issue chanting the chorus of "Gangnam Style" even though the title and phrase are entirely in Korean. As long as there's a catchy point that's easy to follow, there's no need to completely overhaul the Korean lyrics in a song. The real challenge is inventing or identifying what that particular catchy point will be, although that also applies to any pop music producer, regardless of language or country.

Korean lyrics are important to and inherent in K-Pop; in BLACKPINK's collaboration on the Lady Gaga track "Sour Candy" (2020), the girl group incorporates Korean during their featured verses. Some may call this an A&R strategy, but I see this also as a preservation of identity. With more global artists wanting to work with K-Pop artists, perhaps Korean lyrics are one way to identify the "K" in "K-Pop." For example, consider a Lady Gaga fan who's unfamiliar with BLACKPINK (or K-Pop in general) stumbling upon an all-English collaboration track as opposed to one that incorporates Korean. The listener might not know that BLACKPINK was even from Korea or a K-Pop group. By preserving musical identity through Korean lyrics, BLACKPINK can appeal to new listeners by giving them a better idea of who they are.

Think of it in reverse—if a K-Pop act released a collaboration with Beyoncé, would she sing entirely in Korean? Most likely not, since her musicianship and identity are probably better expressed in English. Anyway, expect to see more global collaborations soon. "Sour Candy" will be just one of many in the near future.

It's also undeniable that English lyrics generate wider mainstream appeal. The more English lyrics, the easier it is for newer listeners and existing global fans to recognize and relate to the song, evidenced by BLACKPINK's "Ice Cream" (2020) with Selena Gomez, which is almost entirely in English.

In the specific case of BTS, who have repeatedly declined when Western journalists have asked if they'd start producing an English-only album, they have stayed consistent in musical identity since their earlier years.[274] BTS's music generally contains a balance of both Korean and English lyrics co-written by the members. Their English-only single "Dynamite" (2020) marks a large departure from "ON" (2020) since they decided to outsource the single's production. Interestingly, it became their highest-charting single ever and received ample US radio airplay.[275]

Perhaps if the song's presentation can capture the group's identity without entirely sacrificing what makes them BTS, the language shouldn't matter that much. After all, I believe we've entered a new era in which lyrical languages don't define K-Pop artists' Korean identities.

---

274 Raisa Bruner, "BTS Explains Why They're Not Going to Start Singing in English," *TIME*, March 28, 2019.

275 Lenika Cruz, "BTS's 'Dynamite' Could Upend the Music Industry," *The Atlantic*, September 2, 2020.

I realize this debate gets more complicated when we consider localization strategies and as more K-Pop artists release English or Japanese-only songs, such as Monsta X's all-English album in 2020. Some may ask if this music is still technically K-Pop, to which I answer that the lyrics are just one component; as Professor Gyu Tag Lee mentioned in his interview in Chapter 9, fans today don't want the artists' unique identities to be completely erased for the sake of non-Korean lyrics. I think what really matters is whether the K-Pop act has stayed true to its musical colors and themes that made them who they are, regardless of the languages in which they sing. Musical experimentation will always elicit divided reception, and thus it's up to the artist to either capitalize on a newer direction or stay with the themes that accounted for their initial success. Once again, the idea of K-Pop is continuing to expand. Artists may come from the K-Pop industry, but perhaps it's not productive to put extensive frames on whether their songs are truly K-Pop.

OUTRO

———

While I think there's been a lot of progress in reducing the "All K-Pop songs sound the same" stereotype, I do wonder if K-Pop as a label is restricting people from appreciating the artists and songs for their true worth. K-Pop songs will inevitably have their own unique flair and the Korean lyrics, but I hope that becomes the factor that actually attracts diverse audiences. With an abundance of talent in the scene and savvy strategies that open the door for new collaborations, K-Pop is bound to offer something that caters to most people's tastes. All that's required for this experience is the willingness to explore.

PART 6

THE BUSINESS SIDE

*I don't worry about the future of K-Pop.
I'm really enjoying this job.*

- **CHRIS LEE**,
CEO OF SM ENTERTAINMENT, IN A 2019
BILLBOARD INTERVIEW[276]

---

276 Tamar Herman, "SM Entertainment A&R Chris Lee Talks 'Cultural Technology' & Creating K-Pop Hits," *Billboard*, August 5, 2019.

INTRO

We previously explored the K-Pop industry through the perspectives of trainees, idols, and songwriters. Maybe you've decided that none of these jobs were the right fit, and you'd rather handle the business side of things. This role is essentially taking the pilot's seat in a fancy jet, so I hope you're ready to take on all of the challenges involved in K-Pop business affairs. Both Korean and global executives have realized that K-Pop is quite profitable, and it may seem like everyone ranging from the finance partner to the indie musician wants to take a stab at steering the jet.

Without successful launch and execution, there is no way for K-Pop artists to be sustainable in the long term. Should a project not be financially profitable, the company will likely sit on piles of debt, regretting their investment while the youngsters who were once idols scramble to find new opportunities. Nobody wants this—neither the company, the idols, nor the fans. So, let's explore what has worked directly from the experts themselves.

CHAPTER 22

THE CURRENT SCENE

―――

Just so you don't forget, South Korea is a small country with a lot of talent and capital. Giant conglomerates like Samsung and Hyundai propel the economy and dominate their respective industries. Entertainment is no exception to successful industries; historically, key companies that served as record labels, talent agencies, publishing, and distribution dominated the Korean music market. The industry revolves around these companies to the extent that we may argue it's a competition between companies, not the artists. For K-Pop fans, it doesn't take long before learning about the "Big 3" companies: SM, YG, and JYP Entertainment. In recent years, BigHit Entertainment has also made its way up there as part of the "Big 4."

In the U.S. at least, the general focus is on the artist; I've never heard someone say, "I heard Sony Music just signed this new rookie! Universal better watch out." In fact, most people are probably not even familiar with the Big 3 in the U.S.: Sony, Universal, and Warner. Yet, in South Korea, the Big 4 are highly influential not only in the music business but in the entertainment industry as a whole.

Think back to the K-Pop industry's reliance on idols. The companies' roles include talent recruitment, music production, marketing, and global promotions. Major companies' successful track records over decades in the scene create much buzz every time a new K-Pop act debuts or a comeback occurs.

Let's look at some interesting stories across companies.

SM ENTERTAINMENT: DIVERSIFIED CONTENT

SM is the oldest out of all the major K-Pop companies, and its founder, Lee Soo-Man, is known as the godfather of the industry. Upon producing early idol groups H.O.T and S.E.S. in the 1990s, succeeding acts such as Shinhwa, BoA, TVXQ, Super Junior, Girls' Generation, SHINee, f(x), EXO, Red Velvet, and NCT have all demonstrated both domestic and international success. I really appreciate SM's plethora of music-related ventures, such as the weekly collaborations on SM Station, classical music projects with SM Classics, and stock acquisitions of music entertainment companies like Mystic Story and Million Market.[277]

I want to highlight the interesting business strategy for SM's idol boy band NCT, which is active through multiple subunits and themes (NCT U, NCT 127, NCT DREAM) after debuting in 2016. NCT operates on a rotational system in which members change depending on the album's direction.[278] A

---

277 Soohyun Kim, "[취재파일] 서울시향의 '빨간 맛'...SM이 왜 클래식을?" [[Report File] Seoul City's 'Red Flavor'... Why Is SM Doing Classical Music?], *SBS News*, July 21, 2020; Jiyoung Hwang, "SM, 수란 속한 밀리언마켓 레이블 흡수" [SM, Acquisition of Suran's Label Million Market], *Joongangilbo*, October 2, 2018.

278 SBS PopAsia HQ, "A Beginner's Guide to NCT," *SBS*, July 9, 2018.

2018 Chinese partnership for multi-national boy band WayV expands SM's activity in China, while having WayV members participate in NCT and supergroup SuperM's promotions. No members will be fixed in order to accommodate flexible music business strategy across regions.

SM has also diversified its business strategies outside of the music industry. SM's talent management created subsidiaries including SM C&C to manage actors and comedians, Galaxia SM to manage athletes, and Esteem to manage models and TV personalities, which suggests a plethora of ventures outside of K-Pop. Furthermore, SM invests heavily in a variety of industries including retail, tourism, restaurant, mobile, and technology. SM truly captures the idea that K-Pop entertainment companies are brands in and of themselves. To merely categorize SM as a music label rather than as a diverse entertainment company would be very shortsighted.

In the K-Pop context, gone are the days when producing a well-crafted album would be the end goal. Now, releasing new music implies new content to market and monitor. There's bound to be third-party content, such as YouTube cover dances and lyric videos. There may be an opportunity to create a new mobile game based on the new album. The comeback teasers should incorporate original storylines that best capture the artists' image. Given all of these opportunities, what should the company prioritize when planning for an album comeback, and how should they implement these marketing strategies?

During a chat with Cobb C., former Content Marketing Specialist at SM Entertainment and concert management expert, I learned that data and industry trends are absolutely critical to analyze. For example, if a girl group releases a comeback single, Cobb would need to analyze the viewership trends on the official YouTube music video to determine which countries' viewers respond the fastest and what the increase rate in viewership is. Further, fans will undoubtedly make original YouTube content such as color-coded lyric videos, translations, and cover videos. On Korean online forums, users may discuss, debate, and criticize the single. The artist's team would need to monitor these platforms and forums (even the most malicious ones) for any legal implications including copyright, defamation, or sexual harassment. Cobb notes:

An entertainment content marketer role is more of a lifestyle than a desk job—it doesn't really end when I clock out. I'd need to stay on top of industry trends, because new things are happening all the time.

Idol marketing is a huge challenge due to the difficulties in tracking the factors that account for viewership and sales. Sure, the core fandom exists, but it's very hard to analyze the participation from the general masses. Let's say the aforementioned girl group's newest music video's twenty-four-hour viewership decreased by 5 million from their last single. High overall viewership isn't enough; despite high views, the team would need to figure out why viewership from a particular region declined. Was it regional pop cultural trends, obscure musical experimentation, or even mass power outages? What are the larger factors the company must be aware of? In the particular geographic location in which the decline occurred, the company must analyze consumers' financial spending trends, popular content trends in that region, the investment-to-viewership ratio, and more. Identifying and analyzing which factor caused what data trend is a mind-boggling problem.

Cobb's biggest project was planning and executing EXO's 2018 comeback showcase at a hotel resort. EXO's fifth album *Don't Mess Up My TEMPO* was supposed to be a very important turning point album after their fourth album *The War* had massive success the year before. At the time, the idols were in their late twenties and were soon approaching their mandatory military service—a hurdle for all Korean male entertainers. SM Entertainment had to really solidify EXO's status in the market with this new album before what could be a very long hiatus until all members could be together onstage again.

Cobb was to execute the comeback showcase at the hotel resort, a venue that was more of an open plaza than a formal performance space. Furthermore, Cobb and the team had to entice the audience to come all the way to Yeongjongdo, an island near the city of Incheon, which is quite far from the metropolitan Seoul. The showcase was also a joint project involving the special edition of Samsung's Galaxy Note 9, so the lucky fans who purchased a limited-edition phone also received a VVIP ticket to the comeback showcase. Cobb not only had to successfully execute the showcase marketing plans but also make sure all of the limited editions sold. He admits that ultimately, it was a matter of identifying consumer trends and attracting fans with a side of sleepless nights.

In the end, the showcase concluded successfully, EXO commenced a series of promotional activities, and the limited-edition mobile devices sold out. EXO's fifth album *Don't Mess Up My TEMPO* received over one million preorders and is currently the most successful EXO album to date.[279]

When you think of SM Entertainment, think of its diverse ventures: the albums, the artists, and strategies that may just involve an island showcase.

YG ENTERTAINMENT: INTERNATIONAL COLLABORATION

YG initially started as a smaller hip-hop and R&B-centric label before formally transitioning into more mainstream K-Pop production, as evidenced by their earlier productions in Jinusean, 1TYM, Se7en, and Wheesung in the '90s and '00s. Their idol groups BIGBANG and 2NE1 led the industry from the late '00s to the early-mid '10s, after which YG produced popular idol groups WINNER, iKON, BLACKPINK, and TREASURE. YG's top music producer, Teddy, shapes much of YG's musical direction and is responsible for YG's successful history of in-house production.[280] Recently, BLACKPINK has had incredible international success and a mainstream breakthrough in the West.

During the early-mid 2010s when I was in college, YG Entertainment was arguably doing some of the coolest projects in the entire K-Pop industry. Psy's "Gangnam Style" blew up, BIGBANG

279 Sun-hwa Dong, "EXO Becomes 'Quintuple Million-Seller'," *The Korea Times*, October 31, 2018.

280 Eunjung Lee, "YG 새 걸그룹은 4인조 '블랙핑크'…"테디가 프로듀싱"" [YG New Girl Group Is 4-Member 'Blackpink'… 'Teddy Is Producing'], *Yonhap News*, June 29, 2016.

was unstoppable, 2NE1 continued to break records, and Epik High returned from a long hiatus. Through a unique diversity of skilled acts and strategies, YG Entertainment showed that its artists had all the tools needed to expand K-Pop outside of Asia and receive legitimate recognition in the U.S. market. As a high school senior in 2012, I was confused and shocked when I saw BIGBANG's *Alive* album climb up the Top Albums chart on iTunes. This was iTunes—the most popular platform at the time when music revolved around MP3s—and the main Top Albums chart, not the specific K-Pop/World category.

Alive would proceed to chart at number 150 on the Billboard 200, and BIGBANG would later return to rank at number 172 with their 2016 album *MADE*, making them the first K-Pop act to chart twice.[281] Here was the kicker: YG promoted *Alive* in Korea and in the Korean language. It wasn't an album targeting specific countries at all. BIGBANG simply did what they did best and a bigger, global audience discovered and loved their hits like "Fantastic Baby" and "Bad Boy." Something interesting was happening here; global fans were appreciating K-Pop for what it is and BIGBANG didn't even have to adopt new personas. Could we possibly further bridge the gap between the Korean and the global—especially the U.S.—market?

It's not surprising that American fans loved YG artists who blended very well with the Western aesthetic. In the early 2010s when EDM was influential to popular music around the globe, BIGBANG's leader G-Dragon collaborated with top DJs including Diplo, Boys Noize, and Skrillex. BIGBANG's

---

281 Jeff Benjamin, "BIGBANG Earns 2nd Entry on Billboard 200 with Career-Defining 'Made' Album," *Billboard*, December 19, 2016.

main vocalist Taeyang made his solo career known by working with world-class dance choreographers Lyle Beniga and Shaun Evaristo. 2NE1's CL caught the eyes of Black Eyed Peas' will.i.am and celebrity fashion designer Jeremy Scott. Some said she was even Scott's muse.[282] Interestingly, all these crossovers happened very organically; the Korean artists executed incredible projects, and international artists, choreographers, and designers commended their talents.

I spoke with Peter Chun, who spearheaded these global strategies as the former US Business Director and Publicity/ Marketing Director at YG Entertainment and is the current Head of Marketing at K-Pop tech platform, TheQoos. About the global collaborations, he told me:

> When we first started out, it was really about developing a press kit: "Hey, we're in magazines like *Billboard* or *Complex*... the media is paying attention to us. Our social media following is crazy. Fashion designers like Alexander Wang and Jeremy Scott rock with us and we are working with famous producers and DJs. Not only do we have legit co-signs from the who's who in music and fashion but we also got the YouTube and social media numbers to back it up."

Chun served as a bridge for the YG talent and global brands. He'd convince the casting directors and brand representatives who weren't as familiar with the Asian market to take a look at what YG Entertainment had to offer. The YG artists

---

282 David Yi, "Meet Jeremy Scott's Muse: K-Pop Star CL," *ELLE*, March 21, 2013.

were already at the top of the K-Pop industry and were well equipped for new challenges. By building press step by step, Chun cultivated new global relationships that led to music and fashion collaborations and, ultimately, to larger-scale global advertising campaigns; Taeyang modeled for Calvin Klein, G-Dragon posed on the *Vogue Italia* cover, and both BIGBANG and 2NE1 collaborated with luxury brand Chrome Hearts.

For hip-hop trio Epik High, which was signed to YG Entertainment at the time, Chun recalls a building-block process. He booked them for the 2015 SXSW Music Festival in Austin, Texas, which made a subsequent North American tour possible. Chun invited music promoter Goldenvoice to check out Epik High's act during their sold-out tour, which ultimately led to Epik High's performance at the 2016 Coachella Music Festival.

Chun emphasizes that these business decisions were creative ones to begin with and that everything was organic. For example, at Coachella, he happened to introduce Tablo of Epik High to American R&B singer Gallant. This decision wasn't planned in advance with the intention of a business pursuit; rather, a casual conversation occurred that naturally led to the joint single, "Cave Me In" the next year.

Further, the decisions to pursue these fresh collaborations shaped the public's perceptions toward the YG artists. Even if American casting directors had no idea who BIGBANG was or had never heard of K-Pop, YG Entertainment and their artists' credibility stemmed from their successful track record of collaborations and relationships with recognizable names. Chun states that G-Dragon is linked with top luxury brands Saint Laurent and Chanel because of the creative decisions he made as a talented artist. Today, all four members of BLACKPINK are global ambassadors and models for top luxury brands like Gucci and Saint Laurent and have collaborated with household names such as Lady Gaga and Selena Gomez in 2020 alone.

These collaborations ultimately reinforced the idea that YG artists—and to a larger extent, K-Pop artists—could be perceived as "cool" around the globe.

> It was a personal goal of mine, being born and growing up in America, to show that Asians are dope. My goal was to change people's perceptions of Asians.

Chun's experience bridging the East and the West is something that others need to develop for the K-Pop phenomenon to move forward. With more K-Pop artists gaining recognition on the global stage, I see more work to be done for the industry professionals to ensure that they are marketing properly overseas. Thanks to the efforts of pros like Chun, today the international perception of K-Pop has progressed positively; many global artists and brands now want to work with K-Pop artists. Asians have always been dope, and it's about time that the world recognized it!

JYP ENTERTAINMENT: SPECIFIED MANAGEMENT
JYP Entertainment is the only top company in which the head figure, Park Jin-Young, is still an active entertainer himself

in addition to being an executive producer. Thus, his musical and stylistic influences on the artists are massive—more so than other companies' executive producers. We can see Park's influence in Rain, who is arguably Park's manifestation of his persona, as well as in the countless songs he wrote for JYP Entertainment's artists. As of late, JYP utilizes a blind voting system amongst staff for the lead single selections to ensure the best quality and a fair decision process.[283]

In contrast to SM and YG, which have diversified their modeling and K-Drama ventures, JYP wrapped up its actor management by transferring K-Drama talent to a different company in 2019. After this decision, JYP has been completely dedicated its K-Pop artist roster, which includes groups such as GOT7, DAY6, TWICE, and Stray Kids, all of whom have performed very well commercially. Its new girl group ITZY's second single titled "ICY" (2019) exceeded 40 million YouTube views within four days, breaking the group's own record from the debut single "DALLA DALLA" (2019).[284] The new generation of JYP artists seems to be propelling the company into a new era.

I'd like to explore a new strategy that JYP Entertainment announced at a 2018 corporate briefing. Coined the "4 *bonboo* (본부)(headquarter/HQ)" idea, each headquarter within the company would devote itself to strategizing and executing plans for particular artists. For example, groups GOT7 and TWICE would

283 Hyerin Lee, "[K-POP 제작소] 심은지, JYP에서 작곡가로 일한다는 것" [[K-Pop Production Lab] Shim Eunji, Working as a Songwriter at JYP], *Chosun*, October 16, 2013.

284 Sooyoung Kim, "잘 나가는 빅히트·JYP, 주춤하는 SM·YG … 희비 엇갈린 공룡엔터들" [BigHit and JYP Doing Well, SM and YG Setbacks... Bittersweet Dinosaur Entertainment Companies], *Hankyung*, August 3, 2019.

be under different headquarters with human resources dedicated specifically to them and no one else. Michaela Hahm, former Senior Marketing Manager at JYP, told me that this system facilitated a more efficient division of labor; Hahm could dedicate her sole marketing efforts to her designated artists rather than be responsible for all artists at JYP. Park Jin-Young himself clarified how this strategy differs from traditional Korean company settings, which are usually structured according to individual divisions such as marketing and management:

> Two years ago, I started an experiment… I created a special task force to handle just one artist only. For the past two years, everything related to TWICE was handled by that special task force. The result was amazing—everything was so much faster and efficient. We're trying to make four little companies inside one big company… That's the biggest reason for our company's success within the past year.[285]

This strategy that JYP uses is actually a modified version of the American music business system, in which the personnel revolve around the artists themselves rather than the agency or label. Each artist has their own teams for management, marketing, public relations, and more, rather than the same human resources caring for everyone. The end result is much more tailored to the specific artists and fosters greater communication between the artist and JYP Entertainment. Currently, GOT7 and ITZY are under one headquarter together, while DAY6, TWICE, and Stray Kids are each under their own individual ones. With NiziU (the Japanese girl group

---

285 *JYP Entertainment*, "JYP 2.0," July 26, 2018, video, 24:51.

collaboration), perhaps we may see a new addition or modification to the headquarters system.

Even more so, maybe we'll be seeing more K-Pop industry-wide changes to the existing company structure paradigm and a widespread shift toward the artists rather than the companies.

In our chat, Hahm emphasized that JYP's strategy created a case-by-case experience; her headquarter atmosphere differed from another manager's. Every JYP artist is unique, and naturally, both their business strategies and fandoms differ as well. This idea is the same throughout the industry. Consider the number of strong players in the scene already, and then the diverse strategies amongst companies. No two are completely alike.

BIGHIT ENTERTAINMENT: THE GAME-CHANGER

Today's industry experts and financial analysts herald BigHit Entertainment as a new leader in the industry. As of 2020, an argument can be made for a new entity, the "Big 4."[286] Due to BigHit's rapid ascent to commercial prominence, skeptics contend the company needs a longer successful track record before declaring a Big 4. Yet, BigHit's 2019 annual revenue was 587.9 billion Korean won (roughly $486.3 million USD), which basically doubled from the previous year.[287] In the same year, BigHit's operating profit

---

286 Sungmin Kim, "연예계 빅4 분석...연봉 1위는 '방시혁 회사', 퇴사율 1위는?" [Entertainment Industry Top 4 Analysis... #1 Salary Is 'Bang Shi-Hyuk's Company', Who's Resignation #1?], *Chosun*, January 18, 2019.

287 Sungyeol Yoon, "빅히트, 매출 5879억..전년대비 2배 "사업 다각화 결과"" [BigHit, Revenue 587.9 Million... Double the Previous Year 'Result of Diversified Ventures'], *Starnews*, February 5, 2020.

was 98.7 billion Korean won (roughly $82.8 million USD), a 23.5 percent growth from 2018 and more than the Big 3 combined (in Korean won, SM earned 40.4 billion, JYP earned 43.5 billion, and YG earned 2.0 billion for a total of 85.9 billion).[288] In light of their sheer numbers and growth rate, I think calling BigHit a dark horse of the industry seems under-appreciative. So, where is all this money coming from? Is it all from BTS?

To answer that, let's first take a look at this modified graph courtesy of Professor Anita Elberse of Harvard Business School, who allowed me to present a comparative analysis:

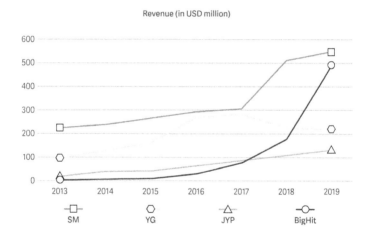

[289] Top 4 K-Pop Entertainment Companies' Revenue (in USD millions)

288 Hyunyoo Kim, "빅히트 엔터테인먼트의 영업이익이 SM·JYP·YG 합친 것보다 많아졌다" [BigHit Entertainment's Operating Profit Exceeds SM·JYP·YG Combined], *Huffington Post*, March 31, 2020.

289 Anita Elberse and Lizzy Woodham, "Big Hit Entertainment and Blockbuster Band BTS: K-Pop Goes Global," Harvard Business School Case 520-125, June 2020.

You can see from the revenue that BigHit has gradually eclipsed YG and JYP to rival SM. But when we compare sole net income, BigHit leads, having earned more than the other three combined.

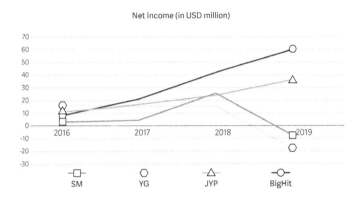

Net Income (in USD million)

[290] Top 4 K-Pop Entertainment Companies'
Net Income (in USD millions)

The focus is indeed on BTS, which generated 97 percent of BigHit revenue in 2019.[291] There are great videos, books, and scholarly materials that solely analyze BTS, so this is a very condensed section. Specifically, I commend the works of music critic Youngdae Kim and Professor Jiyoung Lee.[292]

Fans and experts agree that BTS's global success happened organically. Even after garnering overwhelmingly positive reception at the 2014 L.A. KCON, BTS and BigHit still

290 Ibid.

291 Laure He and Jake Kwon, "Big Hit IPO makes BTS millionaires and their producer a billionaire," *CNN*, September 28, 2020.

292 Youngdae Kim, *BTS: The Review*, (RH Korea, 2019); Jiyoung Lee, *BTS, Art Revolution*, (Parrhesia, 2019).

continued to heavily promote in the domestic market. However, BigHit prioritized authenticity via BTS's transparent fan communication and self-production of music from the onset. In conjunction with slick social marketing strategies, BigHit promoted BTS as one entity instead of having individual members start their own social media accounts, which is still the case as of 2020.

Recently, BigHit has been acquiring smaller yet influential companies; in 2019, BigHit acquired Source Music—the company of popular girl group GFriend—as a subsidiary via stock acquisition. Not only would this acquisition answer skeptics' accusations that BigHit couldn't successfully produce or manage female idols, but BigHit would also be able to expand its creative ventures while diversifying the amount of idol content.[293] In 2020, after much public speculation, BigHit acquired another strong industry player, PLEDIS Entertainment, the home to popular boy bands SEVENTEEN and NU'EST. BigHit announced plans to go public like its Big 3 peers in 2020, and financial experts assessed that the coronavirus pandemic and BTS members' mandatory Korean army enlistment were big factors in this decision.[294] Nonetheless, it was the biggest Korean stock market listing in three years.[295]

293 Jungyeon Lee, "'방탄소년단' 소속사 빅히트, '여자친구' 영입 왜?" ['BTS' Company BigHit, Why Recruit 'GFriend'?], *DongA*, July 30, 2019.

294 Byunghoon Ko, "지체할수록 독?'...빅히트 IPO 어디까지 왔나" ['The More Delay, the More Detriment?'... BigHit IPO So Far"], *Newsway*, May 14, 2020.

295 He and Kwon, *CNN*, September 28, 2020; Julia Fioretti and Shinhye Kang, "K-Pop Superstars BTS's Agency Seeks up to $812 Million in IPO," *Bloomberg*, September 2, 2020.

I'm fascinated by BigHit's massive growth in just a few years. It has invested substantially in its subsidiaries to expand its content, like creating the video game *BTS World*, with Korean gaming company Netmarble and original platforms like Weverse with tech company beNX.[296] Other examples include BigHit IP (character licensing), BigHit Edu (educational content), and Belift Lab (an artist label). The latter, with CJ E&M, debuted the new boy band ENHYPEN in late 2020.[297] BigHit's diverse ventures continue to expand outside of music production and its biannual corporate briefings keep the public updated on its activities.[298]

For a further in-depth discussion on BigHit Entertainment alone, I highly recommend Elberse's Harvard Business School case study, as it provides an in-depth approach to its background and business strategy.

MID-SIZED COMPANIES

There are other companies out there besides the Big 4. In the late 2000s and early 2010s in particular, we saw a boom in the number of idol groups in the industry (recall that 2012 especially was a huge year). This boom involved a lot of mid-sized entertainment companies producing and

---

296 Jungeun Lee, "빅히트엔터테인먼트, 자회사 세워 방탄소년단 활용사업 확대" [BigHit Entertainment, Founds Subsidiary to Expand BTS-Applied Ventures], *BusinessPost*, March 26, 2019.

297 Pansuk Park, "'아이랜드' 글로벌 아이돌 엔하이픈 탄생..대단원 막 내렸다" ['I-LAND' global idol ENHYPEN is born...conclude with final results], *JoongangIlbo*, September 18, 2020.

298 *Big Hit Labels*, "Big Hit Corporate Briefing with the Community (2h 2020)," August 12, 2020, video, 57:43.

launching idol acts of their own, notably Cube, Starship, Jellyfish, FNC, PLEDIS, RBW, and Woolim Entertainment, to name a few. The executives of these companies are usually former employees of the Big 3 or music producers with a success record who decided to take matters into their own hands.

CJ E&M

CJ Group is a mega-conglomerate in Korea, just like Samsung or LG. It created the Entertainment & Media division, CJ E&M, which owns the TV channel Mnet—the home of music programs such as the *Produce* series, *Show Me the Money* (SMTM), *Mnet Asian Music Awards* (MAMA), and many more. In recent years, in addition to its already-existing management wing, CJ has engaged in strategic partnerships with hip-hop labels AOMG and Amoeba Culture.[299] In 2018, CJ established its own subsidiary, Stone Music Entertainment, which handles not only artists' album production and management but also distribution to music streaming services.

So, why exactly is CJ important in today's context? Well, Mnet is a large, influential player in the industry; rising K-Pop acts need exposure on TV so that they may have a chance at the annual MAMA. The network's *Produce* series and SMTM were huge successes that created many new global stars. Further, CJ organizes the aforementioned KCON festivals around the world. Thus, it is beneficial for

299 Mooyeon Kim, "CJ E&M, 다듀·크러시 속한 아메바컬쳐 마저 품는다" [CJ E&M, Harbors Even Dynamic Duo·Crush's Amoeba Culture], *Edaily*, November 13, 2017.

companies—especially smaller ones—to maintain a cordial relationship with TV broadcast networks and an industry titan like CJ.

* * *

In the next chapter, we're going to explore how global companies collaborate with these Korean ones.

CHAPTER 23

GLOBAL STRATEGIC PARTNERSHIPS

———

Today there's an increasing desire for foreign artists and record labels to collaborate with K-Pop artists. The entertainment industry welcomes innovation and collaborations because they foster creativity, whether it be a duet of two singers, a new technology platform, or a successful company acquisition. As K-Pop continues to evolve and diversify, Korean executives have decided their acts would benefit massively from the extra kick that comes from collaborations.

I previously mentioned the U.S.'s "Big 3": Universal, Warner, and Sony Music. Although they're American companies, they're omnipresent in their global reach; each of them owns influential subsidiaries including many famous record labels and music distribution companies.

There's a distinction in the larger global market; for BTS in Korea, the company BigHit Entertainment serves as both the record label (music production) and talent agency (business representation), while a third-party company called Dreamus distributes their music to Korean streaming sites. For U.S. activities, however, BTS works with Columbia Records, a Sony Music subsidiary, for marketing and distribution.[300] For their Japanese activities, BTS is signed to Def Jam Recordings under Universal.[301] As you can see, there are a lot of parties involved that don't overlap for each country's activities.

Let's take a look at a case study. In 2020, the boy band AB6IX took off in Korea. Some of the members already had an existing fanbase, so the public received their singles and albums well and they've earned numerous awards at different award ceremonies. Fans in the Asia-Pacific region were dying for more activities other than a one-time tour, so it was time to test the waters. Fortunately, representatives from Warner Music Asia were very open to the idea, as they saw potential in AB6IX to become globally successful. After many talks behind both open and closed doors, AB6IX's company Brand New Music (BNM) and Warner entered into a strategic partnership.

According to Shin Cho, Senior Marketing Manager and Head of K-Pop at Warner Music Asia, the partnership allowed Warner to spearhead Asian promotional activities including global marketing to regions like Hong Kong and Singapore, which benefitted both parties; BNM could formally cater to audiences outside of Korea while Warner could further tap into the global K-Pop business. If AB6IX really takes off in Asia, then the opportunities for them to branch out for U.S. activities grow even bigger. Warner

---

300 Geoff Mayfield, "BTS Is Headed Straight to No. 1 with New Album 'Map of the Soul: 7'," *Variety*, February 27, 2020.

301 "BTS Signs Contract with Def Jam Recordings," *The Korea Herald*, March 28, 2017.

is the parent company of the well-known Atlantic Records that represents acts like Ed Sheeran, Coldplay, and Sia. If BNM and Atlantic are interested in collaborating someday, negotiations are bound to be a lot smoother due to the previous Warner partnership. After all, this is a tight-knit industry.

Today, many K-Pop stars are increasingly engaging in strategic partnerships with companies for American activities— TWICE with Republic Records (record label), Chungha with ICM Partners (talent agency), and Monsta X with Epic Records (record label) to name a few.[302] Previously, K-Pop artists just signed record deals with Chinese or Japanese companies after strong performances in those markets, but now the opportunities continue to expand around the world.

What is the point of these strategic partnerships? If a K-Pop act sings a duet, remixes a well-known pop song, or invites a well-known pop star to feature on a song, the resulting product will receive more exposure. Recently, we've seen many K-Pop projects with Warner Music alone—Hwasa & Dua Lipa, SEVENTEEN & Pink Sweat$, and Chungha & Christopher. Fresh collaborations stimulate the existing fan and attract new fans, resulting in greater exposure. Companies can coordinate special projects like these, and the pros from A&R, marketing, and management all need to put heads together to determine whether the public will receive the particular collaboration well.

Perhaps the kind of collaborations we've dreamed of in the past are moving closer to reality.

---

302 "More K-Pop Artists Team up with U.S. Labels to Expand Careers," *YonhapNews*, March 11, 2020.

CHAPTER 24

ALTERNATIVE SOURCES OF REVENUE

—

K-Pop is supposed to be a cumulative audiovisual experience; it's not merely enough just to sell albums or gather online streams and downloads. According to investor reports for the Big 3 companies' fiscal year revenues from 2013-2018, the average breakdown—live events were 32.4 percent, recorded music was 25.6 percent, IP licensing, merchandising, etc. was 21.6 percent, and artist appearances in ads, TV, etc. were 19.3 percent.[303] As you can see, pure recorded music sales are only a fraction of the total revenue an artist generates. Let's explore some additional sources of revenue in the K-Pop industry.

LIVE EVENTS

During my high school formal in Korea, the student council somehow got singer IU to come perform "Good Day"

---

303 Bernie Cho, "The Hip Hype Reality of the Korean Wave" (lecture, KAIST College of Business, Seoul, South Korea, October 6, 2020).

(2010) for us. I didn't know why and how she came, but I was awestruck.

I love all live events: concerts tours, showcases, festivals, and local shows. Fortunately for me, a huge portion of K-Pop revenue comes from live events, so they occur pretty frequently (except during the pandemic). Popular idol groups typically perform in Seoul for two or three days, whereas non-idol acts tend to launch nationwide tours adding the cities Busan, Daegu, and Gwangju. For the idols who can have international tours due to a global following, they also have huge merchandise sales while abroad. During a live show, fans can enjoy a special experience while the idols and their company profit.

Like my formal, local events categorized as *haengsa* (행사) are great opportunities, as are university festivals, military events, weddings, and brand promotions. The artists' pay differs depending on popularity; popular idol groups range from 40 to 70 million won ($34,000 to $59,000 USD), but top-tier acts earn much more.[304] If you want them to perform at your house party, be prepared to shell out.

Despite K-Pop's international success and the massive revenues that live events generate, South Korea still doesn't have a proper concert venue solely dedicated to music events. All the concerts take place in sports arenas or university auditoriums, which have neither the seating capacity nor the

---

304 Kyungmi Kim, "아이유는 6000, 송가인은 3500 정말?... 트롯가수 vs 아이돌 행사 '몸값' 차이 얼마일까" [6000 for IU, Really 3500 for Song Ga-In?... Trot Singer V. Idol Haengsa How Big Is the Difference in 'Net Worth'], *Woman Chosun*, June 8, 2020.

optimal sound quality that massive overseas concert stadiums have.[305] I find it a bit strange to think the country hasn't built a music stadium despite its own cultural phenomenon. For BTS's 2018 concert tour, the mere three-day Seoul leg generated one trillion Korean won ($842 million USD), and the group generated a yearly effect of about 5.5 trillion won ($4.6 billion USD) via tourism and merchandising.[306] What if they could perform at even better venues and elevate everyone's concert experience?

Fortunately, Seoul plans to build a proper performance-dedicated arena by 2024 with a 42,000 seat capacity.[307] Yet, for now, the challenge remains—sports arenas obviously prioritize sporting events, so it's difficult for entertainment companies to even reserve a venue.[308] As a result, K-Pop acts greatly rely on international shows at the expense of Korean fans. Proper Korean venues would also imply even greater tourism from global fans. Until then, however, there's a lot left to be desired.

305 Soojin Park, "정부가 2019년 추진하는 '케이(K)' 관광 활성 방안들: '케이팝' 페스티벌, 경연, 전용 공연장" [The Government-Driven 2019 'K' Tourism Enhancement Measures: 'K-Pop' Festival, Competition, Special Venue], *Huffingtonpost*, December 17, 2018.

306 Jongil Kim, "[BTS 혁명] 'BTS 경제효과' 年 5.5조원" [[BTS Revolution] 'BTS Economic Effect' 5.5 Trillion Won per Year], *Sisajournal*, February 21, 2020.

307 "고양 K컬처밸리, 4만2000명 수용 공연장 들어선다" [Goyang K-Culture Valley, Performance Venue for 42,000 People Coming], *DongA*, August 11, 2020.

308 Jaeyong Moon, "K팝 키워놓고...공연수익 해외로 '줄줄'" [Despite Developing K-Pop... Show Revenues Heading Overseas One-after-Another], *MK*, May 3, 2019.

INTELLECTUAL PROPERTY

When I say intellectual property (IP), I'm not referring to specific copyright or trademark laws but rather the industry term that generally refers to the usage of artists' content and likeness. I admit, as a legal professional, that this may be somewhat misleading.

For idol groups, the producers need to set specific art direction based on the individual idols' appearances, strengths, personality traits, and a holistic balance for the group. Prior to the debut, art directors may devise stories, designs, and character traits, which is called "transmedia storytelling."[309] This would often be tied into commercial IP assets for consumption. For example, Cobb C.'s project of EXO's 2018 Comeback Showcase had the limited-edition Samsung smartphones that included EXO's brand identity and trademarked logo.

In 2017, BigHit Entertainment partnered with communications corporation LINE to launch BT21, a collection of original animated characters personally designed by BTS members. BT21 characters would be featured in a line with UNIQLO clothing, Sketchers sneakers, and official BigHit-sponsored merchandise.[310] The subsidiary BigHit IP would execute a new line of animated characters in 2020 titled TinyTAN; this time each character represented each BTS member from real life. Both BT21 and TinyTAN have unique storylines and themes, which companies can

---

309 Korea Foundation for International Cultural Exchange, *Hallyu Now - Global Hallyu Issue Magazine 2020 - 03+04 vol.35*,(KOFICE, 2020), 17-26.

310 BT21, accessed July 22, 2020.

always incorporate into new merchandise for consumers to enjoy.[311]

With headline-grabbing moves like Korean media conglomerate Naver investing 100 billion won into SM Entertainment in 2020, the global role of content intellectual property has expanded exponentially and diversified in the age of live streaming and digital technology.[312] Mobile video game company Netmarble—currently BigHit Entertainment's second-largest stockholder—launched mobile game *BTS World* in 2019 and plans to release a new BTS IP-based online role-playing game titled *BTS Universe Story* in 2020.[313]

Such intellectual property examples provide new, fun layers to audience consumption. The more companies that capitalize on their artists' intellectual property, the more diverse the opportunities for business growth.

MERCHANDISING AND BUNDLING

While I've explained how K-Pop fandoms contribute to physical sales, you may still be curious as to why K-Pop acts still sell so many physical CDs even though they are generally becoming less popular worldwide. I'll explain.

---

311 Jungeun Sung, "빅히트, 방탄소년단 캐릭터 '타이니탄'(TinyTAN)' 론칭" [BigHit, Launches BTS Character 'TinyTAN'], *Startoday*, August 10, 2020.

312 "네이버, SM엔터에 1000억 투자…"글로벌 영상시장 공략" [Naver, Invests 100 Billion Won to SM Ent… 'Global Video Market Strategy'], *DongA*, August 3, 2020.

313 Insuk Kang, "'BTS 유니버스 스토리' 3분기 글로벌 론칭" ['BTS Universe Story' 3-Quarter Global Launch], *The Games Daily*, May 13, 2020.

If a CD is bundled with exclusive merchandise, the customers pay for an experience rather than for the CD itself. Think about all of the various K-Pop items you may have seen in addition to physical CD albums—apparel, glowsticks, posters, trading cards, and more. Let's assume there's an exclusive ticket to a meet-and-greet event that is randomly included in an idol group's comeback album. Resell value for the ticket will be quite high, but you'd also definitely have bragging rights if you can get your hands on it. Even if online streaming may be more convenient, you now have a greater incentive to buy the physical album, especially because many are collectible editions. This is nothing new—K-Pop CDs have been packaged as collectibles since the 1990s.[314]

Album merchandise bundling increases fan participation while raising both support and revenue. After concluding promotional activities, an idol group may also release an album "repackage" or separate versions; the rereleased album could contain a new lead single plus several B-sides in addition to other new merchandise bundling. So, generally, if you wanted to fully support an idol group during a comeback period, you'd better be ready to purchase at least two physical albums in addition to the different bundles available. This is a huge financial commitment, but it's also common fan behavior; in fact, some official events require fans to present their official merchandise to enter.[315]

---

314 Roald Maliangkay, "Defining Qualities: The Socio-Political Significance of K-Pop Collections," *Korean Histories 4.1*(2013): 27-38.

315 Tamar Herman, "For the K-Pop Industry, Merch Is as Important as the Music," *Billboard*, March 16, 2020.

From the industry's perspective, album bundling undoubtedly increases physical sales, which comprise a great portion of chart rankings around the world. Of course, this isn't a recent phenomenon and K-Pop acts are not the only ones to do this. In fact, American acts like Taylor Swift, Travis Scott, and the Backstreet Boys have bundled T-shirts, key chains, smartphone stands, and concert tickets with physical album CDs to make their way to the top of the Billboard charts.[316]

Understandably, in the West, bundling is a dire need in the age of online streaming and generally declining physical sales. However, as part of *Billboard's* most recent reform in July 2020, for the purposes of chart-ranking, albums bundled with merchandise will now only count if the merchandise is an "add-on."[317] This basically means that promoters must disclose the albums' individual pricing instead of the merchandise bundle price as a whole. For K-Pop artists just starting in the U.S. market via newly formed strategic partnerships, these bundling limitations may affect physical sales and, in turn, *Billboard* chart performances. With more K-Pop success in the U.S., I see bundling increasingly becoming a larger factor for companies to consider.

Yet again, we can see that K-Pop is not just about the music—it's an experience.

316 Ben Sisario, "A Billboard No. 1 Is at Stake, So Here's an Album with Your Taylor Swift Hoodie," *New York Times*, June 9, 2019.

317 Chris Eggertsen, "Billboard Announces New Chart Rules: No More Merch & Ticket Bundles," *Billboard*, July 13, 2020.

CELEBRITY ENDORSEMENTS

As much as I love my best friend for endorsing my book, it'd attract more eyes if a K-Pop star did too, right?

In Korea, you can determine the current popular celebrities often by watching a *soju* (Korean alcoholic drink) commercial. Historically, only the A-list singers or actresses would endorse a *soju* brand, supposedly invoking trendy, sexy, or fresh connotations with the nation's drink. Lee Hyori, Lee Minjung, IU, Suzy, Irene, and Song Ga-in are all very popular female figures throughout the country, and the top two *soju* brands fight for their endorsements. There have been recent exceptions such as Psy and Yumdda—two middle-aged, stocky men—who have secured top *soju* brand deals after rising to pop-cultural prominence.

As we can see from *soju* commercials, the impact of celebrity endorsements in Korea are massive; the celebrity's face is displayed on TV in between or during shows, posters are plastered on the walls in restaurants and bars, and cutout placards are placed on the street. Brands vie for the celebrities and compete against one another to boost exposure, popularity, and, in turn, revenue.

Korean TV ads are roughly fifteen seconds long, shown back-to-back between programming, and very often feature celebrities as opposed to unknown actors. The ad must make an immediate impact in fifteen seconds, so the star is "expected to grab attention and make the ad memorable."[318] As a result,

318 James Turnbull, "Just Beautiful People Holding a Bottle: The Driving Forces behind South Korea's Love of Celebrity Endorsement," *Celebrity Studies,* vol.8, no.1 (2017): 128-135.

brands want to hire a figure that everyone knows to promote not only the particular product but also the brand value. If some iPhone users switched to Android because of EXO's endorsement of the Galaxy Note, the consumer retention rate would increase as well.

Perhaps for your next big project or product, consider having a K-Pop star endorse it.

.

OUTRO

———

I think it's very easy to say, "At the end of the day, it's all just showbiz." While this statement is true, it shouldn't detract from the efforts of the artists and fandoms. Yes, most fans understand that K-Pop, just like any other entertainment form, is a business. Writing and performing a good song is only a fraction of the process; how companies present and promote it to the Korean and global audiences is the key. To do so, the K-Pop music business has adapted to the times; it relies on social media, virtual technologies, global fan communication, and overseas exports.

In a tightly knit industry such as that of K-Pop, competition promotes innovation. Information and strategies are bound to circulate and disseminate, while sometimes bridges, unfortunately, get burned in the process. As the Korean companies become more and more intertwined with global counterparts, we as consumers will see never-before-seen content and promotional strategies.

We've explored the two major themes so far: the music and the business. Next, we'll explore the third and equally important theme: the fans.

PART 7

THE FANDOM CULTURE

Without Shinhwa Changjo (fandom), we couldn't have done it for twenty years. Thank you for not leaving and staying with us.

- LEE MINWOO OF SHINHWA,

AT THEIR 20TH ANNIVERSARY CONCERT TOUR[319]

---

319 Dahoon Chung, "[콘서트 종합] 20주년 '신화' 뿐 아니라 '신화창조'도 현재진행형 "젊게 살겠다"" [Concert summary] 20-year continuous progression for not just *Shinhwa* but also *Shinhwa Changjo* "Let's live young"], *SeoulKyungjae*, October, 18, 2020.

INTRO

Although I've been a K-Pop fan for longer than the average person, there are fellow fans out there who have dedicated even more time and effort into fandom activities. There's no universal way to perfectly define everything that goes on within different fandoms, but I'll do my best to give a comprehensive overview of K-Pop fandom culture in this section of the book.

This section will not only provide an introduction into the bigger realm of media and sociology theory but also invoke interesting examples to illustrate how fandoms act and react in the broader scope of the K-Pop phenomenon. The subject of K-Pop fandoms deserves theses and books of their own, so, admittedly, the few chapters here will not be sufficient. Furthermore, I won't be focusing on one sole artist or fandom throughout the next few chapters in order to provide you with a well-rounded introductory knowledge of fandoms.

Fandom culture is a historical phenomenon that we've seen with superstars like Frank Sinatra, Elvis Presley, The Beatles, and Michael Jackson.[320] For K-Pop specifically, without its fandoms, the phenomenon wouldn't be sustainable; K-Pop fandoms are active consumers of content. Yet, to group all K-Pop fans under one giant monolith would be unfair, since they're fans of different artists and engage with unique activities, wordplay, and content specific to each artist. For a quick example, EXO's fandom, EXO-L, often calls members Xiumin and D.O. by birth names "Minseok" and "Kyungsoo" respectively, which would be unfamiliar to someone outside the EXO-L community.

There's some shared culture amongst different K-Pop fandoms as well as some differences. This section will discuss the importance of fandoms to the K-Pop phenomenon while also exploring their legacies. Long gone are the days when fandom activities implied meaninglessly cheering for celebrities. According to journalist Hyun-su Yim, there's a need to consider a problematic widespread notion of assuming and dismissing K-Pop fans as a group of teenage fangirls.[321] Not only is this sexist and misinformed stereotyping, but it also undermines the fandoms' passion and efforts for their artists to succeed.

In short, K-Pop fans are part of the movement themselves and engage in influential, collective action that has transcended the perceived stereotypes and previously common viewpoints toward K-Pop as a whole.

With that, let's explore fandoms beyond the media headlines.

---

320 Dorian Lynskey, "Beatlemania: 'The Screamers' and Other Tales of Fandom," *The Guardian*, September 28, 2013.

321 Hyun-su Yim, "Surprised at Seeing K-Pop Fans Stand up for Black Lives Matter? You Shouldn't Be," *The Washington Post*, June 11, 2020.

CHAPTER 25

THE ARTIST AND
THE FAN

———

PARASOCIALITY AND COMMUNITY

Academia has been analyzing fandoms long before K-Pop's expansion. Consider how we approach celebrities today. You may have heard the term "stan" being thrown around a lot nowadays. The origin of this word comes from Eminem's song "Stan" (2000), which is about an obsessed fan of Eminem who sends him fan letters and eventually commits homicide.[322] The song has resurfaced in recent years, and the song title has become a noun and a verb. The dictionary definition states that a stan is "*noun*—an extremely or excessively enthusiastic and devoted fan; *verb*: to be an extremely devoted and enthusiastic fan of someone or something."[323] Despite originally negative connotations, people use the word stan positively today.

322 Mat Whitehad, "What the Hell Is a 'Stan' and Where Does the Name Come From," *Huffington Post*, October 11, 2017.

323 *Merriam-Webster*, s.v. "stan (n.)," accessed April 13, 2020; *Merriam-Webster*, s.v. "stan (v.)," accessed April 13, 2020.

Here's an example: I stan the R&B/hip-hop singer, Jay Park. I've been a huge fan of his for over a decade, I own and stream all of his albums, talk about him with fellow fans in online forums, and enthusiastically share new projects on my Instagram. I message him directly on Twitter and Instagram, although he has yet to reply. I know that other Jay Park stans out there are more devoted than I am; some attend multiple concerts on the same tour, throw underwear on stage, send him gifts, and make separate fan social media accounts.

It feels as if I've known Jay Park for a long time, since I've watched him establish his career over the years. Yet he has no idea that I exist or that I'm writing this chapter based on my experience as a Jay Park stan. I'm essentially forming a parasocial relationship with Jay; we don't know each other personally, but it's "intimacy at a distance," as I engage primarily through the intermediary of social media.[324] I feel like I can relate to his work ethic and drive as well as his positive outlook on life.[325]

Jay Park collectively addresses his legion of fans. While it's usually a one-sided relationship, he occasionally calls out individual names on live streams and engages in one-on-one video chats. Consequently, sometimes I ponder about the blurry boundary of parasociality upon which we form a fan-artist relationship; even though my impression of his public image comes from what I see on Instagram, he has opportunities to acknowledge my existence as an individual

---

324 Donald Horton and R. Richard Wohl, "Mass Communication and Para-Social Interaction," *Psychiatry: Journal for the Study of Interpersonal Processes,* 19 (1956): 215–229.

325 Annette Choi, "The Parasocial Phenomenon," *PBS,* April 5, 2017.

fan.[326] Nonetheless, I feel appreciated when he thanks the fandom collectively.[327] But in the K-Pop context, how does a fandom form in the first place?

Historically, in South Korea, exclusive fan cafes on Korean search engines like Daum—think of early versions of Facebook groups—systematically organized K-Pop fandoms. Today, K-Pop fandom creation is no longer as organic; the companies actually implement their groups' fandoms. They make a public announcement for potential fans to join and also designate everything from the fandom's name to its official color.

Official K-Pop fandom registration usually occurs within a set period of roughly a month, during which potential members can pay a fixed amount—usually 30,000 won or roughly $25 USD. Upon payment, fans receive exclusive merchandise and benefits such as membership cards, light sticks, priority ticketing for events, and more.[328] Previously, only Korean residents could buy memberships to most official fandoms, so global fans had to rely on unofficial communities on social media. To accommodate those who lived overseas, companies

---

326 P. David Marshall, "The Promotion and Presentation of the Self: Celebrity as Marker of Presentational Media," *Celebrity Studies*, Vol.1, no.1 (March 2010): 35-48.

327 Sean Robinson, "Celebrity Role Models, Social Media, & LGBTQ Youth: Lady Gaga as Parasocial Mentor," in *Contemporary Studies of Sexuality & Communication: Theoretical and Applied Perspectives*, ed. Jimmie Manning and Carey M. Noland, (Dubuque: Kendall Hunt, 2016), 501-518.

328 "Seventeen Official Fan Club 'Carat' 4기 모집 안내" [Seventeen Official Fan Club 'Carat' 4th Cohort Recruitment Announcement], PLEDIS, accessed April 25, 2020.

like SM and BigHit launched the mobile platforms Lysn and Weverse respectively, on which global fans can now pay for membership and receive exclusive benefits.

Fandoms promote a participatory culture in which the fans directly advocate the artists through the online and offline communities.[329] Renowned media scholar, Henry Jenkins, explains that in a participatory culture, members "believe that their contributions matter" and "feel some degree of social connection with one another."[330] Examples of the social and community-driven activities of fandoms are organized mass streaming, hashtag trends, organized protesting, and fan voting for award ceremonies.

Such voluntary collective action reinforces the fans' engagement with not only the artists but with each other as independent communities. For example, ARMYs—BTS's fandom—trended Twitter hashtags and contacted national radio liaisons to help BTS win the 2017 *Billboard* Top Social Artist Award.[331] Social media platforms also allow fans to voice their opinions on specific issues regarding their idols. iKONICs—iKON's fandom—and BLINKs—BLACKPINK's fandom—demanded YG Entertainment be more diligent in promoting comebacks, and Korean ELFs—Super Junior's fandom—demanded two members of Super Junior leave

329 Kwang Woo Noh, "YouTube and K Pop Fan's Tribute Activity," *The Journal of the Korea Contents Association,* Vol.15, No.6 (2015): 25-32.

330 Henry Jenkins, "Confronting the Challenges of Participatory Culture: Media Education for the 21st Century (Part One)," *HENRY JENKINS* (blog), October 19, 2006.

331 Jason Lipshutz, "BTS Thanks Fans for Top Social Artist Win at Billboard Music Awards 2017: Watch," *Billboard*, May 21, 2017.

the group due to scandals.[332] Companies can't just brush off fans' feedback and requests because fandoms generate attention and revenue.

Within the fandoms, some fans even create their own derivative content like fancams, translations, artwork, and fan fiction. Through their creations, fans manifest not only their interests but also their creative talents and fantasies.[333] Fancam and fan fiction subcultures within the larger fandom culture show further intricacies and demonstrate that fandoms cannot be simplified into a single entity.

NOTION OF THE "K-POP FANDOM"

I see another big picture question surrounding K-Pop's global expansion: what exactly is this notion of the K-Pop fandom? Think back to when I suggested that we should appreciate K-Pop artists for who they are rather than grouping them all under a giant K-Pop umbrella. Just because a fan is a Monbebe—a member of Monsta X's fandom—doesn't necessarily imply he's a fan of all other K-Pop acts in the scene. His fan efforts could be solely dedicated to Monsta X, or he may just prefer Monsta X's music over all else.

I find it unfair to outright assume, "Oh, you like Monsta X? So, you're a K-Pop fan! Do you like _____ too?" This is

---

332 Saeron Lee, "앨범 안 내는 소속사에…팬 무시하는 아이돌에…'팬덤'이 뿔났다" [At the Company Not Releasing Albums… at Idols Ignoring Fans… 'Fandom' Is Angry], *Yeongnamilbo*, August 21, 2017.

333 Nam-ok Kim and Suk Seunghye, "그녀들만의 음지문화, 아이돌 팬픽" [Shade Culture of Their Own: Idol Fanfics], *Journal of Korean Culture*, Vol.37 (May 2017): 191-226.

similar to asking a Marvel fan, "Oh, so you're a superhero fan! Do you like DC's Green Lantern too?" Do you see the logic here? It's also strange to assume that a Belieber—a member of Justin Bieber's fandom—is also a Directioner—a member of One Direction's fandom. This is a challenge for any K-Pop fandom; most people still lump K-Pop into a general umbrella category for convenience's sake. The fact that all well-known idol acts share elements in production and promotion further complicate this issue.

The mere ability of someone to say, "I only stan ____, not K-Pop in general," is due in part to the increasing diversity of musical influences and content from various K-Pop artists. Hypothetically, I could be a fan of The Beatles, but other rock bands may not meet my tastes because of how broad the rock genre is. So, am I a rock fan? I think that's for me to decide; how I feel about all other rock bands would be different compared to someone else in the same position. Since each artist has their own style and flair, it's absolutely legitimate to stan an artist but not all K-Pop. On the other hand, it's still possible to be a general fan of K-Pop as a whole and not stan any specific artists.[334]

Fundamentally, K-Pop fandoms aren't different from sports fans or comic book fans. European football fandom culture differs from that of American baseball. While it's possible for someone to belong to both, we recognize that each have different practices, lingo, and norms. The main issue in Western media once again is that they apply the term "the

---

334 Crystal S. Anderson, "K-Pop Fandom 101," *KpopKollective* (blog), December 8, 2013.

K-Pop fandom" to categorize diverse fans and practices into a single monolith. There is no single organization or entity that oversees all respective fans of different K-Pop acts, and it would be impossible for there to be one.

Even a single K-Pop fandom consists of fans from different backgrounds and viewpoints. For example, in the midst of the 2020 Black Lives Matter movement, many Black fans sought to educate unaware fellow fans about the movement's importance.[335] Before I'm a fan of a K-Pop idol, I'm an Asian American with specific viewpoints that may differ from how another fan of a different idol sees the world.[336] So in this context, lumping us into a huge umbrella and assuming we're the same as millions of others is not only inaccurate but also ignorant. Recognize different fandoms of different artists and realize that each fan has its own set of values.

WE ARE TOGETHER—A SYMBIOSIS

The movies *Spider-Man 3* and *Venom* introduce a concept called symbiosis. Both Peter Parker and Eddie Brock contract an extraterrestrial organism that gives them very special powers as well as a sleek black suit. The organism and the body move together in conjunction, creating Symbiote Spider-Man and Venom, respectively.

What am I trying to get at here?

---

335 Hyun-su Yim, "K-Pop Fans: A Diverse, Underestimated and Powerful Force," *The Korea Herald*, June 12, 2020.

336 Raisa Bruner, "How K-Pop Fans Actually Work as a Force for Political Activism in 2020," *TIME*, July 25, 2020.

K-Pop fans, depending on how invested they are in the fandoms, support the culture in various ways, ranging from something as simple as streaming favorite artists on YouTube to waiting outside the airport gates for hours to greet them with fan letters. Sure, this may sound like something that's prevalent in every culture and industry; this happens to sports athletes, Hollywood stars, and even Tiktok influencers. However, K-Pop fans are unique; in fact, they can be passionate to such an extent that they're often portrayed negatively. What makes K-Pop fans different and why do they deserve greater appreciation? What role do they play in the dissemination of content and the longevity of the stars?

Let me suggest one way to think about the fandom-idol dynamic: a harmonious coexistence. A symbiosis.

The idol fandom culture became prevalent in Korea since the early Seo Taiji & Boys days in the '90s. This fandom model further evolved with notably SM Entertainment's H.O.T and their fandom, Club H.O.T. Of course, those were older times when H.O.T. fans—without smartphones or social media—had to rely on a lot of physical activities such as going out to buy cassette tapes, attending concerts, or gathering near the TV broadcast station.[337] Club H.O.T's systemically organized structure and effort to work together with SM Entertainment fostered collective action—donning the fandom's official color and

---

337 Soyoung Jeon, "[팬덤에 빠진 대한민국①] 한국 대중문화 발전의 일등공신은 '빠순이'" [[Korea Immersed in Fandoms①] the 'bbasoon-ee (Fangirl)' Is the Most Meritorious for Korean Pop Cultural Evolution], *Today Shinmun*, May 12, 2018.

merchandise, screaming official fan chants, and representing the idols in public settings.[338]

In 2020, fans still do this all the time. In fact, social media has allowed fans to support their favorite idols on various platforms in addition to the traditional methods and to grow the fandom's global scope exponentially. Examples of what social media has allowed fandoms to do include mass streaming, online voting for awards, and performing charity acts on behalf of artists, which I'll get to later.

Most companies will implement official, coordinated procedures to get an idol group's fandom started. They may designate the official fandom color, provide showcase event details, and have the idols communicate via letter or video to encourage the fans to join. Yet lesser-known companies and idols without as many resources struggle more to generate exposure. Although social media has aided tremendously in building an idol brand and spreading the word about it, some idols still may need to engage in busking—street performances—and performing at smaller local events while even having separate part-time jobs. Without a fandom with shared dedication and collective action, fan support is bound to be uncoordinated. Less support and less exposure equal less results.

With a strong, loyal fandom, however, the idols are financially and emotionally supported on the road to their breakthrough. JiYoung Lee, Professor at Sejong University and an ARMY,

338 Sungmin Kim, 케이팝의 작은 역사 [K-Pop's Small History], (Seoul: Geulhangari Publishers, 2018), 84.

commented on the process of ARMYs' requests to unreceptive U.S. radio stations to finally play BTS's music:

> It was an achievement made by ordinary people through unity and coalition. It was a grassroots movement… In order for BTS to be properly recognized, we needed to fight against such prejudice.[339]

Through the arduous process of collectively contacting U.S. radio stations, ARMYs became aware of and exposed the American industry's prejudiced and xenophobic notions of K-Pop. Thanks to ARMY efforts, today, BTS's physical albums are formally distributed in the U.S. and the radio industry cannot simply ignore the group any longer given the success of "Dynamite" (2020). The fandom's bond becomes further reinforced when BTS credits the fandom, especially during momentous occasions like reaching number one on *Billboard* Hot 100:

> We want to share this honor with you, ARMY. Every step of the way you were there for us. ARMY, you are the reason that keeps us going.[340]

---

339 *Sebasi Talk*, "BTS and Army Grow Together, Fighting Against Prejudice | JiYoung Lee, Professor," September 22, 2019, video, 21:33.

340 *JoseOchoaTV*, "BTS Send Heartfelt Message to Army! [Billboard Hot 100 No.1]," September 2, 2020, video, 1:52.

Support and love go both ways, and a fandom's bond creates something special. *Spider-Man 3* and *Venom* aren't the best movies ever made, but the symbiotic powers in them are pretty awesome. The symbiote becomes engrained in Spider-Man and alters how he acts, both emotionally and physically, as they move as one. For K-Pop fans, the symbiosis idea is the same; the artists influence how fans act, think, and support them while reinforcing each other's existence. Now, *that's* a superpower.

CHAPTER 26

SOUTH KOREA AND THE WORLD

———

Obviously, there's an initial barrier for foreigners when approaching K-Pop: the Korean language. That being said, there are also cultural differences across the Korean and global fandoms. Global fans may only wonder what goes on in Korea and how Koreans perceive K-Pop. There are Korean YouTubers who explain this concept, with videos like "What Koreans Think of _____" or "_____ Explained by a Korean." My goal in this chapter is to give you a cross-comparison of why and how Korean fans consume K-Pop content and how their global counterparts engage with something that's often not part of their primary language or culture.

You see, for an average Korean born in South Korea, K-Pop is just one segment of mainstream entertainment along with K-Dramas, TV variety shows, and online YouTubers. The famous K-Pop tourist locations like a café that idols frequently visit exist, but they're just tourist spots. K-Pop exists but it's not as pervasive as one may expect and fandom activities obviously aren't for everyone. Of course, the Koreans who are actually interested in joining fandoms do so and become very invested. Thanks to the people who gathered together to support Seo Taiji & Boys and H.O.T. in the early days, there's now an institutionalized fandom system for their successors—fan cafes, official relationships with the companies, fanchants, and more.

Now let's picture what a global fan needs to do to fully engage with K-Pop. Actually, think about how everyone engages with entertainment in general. This is as simple as turning on the radio and singing along to a trending song or switching between TV channels to see what program is funnier. It's very simple; content is readily available and all we have to do is tune in.

But what if the content is not immediately understandable because it's in a foreign language? You'd need to go through the process of looking up translations or subtitles and then trying to digest it, not to mention learning to understand the K-Pop industry. As a result, non-native Korean speakers must be much more proactive in their consumption, which isn't the norm. After all, we often turn to entertainment as a source of easygoing fun, relaxation, and excitement. If I'm required to work to better engage with certain media, my efforts better be worth my time.

Put that into context: global K-Pop fans—usually non-Korean speakers—invest a lot of effort into consuming K-Pop content. If they're really hooked and decide to support a specific artist, there will be even more work to do. Unlike Korean fans who receive updates directly from the plethora of Korean outlets, global fans usually have to wait for official translations or rely on fan translators. Fortunately, companies today are very aware of the different fan demographics, so they release content such as official teasers and announcements in both Korean and English for a wide audience to understand.

However, I still don't think receiving some English content provides the same experiences for both groups. If I were to stay updated about a German rock band even though I don't speak German at all, I would need to expend extra effort on researching, and it would definitely help if I started familiarizing myself with some German cultural concepts and basic vocabulary. This learning wouldn't be required, but it would enhance my engagement with the band for sure.

South Korean fans have historically frowned upon and even discouraged the idea of a "multi-stan"—someone who belongs to multiple fandoms at once. Their argument is that it's ironic to openly stan a competitor who isn't your main dedication. K-Pop fandoms often have rivalries or alliances, as we've seen with the Club H.O.T. versus D.S.F. (Sechs Kies) rivalry in the '90s, and a formal alliance across fandoms Ca-T-EL (TVXQ, Super Junior, SS501) in the mid-'00s. The domestic market emphasizes a competitive nature through domestic TV music program charts, Korean online streaming charts like Melon, and V Live popularity rankings, among others.[341]

Globally, multi-stans have historically been more prevalent, especially due to the early international K-Pop events like

341 Bumsoo, "잡덕이면 안 되는 거야?" [Can't I Be a Multi-Stan?], *Brunch* (blog, May 2, 2019.

the SMTown Tour in the early '10s because a lot of fans were just excited to have discovered a new world. Today, however, global fans have increasingly focused on individual fandoms, for several possible reasons such as an abundance of online content for each single artist, the stigma of being a multi-stan from Korean fans, and the relatively new ways to "officially" join a fandom, such as buying a membership on Weverse. Suppose you stan three artists. Realistically, you're unlikely to be as invested in each artist as someone who stans one full-time is. There's just too much content to keep up with, and dedicated K-Pop consumption requires money.

One may argue that the multi-stan concept perpetuates the notion that there is a single K-Pop fandom, but as I mentioned, there is no such single entity. Of course, it's fine to do whatever your heart desires.

According to a 2016 study of Korean fandoms on Twitter from Hankuk University of Foreign Studies, fans frequently expressed both positive and negative reactions toward both the global fandoms and the artist's management. Korean fans were curious and praised the global fans for their efforts in learning Korean and the fanchants, and took pride in seeing their favorite idols succeed in a global context. Korean fans were also excited to see foreign celebrities like Conan O'Brien or Chloe Grace Moretz publicly endorse K-Pop.[342] The sentiment of national pride is very strong within the Korean community as a whole; I experienced this feeling when I saw Psy and BTS make waves around the globe.

---

342 Mathieu Berbiguier and Young Han Cho. "케이팝 (K-Pop)의 한국 팬덤에 대한 연구" [Understanding the Korean Fandom of the K-Pop], *Korean Journal of Communication and Information*, Vol. 81 (2017): 273-297.

Koreans have felt national pride in Korean pop culture expanding outside of the country ever since the initial *Hallyu* Wave, and the current iteration of the K-Pop phenomenon has been no exception. In my discussion with Mathieu Berbiguier, Ph.D. student at UCLA who conducted the aforementioned 2016 study while at Hankuk University, we discussed the duality of Koreans historically seeking Western validation for pop culture with The Grammys, Billboards, and Oscars, as well as having national pride.

Honestly, I get excited whenever Korean content gets globally acknowledged, whether it's Psy setting a YouTube record, BTS topping *Billboard* charts, or the movie *Parasite* sweeping the Oscars. Korean media also celebrated these achievements, calling them "historic" and "the first-ever" for Korea.[343] The media continuously reinforces and validates Korean national pride in this manner, yet I also realize that the excitement has the potential to obscure objective analysis. Of course, within South Korea, there will still always be many skeptics, but I expect more groundbreaking milestones to happen in the near future.

At the same time, some Korean fans do feel that foreigners have invaded their previously exclusive community. Due to K-Pop's global success, the global fandoms' influences and roles have become critical, which leads to a certain uneasiness amongst Korean fans; they feel discomfort over the fact that K-Pop is

---

343 Taeksung Oh, "영화 '기생충' 오스카 수상…K-POP이어 K-FILM 까지 세계 중심 '우뚝'" [Movie 'Parasite' Wins at Oscars… K-Pop and Also K-Film Stands Tall at Center of World], *VoaKorea*, February 11, 2020; Jungmin Seo, "방탄소년단, 한국인 최초로 그래미 시상…'다시 오겠다'" [BTS, First Koreans to Present at Grammys… 'We'll Come Back'], *Hangyeorae*, February 11, 2019.

no longer exclusive to the Korean fandoms. With more and more K-Pop acts focusing on global promotions rather than domestic ones, some Korean fans have also expressed annoyance at the companies for overlooking K-Pop's home.[344] One Korean fan of SEVENTEEN even retired from the fandom after frustrations with the company PLEDIS began focusing much more on Japanese touring than domestic ones.[345]

Global fans—with their more diverse backgrounds and viewpoints than those of their Korean counterparts—are also much more progressive when discussing racial and gender identities within fandom spaces.[346] As a result, sometimes the Korean fans don't mesh with global ones. Furthermore, international fans sometimes have a shared curiosity in the larger Korean society that produces the idols that borderlines on problematic exoticism and even leads to criticisms of the "Koreaboo," a negative term for a fan obsessed with Korean culture.[347] Language barriers can also serve as sources of confusion and conflict; global fans prefer translated content, yet Korean fans dislike when non-Korean speaking fans ask the artists to write in English or for them to translate. Finally, Korean fans often openly criticize global fans for reposting or sharing original content without permission.[348]

344 Berbiguier and Cho, "Fandom," 2017.

345 Kyujin Shin, Heeyoon Im. ""해외 팬클럽과 왜 차별하나요"... 성난 팬덤, 일부는 '탈덕'까지" ['Why Do You Discriminate Us against Global Fanclubs'... Angry Fandom, Some Even 'Unstan'], *DongA*, July 27, 2019.

346 Yim, "K-Pop fans," 2020.

347 Kyungwon Min, "방탄 국내외 팬들 관심사 달라...해외서는 젠더 이슈 주목" [BTS's Global Fans' Interests Are Different...Focus on Gender Issue Abroad], *Joongangilbo*, December 11, 2019.

348 Berbiguier and Cho, "Fandom," 2017.

I believe that as K-Pop continues to attract a diverse demographic of fans, diplomatic relationships and understandings of different perspectives amongst the fandoms are crucial for an inclusive atmosphere. At the end of the day, all fans share their love and passion for their favorite artists, and greater discourse regarding cultural differences is necessary. We all may never fully understand or agree with each other, but we should still promote inclusivity and respect.

CHAPTER 27

THE LASTING LEGACY

———

K-Pop fandoms have lasting legacies. Of course, as active consumers, the fans help propel their artists to stardom and commercial breakthroughs. Furthermore, K-Pop fandoms—as social communities—also engage in positive collective action on behalf of the artists. Not only does this generate artists' exposure, but it also promotes good deeds and rallying behind bigger societal causes. We can see the participatory culture of fandoms when they adopt more active roles in organizing, directing, and advocating causes amongst themselves. Let's take a look at several ways that fandoms are supporters, consumers, and organizers.

Fans engage in their own promotions aside from the official company activities to call attention to particular special occasions. The most notable example of these promotions is the "subway ad" culture in Korea; fans purchase an ad space for their favorite celebrity in a busy, populated subway. The ads often celebrate birthdays or anniversaries, and the target celebrity may even pay a visit to the ad and take a picture with it as a sign of gratitude. Koreans don't only do this for K-Pop idols; it's common to see fan-purchased ads featuring actors, musical stars, professional gamers, and even animated characters. After reality competition shows like *Produce 101* or *K-POP Star* promoted an active consumer-fan voting system, the fans of a designated competitor would encourage others to vote for the artist through these subway ads as well.

To provide some context of their influence, these ads have increased twenty-eight-fold, from only seventy-six in 2014 to 10,468 in 2019.[349] It costs between 1.5 and 4.5 million Korean won ($1,300 and $4,000 USD) pre-tax for a monthly ad space.[350] These ads are the Korean equivalent to seeing your favorite artists (or lawyers and insurance agents) on billboards as you drive down a U.S. highway; whether you like them or not, you're bound to look at them. For fans, subway ads are not only a promotional tactic but also allow communication with the stars to show them love and support.

Additionally, K-Pop fandoms have long engaged in philanthropic behavior for both Korean and global causes. Usually, charity work occurs during a special occasion for the fandom's artist, such as a debut anniversary, birthday, or album release.[351] For example, in South Korea, idol Kang Daniel has often encouraged his fans to donate to charity. In conjunction with Kang's 100th day since his solo

349 Inha Ryu, "아이돌 팬덤문화 인기⊠ 지하철 광고 문화 바꿨다" [Idol Fandom Culture Popularity⊠ Changed Subway Ad Culture], *Kyunghyang*, April 7, 2020.

350 Hyun-su Yim, "K-Pop Ads Taking over Seoul Subway," *The Jakarta Post*, October 16, 2018.

351 Ilyo Moon, ""나의 스타 이름으로 착한 일 할래요" 유행처럼 번진 '팬덤 기부'" ['I Want to Do Something Good on Behalf of My Star' 'Fandom Donation' Trend Spreads], *Chosunilbo*, January 18, 2020.

debut, Korean members of his fandom DANITY raised 9.6 million Korean won and gave 128 blood donations for the Korea Childhood Leukemia Foundation.[352] Kang has since matched fans' donations to various causes, creating a positive synergy effect.

Global fandoms have also specifically engaged in various sociopolitical causes. Notably, in 2020, amidst the Black Lives Matter movement, legions of K-Pop fans on Twitter from various fandoms engaged in collective action to thwart police attempts to arrest peaceful protesters. The fans clogged the application, iWatch Dallas, with fancams and K-Pop video content so that the Dallas Police Department couldn't access uploaded protest footage. They even crashed the app.

In response to racist Twitter posts, K-Pop fans once again clogged the feed with fancams while also tagging #alllivesmatter or #whitelivesmatter to divert attention away. Those seeking to use those hashtags for their agenda were met with unexpected videos of K-Pop idols dancing.[353] K-Pop fans often spontaneously share fancams on Twitter, but this was a coordinated action with a message and purpose.

Another example occurred when Thai K-Pop fans openly criticized the Thai king for disappointing coronavirus reactions

352 Wooyoung Jang, "강다니엘 팬클럽, 소아암 환우 위해 기부…"선한 영향력 힘 믿는다"" [Kang Daniel Fanclub, Donates to Childhood Cancer Patients... 'Believe in Power of Positive Influence'], *Chosunilbo*, November 1, 2019.

353 Kaitlyn Tiffany, "Why K-Pop Fans Are No Longer Posting about K-Pop," *The Atlantic*, June 6, 2020.

with girl group TWICE's lyrics.[354] We also saw such collective action when K-Pop fans and Tiktok users collectively thwarted ticketing and attendance efforts at President Donald Trump's Oklahoma campaign rally in 2020.[355]

The interconnectedness and diversity of K-Pop fandoms really bring into light various regional or race-specific issues around the world. I could list many more, but let's turn to a specific case.

THE CASE OF BTS AND ARMY

Both BTS and their fandom ARMY have displayed fantastic synergy, which amplifies even further for sociopolitical causes. In 2017, BTS launched the "Love Yourself" campaign in a collaboration with UNICEF to curtail violence against youth.[356] The campaign garnered support via Twitter hashtags such as #BTSLoveMyself, which accumulated over 10 million Tweets and attracted fans from 199 countries to the campaign site.[357] BTS subsequently donated 500 million Korean won (roughly $447,000 USD) and by

---

354 Hyun-su Yim, "Thai K-Pop Fans Trending #Dispatch to Vent Frustration at Monarchy," *The Korea Herald*, March 30, 2020.

355 Taylor Lorenz, Kellen Browning and Sheera Frenkel. "TikTok Teens and K-Pop Stans Say They Sank Trump Rally," *The New York Times*, July 11, 2020.

356 "Love Myself 캠페인 상세소개" [Love Myself Campaign Details], LOVE MYSELF, accessed May 2, 2020.

357 Hongkoo Kang, ""BTS 오빠들 덕에 행복해졌다"…'러브 마이셀프' 캠페인 파급력 기대 이상" ['Happier Thanks to BTS Oppas'… 'Love Myself' Campaign Exceeds Expected Ripple Effect], *DongA*, May 2, 2019.

late 2019, they had raised approximately 2.6 billion Korean won in just two years.[358]

As in the case of the 2020 Black Lives Matter campaign, BTS's donation of $1 million USD propelled the ARMY fandom to officially match their amount, raising a total of $2 million in just twenty-four hours. Their actions also spurred pro wrestler and movie star, John Cena, to match another $1 million.[359] ARMYs trended the #MatchAMillion Twitter hashtag, inviting the community to take action and donate. The diversity of the ARMY fandom is a key factor here; Black fans who were at the forefront of the social movement called upon other fans to educate themselves, donate, and protest for the cause.

A variety of factors made this possible on such a massive scale, but BTS's authentic messages through their music and their transparent communication with ARMYs was a main driving factor; intimacy between the artist and fans is very important. What was particularly exciting about the global ARMYs' activities was that their collective action was very organic and systemized despite having no hierarchical structure.[360] Even prior to "Dynamite" (2020)'s release, ARMYs

358 "방탄소년단, 유니세프에 26억 기부..'LOVE MYSELF FESTA'도 함께" [BTS, Donates 2.6 Billion Won to UNICEF... Also 'Love Myself Festa'], *The Korea Times*, October 25, 2019.

359 Mihir Zaveri, "BTS Fans Say They've Raised $1 Million for Black Lives Matter Groups," *The New York Times*, June 8, 2020; Torsten Ingvaldsen, "John Cena Matches BTS' Fans $1M USD Black Lives Matter Donation," *HYPEBEAST*, June 11, 2020.

360 WoongJo Chang and Shin-Eui Park. "The Fandom of *Hallyu*, a Tribe in the Digital Network Era: The Case of ARMY of BTS," *Kritika Kultura* 32 (2019): 260-287.

already had publicized their streaming goals and were more than ready for the single's release.

I discussed ARMYs' preparedness with Nicole Santero, doctoral student at the University of Nevada, Las Vegas, who runs Twitter account @ResearchBTS and has more than 70,000 followers as of October 2020. We talked about the easiness and accessibility of Twitter, as well as how the platform inherently fosters interaction and engagement; like-minded people naturally connect together. In the ARMY context, fans utilize the ability to connect to the fullest, whether it be through setting tangible goals for streaming or trending specific hashtags. Empowered as individuals, they strive to take initiative and collaborate with each other through public Tweets and private chatrooms, which has fostered communities of researchers, translators, statisticians, and more to join the fandom itself.

ARMY boasts huge diversity; the web traffic demographics for BTS's 2020 concert tour tickets included people from all over the world, ranging from minors to those over sixty-five years old, with plenty of male fans.[361] Some ARMY parents would bring their children to concerts to convince *them* to join instead of the reverse; that's a far cry from the stereotypical fandom of just teenage fangirls.[362] If a fan has a great idea they want to share with the ARMY fandom, they could ask an influential account for a retweet, which makes a grassroots movement very possible. Santero is part of the fan-driven

---

361 Aditi Bhandari, "The Mobilizing Power of the BTS Army," *Reuters*, July 14, 2020.

362 *KBStheLive*, "The Real Reason Why BTS Hits No.1 on Billboard," September 4, 2020, video, 8:41.

project *BTS ARMY Census* that analyzes the fandom's global demographics and which has soared well past 350,000 respondents from around the world.

From the examples in this chapter, we can see that a K-Pop fandom is actually an intricate, cohesive community of its own. No longer are fans mere followers of a celebrity; fandoms are communities where fans are not only supporters, but also thinkers, leaders, and organizers. As technology has evolved, so have the fans. Social media has allowed fans to gather and discuss various topics as well as promote discourse and collective action outside of K-Pop. There's a lot of work that goes into an organized, collective movement, but I believe the end results are the fandoms' true legacies.

CHAPTER 28

THE "OTHER" FAN

———

As the K-Pop phenomenon has spread, a wide variety of people have become fans, some of whom have generated widely covered news in both Korea and the rest of the world. Let's discuss two particular categories of these fans.

First, a "*sasaeng* (사생)" fan is someone who invades an artist's personal life. It's basically the equivalent of an obsessed fan beyond socially acceptable norms. In Korea, there's been a history of overly attached and obsessive behavior from *sasaeng* fans. Their activities have included illegally breaking into an idol's house and stealing their possessions, tracking down an idol's phone number and repeatedly calling them, chasing down an idol's car in a taxi, and even reserving first-class flight tickets to sit close to an idol.[363] Why do some people do this, and should they still be considered fans?

Most level-headed fans would criticize and shun *sasaeng* fans for their actions, yet their actual responses have been

---

363 Sungeun Park, ""잠 좀 자고 싶어요"…사생팬에 고통받는 연예인의 호소" ['I Want to Sleep'… Pained Celebrities' Cry Out against *Sasaeng* Fans], *Yonhap News*, January 23, 2018.

interesting. Entire *sasaeng* fan communities or chatrooms exist, in which they share information regarding the stars' whereabouts and plan accordingly. Some *sasaeng* fans feel misunderstood, as they believe the stars rely on their support for money and fame.[364]

This problem has heightened due to K-Pop's globalization; it's not just contained within Korea anymore. Recently, an obsessive German fan claimed that TWICE's Nayeon was his girlfriend and repeatedly tried to approach her. He stalked the locations from Nayeon's photos and even boarded the same airplane she was on. Nayeon publicly requested that he leave her alone, and JYP Entertainment subsequently pressed charges for obstruction of official business and filed a restraining order.[365]

Of course, this has historically been an issue in the general international entertainment industry too; events such as a crazed fan breaking into Chris Brown's mansion in Los Angeles to confess her love or a concertgoer claiming his "life's mission to impregnate" Miley Cyrus happen all too frequently.[366] Sometimes these obsessions turn violent, as we

364 Hyoeun Kim and Hyekyung Cho. "월 100만원 쓰는 女사생팬 '알바·노숙 심지어…'" [Female Sasaeng Spends 1 Million Won per Month 'Part-Time Job, Homelessness, Even…'], *Joongangilbo*, March 15, 2012.

365 Hyojin Rha, "트와이스 나연 스토커로 알려진 남성이 사과 영상을 올렸다" [Man Known as TWICE Nayeon's Stalker Uploads Apology Video], *HuffingtonPost*, January 30, 2020.

366 Ekin Karasin, "'You're Crazy' Terrified Chris Brown Hides as Crazed Fan Tries to 'Break into' His La Mansion and Yells That She's His 'Life Partner'," *The Sun*, March 29, 2020; Verity Sulway, "Miley Cyrus Obsessed Fan Desperate to Impregnate Her Arrested after Terrifying Threats," *Mirror*, September 24, 2019.

saw with the tragic 2016 murder of American singer Christina Grimmie by a crazed fan at a meet-and-greet event.[367]

The extent to which fans should support their stars has always been a gray area, since there's a fine line between supporting and invading. As difficult as it is for some to grasp, the stars do have their own lives outside of their glamorous performances. Sometimes it's difficult for people to know how to appropriately act during an encounter with their favorite singer. Sure, the celebrity may be down to take a selfie, but they would most likely be very unhappy if the same person were to later break into their home to tell them they "love" them. While a healthy dosage of fan activity is not only encouraged but also needed, being a K-Pop idol is still just a job. The stars are here to entertain, not to allow fans to invade their privacy and impact their mental health.

The second type of K-Pop fan that I will discuss is the "anti-fan," which is the opposite of a fan; it's someone who actively hates and disparages a particular artist, their fandom, or both. In the 1990s, the anti-fan culture was prevalent, especially against female celebrities. Interestingly, the anti-fans of these celebrities were often female fans of boy bands. For girl group Baby V.O.X., H.O.T. fans not only sent them hate mail but also sent them razor blades, sprayed them with harmful liquids (which apparently smelled of pepper powder), and threw eggs at them.[368]

367 Chris Stokel-Walker, "What the Murder of Christina Grimmie by a Fan Tells Us about YouTube Influencer Culture," *TIME*, May 3, 2019.

368 Youngrok Kim, "'해투3' 간미연 '안티는 내 잘못...윤은혜, 나 때문에 실명할 뻔'" ['HappyTogether3' Kan Miyeon 'Antis Are My Fault... Yoon Eunhye Almost Went Blind Because of Me'], *Chosunilbo*, March 22, 2018.

In 2006, one crazed anti-fan gave TVXQ's U-Know a bottle of orange juice mixed with superglue. Unaware, U-Know drank the bottle and was immediately sent to the hospital. Subsequently, he suffered from mental trauma. Both U-Know and SM Entertainment decided not to file charges due to the perpetrator's young age of twenty.[369]

Today, a greater social awareness of idol fandom culture as well as quick dissemination of information via social media helps dissuade potential perpetrators from such violent actions. However, in present context, anti-fans are still very prevalent online, especially thanks to the anonymous commenting culture. Further, cancel culture and doxing are rampant in the global context, especially when someone states something contrary to or offensive to a fandom's ideals and values. While there are always bad apples, there's no way to accurately measure how much toxic behavior occurs in a particular fandom, specifically.

So, how do we promote a fun but respectful global K-Pop fandom culture? Well, fans should consider whether their idols would be proud of their actions. Fans represent the idols as supporters and ambassadors; in turn, the idols should serve as respectable role models.

Again, I urge you to recognize that showbiz works similarly everywhere and that crazed K-Pop fans are just one aspect of a much larger problem in entertainment as a whole. Should fandom culture address toxic fans or anti-fans? Absolutely. Do they represent K-Pop fandoms as a whole? Absolutely not.

---

369 Kyungran Lee and Inkyung Lee. "동방신기 독극물 테러범 ' 우발적 범행' 진술" [TVXQ's Poison Terrorist Alleges 'Accidental Crime'], *Joongangilbo*, October 15, 2006.

OUTRO

———

Fandoms have evolved as K-Pop has grown exponentially. It's quite easy today to get plugged into a fandom on social media. The degree of dedication and commitment to fandom activity obviously differs per person, but it's something special to see individual fans come together in unity for a specific reason. In the K-Pop context, the fans are vital in advocating for their artists' rights, engaging in discourse and criticism, and supporting artists emotionally and financially. There's an important role to play as a fan beyond being a mere cheerleader; how each person becomes involved is up to them. What will *you* do?

PART 8

THE FUTURE OUTLOOK

We are the Future.

- H.O.T,

IN THEIR 1997 SINGLE, "WE ARE THE FUTURE"[370]

---

370 *MBCkpop*, "H.O.T - We are the future, HOT - 위 아더 퓨처, MBC Top Music 19971122," June 19, 2012, video, 3:36.

CHAPTER 29

THE ODYSSEY OF HENRY LAU

———

Instead of giving you a full summary of the main topics we've discussed in this book, I want to tell you the story of K-Pop-idol-turned-international-sensation, Henry Lau. Singing, dancing, instrumental performances, Korean variety TV programs, Hollywood and Chinese films, viral Tiktok videos—you name it, he's done it. My parents don't watch a lot of Korean TV, but even they are big fans of Henry.

To bring you up to speed, Henry debuted as a special violinist for Super Junior's "Don't Don" (2007). As a Chinese Canadian, he officially joined the Chinese subunit Super Junior-M the next year and subsequently released solo albums with SM Entertainment. In recent years, Henry has captured both Korean and global audiences through fantastic musical performances and an approachable personality on variety TV programs. He is currently signed to Monster Entertainment Group as a solo artist and works with his brother and the company's CEO, Clinton.

When I first asked how he feels when reflecting on this thirteen-year career, Henry responded:

It's something I never expected to do. I don't think anyone really plans on being a pop star. I feel very fortunate that I'm doing something that I love and that I can do it all around the world.

He's grateful to his parents for the sacrifices they made for him to start his music career, as they ensured that he and his siblings became classically trained musicians at a young age. Henry remembers how his mother learned to cut her own hair instead of visiting hair salons and spending the saved money on their high-level music lessons. Thanks to these sacrifices, Henry could fully devote himself to his passion for music and pass SM Entertainment's global audition in Canada in 2006.

Since he was a young musician, Henry has looked up to Paganini, Liszt, and Mozart as role models and tried to envision how these classical musicians would have approached theory and performances. As a result, Henry has always tried to hold himself to a high standard of what he thinks a successful K-Pop idol should be. However, it was this mindset rather than the company or fans that pressured him to conform to the existing K-Pop framework.

It wasn't until he developed his own color—in music, TV appearances, and artistic pursuits—that he developed his own identity and standard as an entertainer.

Critics have called Henry a "musical genius" after garnering the public's attention through many legendary performances on Korean TV, especially violin-dancing and vocal-instrumental covers on *Begin Again*.[371]

In the context of his music, Henry believes that it doesn't matter whether "it's inside or outside the box, as long as the music is good." Henry not only keeps an open mind but also loves thinking about every aspect of a performance—"the lights, sound, camera angles, music, and how I'm performing it." You can see Henry's attention to detail on his social media channels like Tiktok and YouTube, where he has translated his creative skills into viral videos. With this approach, Henry has been able to collaborate with many talented people worldwide.

Beneath the flashy, large-scale performances in Korea, China, and other countries, however, lies huge amounts of "preparation and training. It's something that no amount of talent can replace." Even as a famous entertainer, Henry regularly dedicates time for vocal, dance, and classical violin lessons.

---

371 *SBS NOW*, "[스타킹] 모두를 놀라게 한 헨리(Henry Lau) 바이올린과 함께 춤을!! / StarKing' Review" [[Star King] Henry Lau Dancing with the Violin Surprising Everyone!! / StarKing' Review], March 31, 2014, video, 2:35; *Beginagain*, "[Full.ver] 제철소의 색다른 사운드로 재창조된 헨리(Henry) - Believer" [[Full.ver] Henry - Believer Recreated with Fresh Sounds of the Ironworks], July 12, 2020, video, 3:22.

It's not always something I want to do, but this is my profession. I'm an artist and I need to hone my craft.

With a strong supporter in Monster Entertainment Group, Henry can further bring his inspirations and ideas to life. The incredible team that Clinton has built values him as an artist and pushes him when he needs it; "most people underestimate the amount of support, planning and passion that a company needs to have" for this synergy. Since signing with Monster, Henry has starred in a Spielberg studio-produced film *A Dog's Journey* (2019) and an award-winning Chinese film *Double World* (2020), which have contributed massively to Asian representation in global media. As we've discussed before, a strong company-artist relationship founded in trust and support is crucial for success.

From debuting as a K-Pop idol from a top company to pursuing unique creative ventures to performing worldwide as a solo artist, Henry embodies the idea behind the odyssey. His lengthy career journey has involved awards, challenges, and inspirations, but none of them happened overnight. Even though his trajectory was unpredictable at times, Henry was always prepared for new endeavors.

This past year, I worked very closely with Monster Entertainment Group to focus on and develop my musical sound. I'm excited to show the world a different color in my music.

Henry's odyssey shall continue as the fans stay tuned for more.

CHAPTER 30

WHAT'S NEXT?

While I don't have one specific answer for what's next in K-Pop, I do have a few important notes on the topic for you to consider as we conclude.

THE STATE OF THE U.S. LANDSCAPE

To recap, K-Pop acts venture to the U.S. for more business opportunities and exposure in the world's biggest music market. For example, BTS reached the coveted number one spot on the *Billboard* Hot 100 chart with their all-English single "Dynamite" (2020) and received full fan support as well as ample radio coverage. It's unclear whether the U.S. radio will be equally as receptive to a future Korean-language single, but I'm optimistic. Grammy Award contention is now a reality, too.

While more K-Pop acts may "make it" in the U.S., I think it's unlikely that a successor will replicate the exact same strategies as BTS for commercial success and public recognition. Recently, Monsta X, NCT 127, SuperM, and BLACK-PINK have all successfully engaged in U.S. promotions. With the increase in strategic partnerships between Korean and

American companies for TWICE, Chungha, and (G)I-DLE, newer contenders are arriving. If the American industry and consumers demand K-Pop, then the Korean companies have no reason not to supply it to them.

K-Pop is already a successful global phenomenon; there are fewer barriers to entering the U.S. market today than there were ten years ago. Don't be surprised to see more K-Pop in the American media going forward.

CULTURAL APPROPRIATION DEBATE

Let's address the elephant in the room. Today, there is no delay in online content distribution and audiences are more diverse than ever. Plenty of case-specific controversies have occurred in the industry, such as racial slurs, the usage of religious items, culturally insensitive attire, and ignorant statements on TV. Voices are more amplified than ever; for example, viewers have only recently criticized T-ARA's "YAYAYA" (2010) for stereotyping Native Americans.[372]

Cultural appropriation in K-Pop is a very nuanced topic. The industry is aware that K-Pop reaches far beyond the domestic market, and since the entertainment business intends to profit off of global consumers, feedback is warranted. The inclination for those outside of Korea may be to call for Koreans' greater awareness of different cultures, but in reality, it's not so easy.

In a historically homogenous society, it's difficult for Koreans to fully understand and empathize with different cultures. To what

---

372 1theK, "[MV] T-ARA - yayaya," November 26, 2013, video, 4:49.

extent should artists pay respect and homage to cultures they seek to utilize and profit from? If Asian Americans take issue with a music video that Asians applaud, whose word should we take? Is it possible to appropriate K-Pop itself, as a part of Korean culture? The line between cultural appropriation and appreciation is very blurry.

K-Pop started by incorporating and experimenting with other cultures' audiovisual elements. Even though companies are becoming warier of the issues and hiring expert consultants, I think becoming less problematic in the global audience's eyes will be a gradual process, and in order to do so, Korean society will need to discuss the idea of cultural appropriation more frequently. Global fans' roles are also absolutely critical to getting more conversations started and shaping K-Pop content's trajectory.

Here's to more cultural understanding and diversity.

CHANGES TO THE INDUSTRY PARADIGM

As with EXP Edition and Kaachi, will we see more industry-independent K-Pop acts? Remember that the K-Pop industry generally revolves around companies, and rookie talents don't get to assemble their own teams. Perhaps aspiring idols can start to recruit coaches and train on their own like EXP Edition did. However, it's unclear whether they can fully compete with the rest of the industry.

In 2018, solo artist Holland debuted under his own management as K-Pop's first openly gay idol.[373] Despite not appearing

---

373 Inha Ryu, "[인터뷰]'성소수자 신인가수 홀랜드입니다'" [[Interview] I'm LGBTQ Rookie Artist Holland], *Kyunghyang*, February 4, 2018.

in Korean mainstream media, Holland amassed a huge following on social media from global fans, and he suggests a new alternative to the company-driven paradigm.[374] Again, the competitiveness of such artists is a separate topic.

I've also discussed K-Pop idol acts that encountered more success overseas first and then in Korea. Many recent popular groups such as LOONA, Stray Kids, ATEEZ, and Everglow are following this pattern. It's shrewd business strategy to capitalize on such global reception since idols are generally driven by dedicated fandoms. Korean public recognition is no longer an absolute requirement for international fame. However, keep in mind that K-Pop is ultimately intended to cater to both domestic and global audiences.

Times have changed and more players are entering the scene, so strategies must adapt as well.

---

374 Tamar Herman, "Holland on 'Nar_C,' Depicting LGBTQ Love Stories in K-Pop & Making His Own Way," *Billboard*, May 2, 2019.

OUTRO

After reading this book, I hope you now understand that K-Pop is a legitimate pop-cultural phenomenon that impacts millions worldwide. I don't expect you to remember everything, but hopefully, you've learned a thing or two by now.

In this age of social media, the symbiotic bond between artists and fans is more amplified than ever before, and as the diversity of K-Pop fandoms grows, fans become more outspoken on behalf of the artists. I hope that the general public's stereotypes of K-Pop will gradually shift because of these modern developments. Of course, we also need accurate and informed representation in the media; it won't be an overnight process in which everyone suddenly loves and respects K-Pop.

We're living in an era during which K-Pop has expanded into topics and discussions never before imaginable. No longer is it just about music in a foreign language; now, K-Pop is both a phenomenon and a community, and its expansiveness as a pop-cultural form increases every year. K-Pop may not be for everyone, but it certainly is for many people.

You may have noticed throughout this book that certain people I've discussed—primarily Clyde Kelly, the global ARMY fandom, and Henry Lau—aren't even from South Korea; yet, they still have propelled the global K-Pop phenomenon in their own ways through a combination of music, industry, and culture. K-Pop's odyssey would be directionless without people from around the world contributing in both serendipitous and organic ways.

People often ask me where I see K-Pop going from here. I confidently believe that we're going to be seeing this odyssey for a long time. Technology grows at such a rapid rate and fans continue to become even greater collective forces. New rookies capture the scene while many veterans still dominate. So much has changed in the past several years, and there are so many factors that keep progressing K-Pop. As fans and consumers, let's just enjoy the ride.

I hope this book inspires you to go out and explore, engage, and discuss.

The odyssey continues.

ACKNOWLEDGMENTS

It truly takes a village to write a book but an even more special one to write a book on K-Pop.

I'd like to first thank my interviewees who have served as consultants and mentors as I navigated the many layers of K-Pop:

Hyuk Shin (153/Joombas Music Group), whom I have been following for a decade and has been a huge inspiration and supporter throughout the scope of this project. **Peter Chun (theQoos)**, who was behind all of the cool YG projects I've fanboyed over and also inspires me to be a bridge between the East and West. **Tamar Herman** and **Shin Cho (Warner Music Asia)** for incredibly helpful industry insights early on in my brainstorming phase that helped me stay on track. **Brian Nam (DIVE Studios)** and **Evan Ghang (KAI Media)**, whose creative content I've loved and who will further pioneer the K-Pop content space. **Bernie Cho (DFSB Kollective)**, who provided wisdom and guidance in the eleventh hour.

Cobb Cho and **Michaela Hahm** for sharing their unique insights into the industry through the important projects they've spearheaded. **Han Kim (Sheppard, Mullin, Richter & Hampton LLP)** and **Cass Song (ISA)**, whom I look up to as career mentors and for their diverse insights through the span of their legal and industry careers. **Darren Won**, who wholeheartedly supplemented my research with fascinating, direct experiences. **Nayoon Kim**, who's a star and was super helpful in explaining her experiences over the years. **Clyde Kelly,** whose crazy talents, professionalism, and creativity motivate me.

Another special thanks to the academic scholars who have provided much-needed guidance:

Gyu Tag Lee (George Mason University), whose fantastic books, interviews, and responses to my inquiries have been a huge inspiration for me to work on a book of my own. **Stephanie Choi (UC Santa Barbara)**, who has been my teacher throughout the year, encouraging me to explore the academic and social aspects of K-Pop fandoms. **Cedar-Bough Saeji (Indiana University Bloomington)**, whose awesome passion for K-Pop rang through our phone chat, which could've easily continued for another hour. **Mathieu Berbiguier (UCLA)**, whose research, side projects, and YouTube videos I'm always excited for. **Nicole Santero (University of Nevada, Las Vegas)**, who continues to amaze me with her BTS & ARMY projects and keeps me excited with her innovative ideas.

Also, a big thank you to the many additional industry insiders, scholars, and fellow fans whose contributions, viewpoints, and experiences have inspired and motivated me write this book in the first place.

A very special thanks to **Henry and Clinton Lau of Monster Entertainment Group**, both from a huge fan and a professional. I can't wait for everything you guys will do in both the East and the West, and I respect the importance of your work that helps Asian representation in global entertainment. Thanks to **James Kwon** for connecting us.

Characters on the cover based on design by Pikisuperstar.

Special shoutouts to **JinYoung Cho, Brandon Toy, Julie Yi, Ashley Xu,** and **Serra Park** for providing me with the initial encouragement and insights to start this book when I didn't think it was possible.

I'd also like to acknowledge my fantastic team, who ensured that my idea for this book became a reality, including **New Degree Press, Eric Koester, Brian Bies**, **Rob Alston, Lyn Solares, ChandaElaine Spurlock, Sherman Morrison, Jennifer Psujek, Jamie Tibasco, Heather Gomez, Leila Summers, Gjorgji Pejkovski, Agata Wawryniuk, Amanda Brown, Zoran Maksimovic, Kash Aboud,** and **John Chancey.**

Last but not least, I thank all of you who have supported me along the way both, on and off social media platforms, including friends, colleagues, and strangers-turned-friends.

SPECIAL THANKS

I'd like to gratefully acknowledge the following people for making this book come to reality. We did this together.

Aika Toriyama	Ashley Bang
Alan Q Tang	Ashley Xu
Albert Jo	Audrey Youn
Alex Kwon	Austin Nguyen
Alex Majors	Ben Choi
Allison Ko	Ben Gilberg
Amanda Lopez	Beth Hightower
Andie Estella	Bhavin Shah
Andrew Eom	Bic Pentameter
Andrew Jeon	Blake Pittell
Angie Seo	Bolin Z.
Anna Park	Bradford Park
Anna Sheu	Brandon Toy

Brian Calla

Brian Shim

Casey Pao

Catherine Chung

Cesare Mario Viacava

Chae Yoon Lee

Chrissy H. Pak

Christine Jeong

Christine Kim

Christopher Chew

Claire Kim

Colette Balmain

Connie Zhang

Courtney Lazore

Cynthia Wu

Dafna M.

Daniel Choe

Daniel Z Anderson

David Lim

David Moon

Dennis Park

Derek Minwoo Jung

Donghyeok Han

Dongseob Kim

Dui Lee

Edwina Yuan

Eileen Tran

Elmer Min

ENJOY DANCE STUDIO

Eric Koester

Eric Paik

Eunice Kim

Fred Lee

Gabrielle Oh

Godwin Chan

Han C. Choi

Han Soo Kim

Hana Kim

Hwajin Kang

Hyewon Son

James Arias

James Lee

James Steiner-Dillon

Jane Kim

Janice Ji

Jeffrey Tang

Jeffrey Wang

Jennifer Jeong

Jennifer Kim

Jennifer Lee

Jenny Lee

Jeong Lee

Jeremiah Kim

Jeremy Valencia

Jessica Shieh

Jiayi Xu

Jieun Gina Hong

Jihu Kim

Jim Won

JinYoung Cho

Jin Soo Lee

Jina Moon

Jinlin Ye

Jinsoo Chung

Jinsuk Kim

Joey Choi

John Yoon

Johnathan Sargent

Joo Won Jang

Joyce Kwon

JP Prusakowski

Julie Yi

Jun Lee

Junny Lee

K. Lyn Baker

Kathy Hoa

Kathy Wang

Kay Kim

Kelly Yen

Kevin Yu

Kwanghyun Lee

Kyo Young Koo

Kyung H Soung

Lauren Kim

Laurie Villar

Lawrence Bai

Liat Shapiro

Lilly Tang

Lydia Lim

Lynn Shiung

Lynnewood Jeff Shafer II

Margaret Garibaldi

Mariana Guardado

Matthew Moon

Matthew Park

May Do

Melissa Natividad

Michelle Shin

Min Jae Kim

Min Oh

Min Seok Kang

Mina Seo

Minho Park

Nai Ming (Norman) Chen

Natalie Ma

Nayeon Kim

Nicole Gildea

Nicole H.

Nicole Shim

Peter Lee

Rachel Ahn

Raja Sutherland

Ramandeep Mann

Rebecca Kah

Rebecca Myers

Rio Luo

Rosemond Perdue

Roy Jung

Ruiling Wen

Ryan Gu

Ryan Tanny Kang

Sang Yun Lee

Sara Merican

Sarah Bernardo

Sean Kim

Seoiyoung Ahn

Seo Ho Moon

Seo Hyung Koo

Seok Whee Jason Nam

Seung Joo Ahn

Simon Shahinian

Simone Lamont

Sinporion Phuong

Sky Gu

Sofia Bonfiglio

Sohyun Kim

SokHui Zybura

Somin Lim

Sonya Eom

Soojin Lee

Sophie Park

Sophie Seojeong Lee

Soyeon Kim

Soyoung Jung

Sujin Hong

Sun Ho Song

Sung Jun Kim

Suzi Hyun

Taehyung Kim

Taeyong Shin

Terry C.

Thomas Seo

Tiffany Sam

Tijana Miljkov

Tom Lee

Toni Lee

Wan-Mo Kang

Wallea Eaglehawk

Won Jae Jeong

Xinyue Wang

YeJi An

Yong Bin Cho

Yoolim Jeon

Yoon Duk Kim

Yumi Lee

Yun Jee Lee

Zhiqi Liu

Ziqian Tao

APPENDIX

PART 1 – WHAT IS K-POP?

Ahn, Joongho, Sehwan Oh, and Hyunjung Kim. "Korean Pop Takes Off!: Social Media Strategy of Korean Entertainment Industry." *2013 10th International Conference on Service Systems and Service Management*, Hong Kong (2013).

Berbiguier, Mathieu, and Younghan Cho. "Understanding the Korean Fandom of the K-Pop: Focusing on Its Perspectives on Foreign Fans." *Korean Journal of Communication and Information*, no.81 (2017).

Bugs. "국내 장르" [Korean Genres]. Last accessed August 3, 2020. https://music.bugs.co.kr/genre/home.

Byrne, Brian Patrick and Ahir Gopaldas. "Radio, Why Won't You Play BTS?" *NowThisNews*. April 3, 2020. https://nowthisnews.com/pop/radio-why-wont-you-play-bts.

Chad Future. "What I Learned from Living in Korea - [CFTV] EP.10." September 24, 2016. Video, 7:04. https://www.youtube.com/watch?v=RU_H4nm5sMk.

Chen, Aria. "'Korean Music Is Amazingly Vibrant.' Time Talks to Seoul Hip-Hop Sensation Epik High." *Time.*July 14, 2019. https://time.com/5625205/epik-high-south-korea/.

Cho, Byung-Chul, and Sim Hichul. "Success Factor Analysis of K-Pop and a Study on Sustainable Korean Wave - Focus on Smart Media Based on Realistic Contents," *The Journal of the Korea Contents Association*, Vol.13 No.5 (2013).

Cho, Si-hyun. "문재인 대통령 "우리 콘텐츠가 세계를 이끌게 될 것"" [President Moon Jae-In 'Our Content Business Will Lead the World']. *NewBC*. September 17, 2019. https://www.newbc.kr/news/articleView.html?idxno=6795.

Choi, Moon-Hee. "K-Pop Group BTS Induces Production Worth 4 Tril. Won per Year." *BusinessKorea*.December 19, 2018.
http://www.businesskorea.co.kr/news/articleView.html?idxno=27583.

Chong, Elaine. "'I Could Have Been a K-Pop Idol - but I'm Glad I Quit'." *BBC*. February 13, 2020.
https://www.bbc.com/news/stories-51476159.

DKDKTV, "Is Kaachi Kpop? Koreans Define Kpop." August 8, 2020. Video, 9:21.
https://www.youtube.com/watch?v=rC7I-Az8mFY.

Encyclopedia of Korean Culture. s.v. "Daejoong-Eumak" [Popular Music]. Accessed March 2, 2020.
https://encykorea.aks.ac.kr/Contents/Item/E0014806.

Herman, Tamar. "BTS & Halsey's 'Boy with Luv' Goes Platinum." *Billboard*. June 24, 2019.
https://www.billboard.com/articles/columns/k-town/8517197/bts-halsey-boy-with-luv-certified-platinum.

Hong, Dam-young. "How K-Pop Is Becoming Mainstream on Us Talk Shows." *The Korea Herald*. March 27, 2020.
http://www.koreaherald.com/view.php?ud=20200326000961&fbclid=IwAR24HgV
WiziKPh-yi4j9DUSwmWXz9sasU-vFF6G-sSOhC-ZaMEpZIO-4pnU.

IFPI. "Global Music Report: The Industry in 2019." Accessed June 13, 2020.
https://www.ifpi.org/wp-content/uploads/2020/07/Global_Music_Report-the_
Industry_in_2019-en.pdf.

JTBC News. "[인터뷰] 박진영 "기획사 시스템 아니면 해외경쟁 어려워"" [[Interview] Park Jin-Young "International Competition Difficult without Agency System"]. May 5, 2015. Video, 19:05.
https://www.youtube.com/watch?v=dOgkTvYxHsU.

KCON TV. "I Am Chad Future (Special)." April 8, 2014. Video, 22:10.
https://www.youtube.com/watch?v=pcWiI2jeHyE.

Kim, Hyung-won. "문체부, 세계 25개국에 '케이팝 아카데미' 사업 추진" [MCST, Pursues 'Kpop Academy' Business in 25 Countries]. *IT Chosun*. May 7, 2019.
http://it.chosun.com/site/data/html_dir/2019/05/07/2019050701004.html.

Kim, Jung-sook. "[글로벌 칼럼] 케이팝의 시작과 문제점은 무엇인가?" [Global Column: What Are the Beginnings and Problems of K-Pop?] *The Korea Post*. March 23, 2017.
http://www.koreapost.co.kr/news/articleView.html?idxno=22348.

Kim, Suk-Young. *K-Pop Live: Fans, Idols, and Multimedia Performance*. Stanford: Stanford University Press, 2018.

Kim, Sungmin. 케이팝의 작은 역사 [K-Pop's Small History]. Seoul: Geulhangari Publishers, 2018. Adobe Digital Editions.

Kim, Tae Hoon. "BTS 10년이면 경제효과가 56조원" [56 Trillion Won in Economic Effect for 10 Years of BTS]. *Kyunghyang*. December 7, 2019. http://news.khan.co.kr/kh_news/khan_art_view.html?art_id=201912071136001.

Kimjakga. "케이팝이란 무엇인가: Z-Girls, Boy Story, EXP 에디션 사례 연구를 중심으로" [What is K-Pop: Focusing on Research from Z-Girls, Boy Story, EXP Edition]. *Donga*. June 28, 2019. https://weekly.donga.com/3/all/11/1774465/1.

Korea Foundation for International Cultural Exchange. *2019 한류의 경제적 파급효과 연구* [Research on Economic Ripple Effects of Hallyu]. Seoul: KOFICE, 2020.

Korea Times. "K-Pop's Global Popularity Draws Foreign Students to South Korea Universities." *South Asia Morning Post*. April 18, 2018. https://www.scmp.com/culture/music/article/2141651/K-Pops-global-popularity-draws-foreign-students-south-korea.

Lee, Gyu Tag. "De-Nationalization and Re-Nationalization of Culture: The Globalization of K-Pop." PhD diss., George Mason University. 2013.

Lee, Gyu Tag. 갈등하는 *K, Pop* [K-Pop in Conflict]. Seoul: Three Chairs Publishing Company, 2020. https://www.bookjournalism.com/contents/10433.

Lee, Gyu Tag. 케이팝의 시대 [The K-POP Age]. Seoul: Hanwool Academy, 2016.

Lee, Sara. "유럽 최초 K POP 걸그룹 KAACHI, 런던에서 첫 데뷔" [Europe's First K Pop Girl Group Kaachi, Debuts in London]. *NewsA*. April 30, 2020. http://www.newsa.co.kr/news/articleView.html?idxno=249040.

Lie, John. *K-Pop: Popular Music, Cultural Amnesia, and Economic Innovation in South Korea*. Oakland: University of California Press, 2015. http://ebookcentral.proquest.com/lib/upenn-ebooks/detail.action?docID=1711046.

Liu, Marian. "Do You Need to Be Korean to Be K-Pop?" *CNN*. June 13, 2017. https://www.cnn.com/2017/06/12/asia/exp-edition-non-korean-K-Pop-band/index.html.

Melon. "한국대중음악" [Korean Mainstream Music]. Last accessed August 3, 2020. https://www.melon.com/genre/song_list.htm?gnrCode=GN0100.

Merriam-Webster.com Dictionary. s.v. "K-Pop." Accessed August 21, 2020. https://www.merriam-webster.com/dictionary/K-Pop.

Moon, Kate. "Eric Nam Made It as a K-Pop Star. Now He Wants to Make It Back Home in America." *TIME*. November 26, 2019. https://time.com/5739662/eric-nam-interview/.

Moon, Wansik. "방탄소년단 뷔, 'Sweet Night' 아이튠즈 88개국 1위..8년만 싸이 기록 경신" [BTS V, 'Sweet Night' #1 on iTunes in 88 Countries...Breaks Psy's Record in 8 Years]. *Naver*. May 25, 2020. https://n.news.naver.com/entertain/article/108/0002865290.

MTV. "Vote Now – Nominees for 2020 MTV Video Music Awards." Accessed August 10, 2020. http://www.mtv.com/vma/vote/.

Netflix. "K-Pop | Explained | Netflix." May 31, 2018. Video, 0:45. https://www.facebook.com/netflixus/videos/10155584095328870.

Ochoa, John. "BTS Talk New Album 'Map of the Soul: 7': 'the Genre Is BTS'." *Grammys*, February 22, 2020. https://www.grammy.com/grammys/news/bts-talk-new-album-map-soul-7-genre-bts.

Park, Young-mi. "문체부, 외국인 80% "한국 이미지 긍정적"…대표 이미지 한식·K팝" [MCST, 80% Foreigners 'Positive Image of South Korea'... Main Image Korean Food/Kpop]. *Koreailbo.* January 22, 2019. http://www.koreailbo.co.kr/news/articleView.html?idxno=1636.

Pickles, Matt. "K-Pop Drives Boom in Korean Language Lessons." *BBC.* July 11, 2018. https://www.bbc.com/news/business-44770777.

Schulman, Alissa. "2019 MTV VMA Winners: See the Full List." *MTV.* August 26, 2019. http://www.mtv.com/news/3136861/2019-mtv-vma-winners/.

Shin, Hyun-joon. 가요, 케이팝 그리고 그 너머 [Gayo, K-Pop and Beyond]. Paju: Dolbaegae, 2013.

Singh, L. "Jay Park on K-Pop and Cultural Appropriation." *Vice.* November 29, 2019. https://www.vice.com/en_in/article/7x5gb9/jay-park-interview-K-Pop-cultural-appropriation.

Suarez, Gary. "Cardi B, Bad Bunny, and the Perils of Latin Novelty." *Vice.* April 27, 2018. https://www.vice.com/en_us/article/pax5w8/cardi-b-bad-bunny-j-balvin-i-like-it-essay-cultura.

The Korea Society. "The Economy of Kpop." August 27, 2018. Video, 42:43. https://youtu.be/en5j684QsV0.

Trust, Gary. "BTS Sets New Career Best on Hot 100 as 'on' Blasts in at No. 4; Roddy Ricch's 'the Box' Rules for Eighth Week." *Billboard.* March 2, 2020. https://www.billboard.com/articles/business/chart-beat/9326707/roddy-ricch-the-box-number-one-eighth-week.

Yim, Hyun-su. "Is There a Media Double Standard for K-Pop?" *The Korea Herald.* June 18, 2020. http://www.koreaherald.com/view.php?ud=20200618000951.

Yoo, Dong-gil. *K-POP 뮤직비즈니스의 이해* [Understanding K-Pop Music Business]. Seoul: AXIMU, 2017. Adobe Digital Editions.

Zaugg, Julie. "The Hothouse Academies Offering Kids a Shot at K-Pop Stardom." *CNN.* October 5, 2018. https://www.cnn.com/2018/10/05/asia/kpop-schools-south-korea-intl/index.html.

PART 2 – GLOBALIZATION

An, Jinyong. "박진영 "윌 스미스에 곡 줄때 가장 행복했다"" [Park Jin Young "Giving My Song to Will Smith Was My Happiest Moment]. *Munhwailbo*, November 5, 2014. http://www.munhwa.com/news/view.html?no=2014110501073612069001.

Benjamin, Jeff. "Girls' Generation Makes Big U.S. Debut on 'Letterman': Watch." *Billboard*, February 1, 2012. https://www.billboard.com/articles/columns/viral-videos/508237/girls-generation-makes-big-us-debut-on-letterman-watch.

Benjamin, Jeff. "Girls' Generation Reacts to YouTube Music Awards Win, Talks New Music: Exclusive." *Billboard*, November 4, 2013. https://www.billboard.com/articles/columns/k-town/5778185/girls-generation-reacts-to-youtube-music-awards-win-talks-new-music.

Benjamin, Jeff. "Girls' Generation Splinter Group Enters Billboard 200." *Billboard*, May 4, 2012. https://www.billboard.com/articles/news/489102/girls-generation-splinter-group-enters-billboard-200.

Billboard Music Awards. "BTS Wins Top Duo / Group - BBMAs 2019." May 1, 2019. Video. 1:26. https://www.youtube.com/watch?v=pE7Hjuz8LCM.

Brown, August. "K-Pop Brings Superfans and Diversity to KCON L.A. 2019." *Los Angeles Times*, August 18, 2019. https://www.latimes.com/entertainment-arts/story/2019-08-18/kcon-la-concert.

Bruner, Raisa. "BTS Explains Why They're Not Going to Start Singing in English." *TIME*, March 28, 2019. https://time.com/5560818/bts-singing-english/.

Caulfield, Keith. "SuperM Debuts at No. 1 on Billboard 200 Albums Chart with 'the 1st Mini Album'." *Billboard*, October 13, 2019. https://www.billboard.com/articles/business/chart-beat/8532879/superm-the-1st-mini-album-billboard-200-no-1.

Cho, Byung-Chul, and Sim Hichul. "Success Factor Analysis of K-Pop and a Study on Sustainable Korean Wave - Focus on Smart Media Based on Realistic Contents," *The Journal of the Korea Contents Association*, Vol.13 No.5 (2013).

Cho, Wooyoung. "SM 파리 공연 후 1년..가요계 빅3가 말하는 K팝" [1 Year after SM's Paris Show... K-Pop as Told by the Industry 'Big 3']. *eDaily*, June 11, 2012. https://www.edaily.co.kr/news/read?newsId=01121766599560736&mediaCodeNo=258.

Dong, Sun-hwa. "K-Pop Artists' China Virus Gig Invite No Ban Lift: Experts." *The Korea Times*, April 2, 2020. https://www.koreatimes.co.kr/www/art/2020/04/732_287257.html.

Friedman, Megan. "Korean Pop Star Rain Wins Time 100 Poll — Again." *TIME*, April 15, 2011. https://newsfeed.time.com/2011/04/15/korean-pop-star-rain-wins-time-100-poll-again/.

Haasch, Palmer. "Grimes Says That X æ a-XII's Godmother Is a K-Pop Idol She Collaborated with in 2018." *Insider*, May 26, 2020. https://www.insider.com/grimes-x-ae-a-xii-baby-elon-instagram-loona-gowon-2020-5.

Han, Sang-hee. "BoA to Make US Debut through MTV." *The Korea Times*, November 30, 2008. http://www.koreatimes.co.kr/www/news/special/2008/12/178_35301.html.

Harvard University. "'Gangnam Style' Singer PSY Visits Harvard." June 19, 2013. Video. 1:18:36. https://www.youtube.com/watch?v=wJKjsb_A8M4.

Im, Daegeun. "중국의 '뒤끝 작렬' 한한령, 한류의 미래는 있는가" [China's Holding Grudge *Hanhanryung*, Does Hallyu Have a Future?] *Joongangilbo*, February 26, 2019. https://news.joins.com/article/23395548.

Im, Yoosub. "지난 10년간 데뷔한 걸그룹들서 살아남은 그룹들" [The Debuted Girl Groups of the Past Decade That Are Still Active]. *Joongangilbo*, February 27, 2017. https://news.joins.com/article/21320263.

Jung, Ho jae. "유럽소녀 흥분 그 후 케이팝의 불편한 진실" [K-Pop's Inconvenient Truth after European Girls' Excitement]. *Donga*, July 8, 2011. http://www.donga.com/news/article/all/20110710/38651745/2.

Kang, Youngwoon. "한국인은 아니지만…"우리도 K팝 아이돌"" [Not Korean…'but We're Also K-Pop Idols']. *MK*, February 28, 2020. https://www.mk.co.kr/news/culture/view/2020/02/210495/.

Kim, Eunwoo. "[미국음악일기] 보아·세븐·원더걸스, 3대 기획사의 미국 진출 실패담" [[US Music Diary] BoA, Se7en, Wonder Girls, the Big 3 Labels' Failed US Promotions]. *BizHankook*, November 9, 2017. http://www.bizhankook.com/bk/article/14343.

Kim, Joohee. "美 타임지, 방탄소년단 글로벌 성공 비결 집중 조명.."가장 중요한 건 음악"" [US TIME, Sheds Light onto BTS's Success Factors…'the Most Important Is the Music']. *Seoul Kyungjae*, October 10, 2019. https://www.sedaily.com/NewsVIew/1VPGUGPJS1.

Kim, Myungshin. "동방신기, '*Purple Line*' 오리콘 싱글 차트 1위!"" [TVXQ, 'Purple Line' Oricon Single Chart #1!]. *Hankookkyungjae*, January 17, 2008. https://www.hankyung.com/life/article/2008011755857.

Kim, Sooah. "K-POP 과 신한류의 대한 텔레비전 담론" [Television Discourse on K-Pop and K-Pop Idol Stars' Passion]. *Seoul National University Journal of Communication Research*, vol.50, no.1 (2013): 67-73.

Kim, Sunghyun. "댄스음악이 케이팝의 전부 아냐.. 또 한번 진화할 것" [Dance Pop Isn't All of K-Pop...it Will Evolve Again]. *Chosun*, February 24, 2020. https://news.chosun.com/site/data/html_dir/2020/02/24/2020022400155.html.

Kim, Sungmin. 케이팝의 작은 역사 [K-Pop's Small History]. Seoul: Geulhangari Publishers, 2018. Adobe Digital Editions.

Kim, Yoon-mi. "Big Bang wins Best Worldwide Act." *The Korea Herald*, November 7, 2011. http://www.koreaherald.com/view.php?ud=20111107000691.

Kim, Youngdae, and T.K. Park, "What the Rise of Black Pink and BTS Says about the Future of K-Pop." *Vulture*, August 28, 2018. https://www.vulture.com/2018/08/bts-black-pink-and-the-continued-success-of-K-Pop.html.

Ko, Kyudae. "원더걸스 사태로 본 아이돌 가수 미국 진출의 실상" [The Reality of Idol Stars' US Promotions, from the Wonder Girls Incident]. *Donga*, March 03, 2010. https://shindonga.donga.com/3/all/13/109230/3.

Korea Creative Content Agency (KOCCA). "Content Industry Trend of Thailand (2019 Vol.9)." Naju, KOCCA: 2020.

Korea Foundation for International Cultural Exchange. "2020 해외한류실태조사" [2020 Research on Hallyu's Global Reality]. Seoul: KOFICE, 2020.

Lee, Alicia. "K-Pop Fans Are Taking over 'White Lives Matter' and Other Anti-black Hashtags with Memes and Fancams of Their Favorite Stars." *CNN*, June 8, 2020. https://www.cnn.com/2020/06/04/us/kpop-bts-blackpink-fans-black-lives-matter-trnd/index.html.

Lee, Dongyeon. "SM 엔터테인먼트 LA 공연의 진실" [The truth behind SM Entertainment's LA show]. *Pressian*, January 25, 2012. https://www.pressian.com/pages/articles/37975.

Lee, Gyu Tag. 케이팝의 시대 [The K-POP Age]. Seoul: Hanwool Academy, 2016.

Lee, Hyerin. "보아 "미국진출, 난 물 만난 고기였다"" [BoA 'US Promotions, I Was a Fish in the Water']. *AsiaKyungjae*, September 10, 2008. https://www.asiae.co.kr/article/2008091014383936983.

Lee, Kyungran. "슈주 차이나, 8일 중국서 데뷔 무대" [SuJu China, Chinese Debut Stage on the 8th]. *Joongangilbo*, April 8, 2008. https://news.joins.com/article/3103210.

Lipshutz, Jason. "BTS Thanks Fans for Top Social Artist Win at Billboard Music Awards 2017: Watch." *Billboard*, May 21, 2017. https://www.billboard.com/articles/news/bbma/7801216/bts-video-top-social-artist-win-billboard-music-awards-2017.

Maeng, Joonho, and Youngmok Lee. "세계를 깜짝 놀라게 한 작곡가 박진영" [Songwriter Park Jin Young Who Shocked the World]. *Joongangilbo*, April 13, 2005. https://news.joins.com/article/2056347.

MBCEntertainment. "[라디오스타] 이제는 말할 수 있다! 박진영의 미국병(?) 해명 20200812" [[Radio Star] He Can Say It Now! Park Jin Young's US-Fever Explanation 20200812]. August 12, 2020. Video. 2:59.
https://www.youtube.com/watch?v=QsxdH8jLaWU.

Ministry of Sports, Culture and Tourism. "K-Pop 월드페스티벌 2011 창원서 열려" [K-Pop World Festival 2011 Commences in Changwon]. Last modified December 12, 2012.
http://www.kocis.go.kr/promotionContent/view.do?seq=3090.

officialpsy. "Psy - Gangnam Style M/V." July 15, 2012. Video. 4:12.
https://www.youtube.com/watch?v=9bZkp7q19fo.

officialpsy. "Public Announcement - Scooter Braun Regarding PSY." September 3, 2012, video, 1:23.
https://youtu.be/sOn3aWDHlsE.

Ryzik, Melena. "His Style is Gangnam, and Viral Too." *The New York Times,* October 11, 2012.
https://www.nytimes.com/2012/10/14/arts/music/interview-psy-the-artist-behind-gangnam-style.html.

Savage, Mark. "BTS Are the First Korean Band to Headline Wembley Stadium." *BBC,* June 2, 2019.
https://www.bbc.com/news/entertainment-arts-48487862.

SCMP Reporter, "BTS Singer RM's English Skills Criticised by the Times. BTS Army Go on the Offensive on Social Media." *South China Morning Post,* October 9, 2018.
https://www.scmp.com/culture/music/article/2167600/bts-singer-rms-english-skills-criticised-times-bts-army-go-offensive.

SMTOWN. "'The Star of Asia' BoA, the Star of Asia, Unveils a Teaser Image That Makes a Difference! Focus Your Attention!" Last modified June 1, 2019.
https://www.smentertainment.com/PressCenter/Details/3105#.

Song, Eunkyung. "KBS '뮤직뱅크' 다음달 두바이서 열려...백현.트와이스 등 출연" [KBS 'Music Bank' to Launch in Dubai Next Month... Baekhyun, TWICE, Etc. to Perform]. *Yonhap,* February 1, 2020.
https://www.yna.co.kr/view/AKR20200201041400005.

Sun, Mikyung. "[공식입장] TWICE, 韓 앨범으로 日 오리콘 차트 2위...'원톱인기'" [[Official] TWICE, Korean Album Charts #2 on Japanese Oricon Chart...'One-Top Popularity']. *Chosun,* April 18, 2018.
https://news.chosun.com/site/data/html_dir/2018/04/18/2018041801414.html.

Trust, Gary. "BTS' 'Dynamite' Blasts in at No. 1 on Billboard Hot 100, Becoming the Group's First Leader." *Billboard,* August 31, 2020.
https://www.billboard.com/articles/business/chart-beat/9442836/bts-dynamite-tops-hot-100-chart.

World Population Review. "South Korea Population 2020 (Live)." Accessed April 2, 2020.
https://worldpopulationreview.com/countries/south-korea-population.

Yang, Jiwon. "싸이 "군대를 두 번 간게 아니고 훈련소 두 번"" [Psy 'I Went to the Army Training Facility Twice, Not the Army Itself Twice]. *Joongangilbo*, April 8, 2010. https://news.joins.com/article/4102464.

Yang, Yoochang. "'빌보드 1위' 새 역사 쓴 방탄소년단의 4가지 성공 비결" ['Billboard #1' The 4 Success Strategies of History-Writing BTS]. *MK*, May 29, 2018. https://www.mk.co.kr/news/culture/view/2018/05/340318/.

Yoo, Eunyoung. "빅뱅, 3월 중국 투어...총 8개 도시 18만 2천 관객" [BIGBANG, March Chinese Tour... Total 8 Cities, 182,000 Attendees]. *Busanilbo*, February 5, 2016. http://www.busan.com/view/busan/view.php?code=20160205000259.

Yoon, So-yeon. "BTS Sells Most Records for Male, Foreign Act in First Week of Release: Oricon." *Korea JoongAng Daily*, July 21, 2020. https://koreajoongangdaily.joins.com/2020/07/21/entertainment/kpop/BTS-ORICON-MAP-OF-THE-SOUL/20200721165500407.html.

Yoon, So-yeon. "JYP's Newest Girl Group NiziU Release Pre-debut EP." *Korea JoongAng Daily*, June 30, 2020. https://koreajoongangdaily.joins.com/2020/06/30/entertainment/kpop/NiziU-Nizi-Project-JYP-Entertainment/20200630171100299.html.

Yoon, Sukmin. "빅뱅, 한국가수 최다 중국 11개도시 18만명 동원 투어 성료" [BIGBANG, Korean Artist Record for Biggest Chinese Tour with 11 Cities and 180,000 Attendees]. *Hankookkyungjae*, August 31, 2015. https://www.hankyung.com/entertainment/article/2015083153174.

YouTube. "Music Charts & Insights - BLACKPINK." Accessed August 25, 2020. https://charts.youtube.com/artist/%2Fg%2F11byzf3gtr.

YouTube. "Music Charts & Insights - BTS." Accessed August 25, 2020. https://charts.youtube.com/artist/%2Fm%2F0w68qx3.

YouTube. "Music Charts & Insights - TWICE." Accessed August 25, 2020. https://charts.youtube.com/artist/%2Fg%2F11btzyw8k4.

PART 3 – ONLINE TECHNOLOGY & CONTENT

"More K-Pop Artists Team up with U.S. Labels to Expand Careers." *YonhapNews*, March 11, 2020. https://en.yna.co.kr/view/AEN20200311008300315?section=culture/K-Pop.

"TVXQ in Guinness World Record," *KBS World*, March 24, 2009. https://libguides.westsoundacademy.org/c.php?g=457482&p=3156335.

[Ailee OFFICIAL] aileemusic. "Ailee Singing the Climb by Miley Cyrus." August 7, 2009. Video. 3:51. https://www.youtube.com/watch?v=oEDZotuzygk.

Ahn, Heejeong. "네이버 브이라이브, 글로벌 유료 멤버십 '팬십' 출시" [Naver Vlive Launches Global Paid Membership 'Fanship']. *ZDNet Korea*, March 26, 2019. https://zdnet.co.kr/view/?no=20190326102435.

and2jw. "Berkeley Style: PSY- Gangnam Style Global Parody Cover Full [J.Won.K]."
August 25, 2012. Video. 4:11.
https://www.youtube.com/watch?v=UNrqx6eZgj4.

Aoimirai's KPOP. "K-Pop - YouTube Ads Spell the End of Meaningful View
Counters." Last modified May 2, 2020. Accessed May 15, 2020.
http://kpop.aoimirai.net/youtube_ads_spell_the_end_of_meaningful_view_
counters.html.

Baek, Jongmo. "방탄소년단·싸이는 왜 유튜브에 영상을 계속 올리나" [Why Do
BTS/Psy Continue to Upload YouTube Videos?]. *DailySmart*, July 1, 2018.
http://www.dailysmart.co.kr/news/articleView.html?idxno=1598.

Baek, Yujin. "[혼돈의 음원시장]①글로벌 공룡이 달려든다" [[Chaotic Digital
Music Market] ① Global Dinosaurs Are Coming]. *BusinessWatch*, March 3, 2020.
http://news.bizwatch.co.kr/article/mobile/2020/03/03/0021.

BBC News. "The Dark Side of K-Pop Clubs - BBC News." June 25, 2019. Video. 8:31.
https://www.youtube.com/watch?v=l-YAUL4qgmU.

BBC Radio 1. "K-Pop: Korea's Secret Weapon?" January 18, 2018. Video. 27:28.
https://www.youtube.com/watch?v=clXOslwjPrc.

BBC. "K-Pop Idols: Inside the Hit Factory." October 25, 2019. Video. 60:00.
https://www.bbc.co.uk/programmes/m0009m8g.

Bevan, David. "Seoul Trained: Inside Korea's Pop Factory." *SPIN*, March 26, 2012.
https://www.spin.com/2012/03/seoul-trained-inside-koreas-pop-factory/.

BuzzFeed Celeb. "EXID Plays 'Would You Rather.'" May 29, 2018. Video. 5:48.
https://www.youtube.com/watch?v=hxYK2Idd0ZU.

Cho, Junhyuk. "트위터, '케이팝' 내세워 전 세계 3억 유저 사로잡는다"
[Twitter, Captures 3 Million Worldwide Users with 'Kpop' at
Forefront]. *HankookKyungjae*, November 7, 2019.
https://www.hankyung.com/it/article/201911071348H.

CollegeHumor. "Mitt Romney Style (Gangnam Style Parody)." October 8, 2012.
Video. 2:51.
https://www.youtube.com/watch?v=yTCRwi71_ns.

GAON Chart. "국내 음악시장 현황" [Status of the Domestic Pop Market]. Last
modified March 5, 2019.
http://gaonchart.co.kr/main/section/article/view.
gaon?idx=15104&sgenre=thema&search_str=

Graham, Jefferson. "Coronavirus: From Facebook to YouTube, Live Video Is Back.
How the Apps Compare." *USA Today*, March 26, 2020.
https://www.usatoday.com/story/tech/2020/03/26/how-do-facebook-twitter-
youtube-and-instagram-live-compare/2901775001/.

GW IKS. "CedarBough T. Saeji, "Parasitic or Symbiotic?: The Rise of the K-Pop Adjacent Industries." November 12, 2019. Video. 24:49. https://www.youtube.com/watch?v=PKusT1Ip2jQ.

Herman, Tamar. "SuperM's Virtual K-Pop Concert Sees Major Earnings." *Forbes*, April 26, 2020. https://www.forbes.com/sites/tamarherman/2020/04/26/superms-virtual-K-Pop-concert-sees-major-earnings/#56bbfe6293ef.

Hulu. "K-POP Machine." Last accessed March 30, 2020. https://www.hulu.com/series/investigations-by-vice-14464f32-95a3-4266-8193-d7c5e1b577f2.

Jeon, Jinyong. "언택트 시대 온다?" [Is the Untact Age Coming?], *NextEconomy*, April 6, 2020. http://www.nexteconomy.co.kr/news/articleView.html?idxno=13312.

JTBC. "StageK." Last accessed April 2, 2020. http://tv.jtbc.joins.com/stagek.

Judson Laipply. "Evolution of Dance." April 6, 2006. Video, 6:00. https://www.youtube.com/watch?v=dMHobHeiRNg.

Kang, Ilyong. "*SNS, Kpop-eh bbajida*" [SNS Is Obsessed with Kpop]. *AjuKyungjae*, April 9, 2019. https://www.ajunews.com/view/20190409143503852.

KCON. "KCON:TACT 2020 Summer Brings KCON to Fans Worldwide." Last accessed June 1st, 2020. http://www.kconusa.com/kcontact-2020-summer-brings-kcon-to-fans-worldwide/.

Kim, Eun-hyung. "빈곤한 가요, 무너진 시장" [Poor *Gayo*, Crashing Market]. *Hangyeorae*, January 20, 2000. http://legacy.h21.hani.co.kr/h21/data/L000110/1pbc1a01.html.

Kim, Hyojung. "날개 단 음반 판매...상반기에만 밀리언셀러 3팀" [Physical Sales Soar...3 Million Seller Acts in First Half Alone]. *YonhapNews*, July 2, 2020. https://www.yna.co.kr/view/AKR20200702153600005.

Kim, Jisun. "K팝 기획사들 "오프라인 공연 못해 어려워"...문체부 "하반기부터 준비"" [Kpop Companies 'Difficult without Offline Performances'... MCST 'Preparation Starting Second Half of Year']. *KBS News*, June 19, 2020. http://mn.kbs.co.kr/mobile/news/view.do?ref=A&ncd=4474874.

Kim, Kyung-jin. "Koreans Spend Hours Plugged into YouTube." *Korea JoongAng Daily*, September 11, 2019. https://koreajoongangdaily.joins.com/news/article/article.aspx?aid=3067896.

Kim, Pogeuni. "1곡 재생때 0.4원...이효리도 "음악으로 먹고살기 힘들어"" [0.4 Won for 1 Song Played...Even Lee Hyori Says "It's Hard to Make a Living off of Music"]. *Hangyeorae*, November 12, 2017. http://www.hani.co.kr/arti/culture/culture_general/818581.html.

Kim, Sungmin. 케이팝의 작은 역사 [K-Pop's Small History]. Seoul: Geulhangari Publishers, 2018. Adobe Digital Editions.

Kim, Yeonjeong. "In-Stream Video Ads and Sponsorships to Include K-Pop Content Worldwide." *Twitter* (blog), *Twitter*, February 7, 2019. https://blog.twitter.com/en_sea/topics/product/2019/Instream-videoads-and-sponsorships-to-include-kpop.html.

Kim, Yong Hwan, Dahee Lee, Nam Gi Han, and Min Song. "Exploring Characteristics of Video Consuming Behaviour in Different Social Media Using K-Pop Videos," *Journal of Information Science*, Vol 40(6) (2014): 806-822.

King, Ashley. "Did Tiktok Crash during Its 30-Second BTS Exclusive?" *Digital Music News*, February 21, 2020. https://www.digitalmusicnews.com/2020/02/21/tiktok-crash-bts-exclusive/.

Korea Creative Content Agency (KOCCA). "2019 음악 산업백서" [2019 Music Industry White Paper]. Naju, KOCCA: 2020.

Koreaboo. "'9 Muses of Star Empire' BBC Documentary." September 20, 2014. Video. 47:34. https://www.youtube.com/watch?v=4s3p15YAVF0.

Korean Foundation for International Cultural Exchange (KOFICE). "Interview with Susan Kang, Founder of 'Soompi'." Last modified March 15, 2017. Accessed April 3, 2020. http://eng.kofice.or.kr/c00_hallyuInsights/c00_hallyuInsights_01_view.asp?seq=7910.

KpopRadar. "YouTube Viewcount." Last modified August 24, 2020. https://www.kpop-radar.com/viewcount.

Lau, Jack. "BTS Army Makes Jungkook Video Twitter's Most Retweeted Tweet in 2019; 'World Record Egg' Well and Truly Beaten." *South China Morning Post*, December 11, 2019. https://www.scmp.com/lifestyle/entertainment/article/3041648/bts-army-makes-jungkook-video-twitters-most-retweeted-tweet?utm_source=TodayOnline&utm_medium=partner&utm_campaign=contentexchange.

Lee, Dakyeom. "'세계지식포럼' 이수만이 꿈꾸는 미래 #CT #슈퍼엠 #컬처 유니버스(종합)" ['World Knowledge Forum' the Future Lee Soo Man Envisions #Ct #Superm #Culture Universe]. *StarToday*, September 26, 2019. https://www.mk.co.kr/star/hot-issues/view/2019/09/767441/.

Lee, Gyu Tag. 케이팝의 시대 [The K-POP Age]. Seoul: Hanwool Academy, 2016.

Lee, Hoyeon. "[HI★리뷰] "팬들과 함께 있는 듯" 슈퍼엠, 신개념 온라인 콘서트 성료." [[Hi★Review] "Feels like We're with the Fans" SuperM, Successfully Completes Innovative Online Concert]. *Hankookilbo*, April 26, 2020. https://www.hankookilbo.com/News/Read/202004261669069627.

Lee, Hyein and Heejin Ko. "SNS 중심에 있는 그들, 한류의 중심이 된다" [Those at the Center of SNS, Become the Center of Hallyu], *Kyunghyang*, December 31, 2017. http://news.khan.co.kr/kh_news/khan_art_view.html?art_id=201712312123015.

Lee, Jaehoon. "세븐틴, BTS 소속사 '빅히트'가 만든 위버스 입점" [Seventeen Enters BTS's company BigHit's WeVerse]. *Newsis*, March 12, 2020. https://newsis.com/view/?id=NISX20200312_0000953027.

Lee, Jeongyeon. "방탄소년단 첫 온라인 콘서트 '방방콘 더 라이브'…전 세계 아미들 열광" [BTS first Online Concert 'BangBangCon the Live'… ARMYs Enthusiastic Worldwide]. *Donga*, June 15, 2020. https://www.donga.com/news/Entertainment/article/all/20200614/101504508/5.

Leskin, Paige. "Finally: Google Just Revealed YouTube's Ad Revenue, 14 Years after Acquiring It, and the Video Site Brought in $15 Billion Last Year." *BusinessInsider*, February 3, 2020. https://www.businessinsider.com/youtube-ad-revenue-15-billion-2019-google-breakout-2020-2.

Lewis, Isobel. "BTS: More Than 50 Million Tune into Bang Bang Con Virtual Concert Series." *Independent*, April 20, 2020. https://www.independent.co.uk/arts-entertainment/music/news/bts-bang-con-virtual-concert-watch-online-coronavirus-a9474471.html.

M2. "[MPD직캠] 방탄소년단 지민 직캠 4K 'FAKE LOVE' (BTS JI MIN FanCam) | @MCOUNTDOWN_2018.5.31" [MPD Fancam] BTS Jimin Fancam 4K 'Fake Love' (BTS JI MIN FanCam) | @Mcountdown_2018.5.31]. May 31, 2018. Video. 4:07. https://www.youtube.com/watch?v=GfX62fI1NyA.

Messerlin, Patrick, and Wonkyu Shin. "The Success of K-Pop: How Big and Why So Fast?" *Asian Journal of Social Science* (January 2017): 4.

Min, Kyungwon. "전 세계 아미 방구석 찾아간 BTS 방방콘…이틀간 5059만뷰" [BTS BangBangCon Visits Worldwide Army…50.59 Million Views]. *JoongangIlbo*, April 20, 2020. https://news.joins.com/article/23758260.

MIT Gangnam Style. "MIT Gangnam Style." October 27, 2012. Video. 5:02. https://www.youtube.com/watch?v=lJtHNEDnrnY.

Mnet K-POP. "[BTS - Fake Love] Comeback Stage | M Countdown 180531 EP.572." May 31, 2018. Video. 4:02. https://www.youtube.com/watch?v=x5ZeAfz4G3s.

Moon, Sungho. "데뷔 확률 0.1%, 그들이 아이돌에 도전 하는 이유" [Debut Possibility 0.1%, the Reason Why They Continue to Try Become Idols]. *SeoulTV*, March 10, 2020. http://stv.seoul.co.kr/news/newsView.php?id=20200310500023.

Netflix. "Explained." Last accessed March 30, 2020. https://www.netflix.com/title/80216752.

Oh, Ingyu, and Gil-Sung Park. "From B2C to B2B: Selling Korean Pop Music in the Age of New Social Media." *Korea Observer* 43.3 (Autumn 2012): 365-397.

Oh, Ingyu, and Hyo-Jung Lee. "Mass Media Technologies and Popular Music Genres: K-Pop and YouTube." *Korea Journal*, vol. 53, no.4 (Winter 2013): 34-58.

Park, Hyemyoung. "팬클럽과 팬문화" [Fanclubs and Fan Culture]. *cine21*, November 9, 2006. http://www.cine21.com/news/view/?mag_id=42526.

Park, Jinwoong. "아이돌 팬덤, 당당한 문화로 자리잡다" [Idol Fandoms Confidently Find Own Cultural Ground]. *KUNews*, May 12, 2019. https://www.kunews.ac.kr/news/articleView.html?idxno=30376.

Park, Joonhyung. "빅히트 대표 "정답은 콘텐츠입니다"" [Bighit Rep 'the Answer Is Content']. *MK*, April 19, 2020. https://www.mk.co.kr/news/business/view/2019/04/243039/.

pharkil. "[직캠/Fancam] 141008 EXID(하니) 위아래 @ 파주 한마음 위문공연" [[Fancam] 141008 EXID (Hani) Up & Down @ Paju Hanmaeum Consolation Performance]. October 9, 2014. Video. 3:15. https://www.youtube.com/watch?v=cmKuGxb23z0.

Recording Industry Association of America (RIAA). "RIAA 2018 YEAR-END MUSIC INDUSTRY REVENUE REPORT." Last modified 2020. Accessed September 2, 2020.

Regan, Helen. "This Video of a K-Pop Singer Falling 8 Times in 1 Song Will Inspire You to Keep Going No Matter What." *TIME*, September 7, 2015. https://time.com/4024228/K-Pop-gfriend-fall-korea-yuju/.

Ruiz, Marah. "EXO's Baekhyun performs "sweet" and "spicy" versions of 'Candy' in live showcase." *GMA Network*, May 27, 2020. https://www.gmanetwork.com/entertainment/showbiznews/news/64003/exos-baekhyun-performs-sweet-and-spicy-versions-of-candy-in-live-showcase/story.

Seoul Kyungjae Shinmoon. "[#복세편살] <14> '오늘의 떡밥은 뭘까?' 아이돌계의 큰손 '직캠' 문화" [[#Boksaepyunsal] <14> "What's Today's Gossip?" Idol Industry's Big Hand, 'Fancam' Culture]. *Naver*, August 19, 2019. https://m.post.naver.com/viewer/postView.nhn?volumeNo=23606997&memberNo=22213349&searchKeyword=%EC%95%84%EC%9D%B4%EB%8F%8C&searchRank=258.

Shim, Seohyun. "브이라이브 강화하는 네이버, 이번엔 SM과 '언택트 팬관리'" [Naver Strengthening V Live, This Time with SM 'Untact Fan Management']. *Joongangilbo*, April 14, 2020. https://news.joins.com/article/23754271.

Shin, Daeun. "동남아 공략하는 브이라이브…현지 연예인과 맞손" [Vlive Targeting Southeast Asia… Collaborations with Local Celebrities]. *Hangyeorae*, June 27, 2019. http://www.hani.co.kr/arti/economy/it/899560.html.

smile -wA-. "150905 여자친구(GFRIEND) - 오늘부터 우리는 (Me gustas tu) @인제 SBS 라디오 공개방송 직캠/Fancam by -wA-" [150905 GFRIEND - Starting Today We (Me Gustas Tu) @ Inje SBS Radio Public Show Fancam by -wA-]. September 5, 2015. Video. 4:02. https://youtu.be/Ag2R7Mt8yI8.

SMTOWN. "TVXQ! 'Rising Sun' MV." November 23, 2009. Video, 5:19.
https://www.youtube.com/watch?v=2ZxK6ohbX-s.

Song, Seung-hyun. "K-Pop Powerhouses Ask for Financial Support from
Government." *The Korea Herald*, June 21, 2020.
http://www.koreaherald.com/view.php?ud=20200621000146.

StarshipTV. "[MV] Monsta X – Pepsi For The Love Of It (Korean Version)."
September 9, 2019. Video, 2:45.
https://www.youtube.com/watch?v=IPxSQTRLss0.

TWICE. "Ep 1. First Step Towards Our Dream | TWICE: Seize the Light." April 29,
2020. Video, 15:46.
https://www.youtube.com/watch?v=mEtUkIDqbog.

V Live. "Channels." Last accessed May 3, 2020.
https://www.vlive.tv/channels.

Woo, Bin. "'슈퍼엠이 언다'…SM X 네이버, 라이브 콘서트 스트리밍 서비스
시작" ['SuperM the Opening Act'... SM X Naver, Starts Live Concert Streaming
Service]. *10asia*, April 21, 2020.
https://tenasia.hankyung.com/music/article/2020042160704.

Yang, Seungjun and Jung-geun Song. "아이돌 파는 상술 덕에 CD시장 '웃픈' 부활"
[CD market's bittersweet revival after trick of the trade via idol sales]. *Hankookilbo*,
December 18, 2018.
https://www.hankookilbo.com/News/Read/201812171696325599.

YonhapNewsTV. ""K팝 좋아요"…트위터·인스타그램 CEO 방한 / 연합뉴스
TV (YonhapnewsTV)" ['I like KPOP'... Twitter ·Instagram CEO visits Korea /
YonhapNewsTV]. March 22, 2019. Video, 1:52.
https://www.youtube.com/watch?v=SweIVzxSpHk.

YouTube. "hello82." Last accessed March 15, 2020.
https://www.youtube.com/channel/UC1HHeTLXHMM5FiEyQpS1toA/videos.

PART 4 – THE IDOL SYSTEM

"Flowerboys and the Appeal of 'Soft Masculinity' in South Korea." *BBC*, September 5, 2018.
https://www.bbc.com/news/world-asia-42499809.

"세정, 가슴아픈 가족사고백 "형편 어려워 결식아동 급식카드로 끼니 해결""
[Sejung, Heart-Wrenching Family Story Confession 'Had to Eat with Meal Vouchers
for Low-Income Youth']. *Joongdoilbo*, March 2, 2018.
http://www.joongdo.co.kr/web/view.php?key=20180302001219171.

"악플에 아팠던 구하라…"연예인, 말못할 고통 앓아" 호소하기도" [Goo Hara Hurt
from Malicious Comments... Appealed 'Celebrities Suffer from Indescribable
Pain']. *DongA*, November 24, 2019.
http://www.donga.com/news/Top/article/all/20191124/98513429/1.

1theK. "[MV] GFRIEND _ Glass Bead." November 2, 2017. Video, 3:43.
https://www.youtube.com/watch?v=GU7icQFVzH0.

BLACKPINK. "BLACKPINK - Boombayah M/V." August 8, 2016. Video, 4:03.
https://youtu.be/bwmSjveL3Lc.

Chae, Hyeseon. "'아이돌'에 대한 지드래곤의 생각" [G-Dragon's Thoughts on
"Idol"]. *Joongangilbo*, February 17, 2017.
https://news.joins.com/article/21275790.

Chae, Hyeseon. "'너만 없었다면 예쁜 그룹이었을 텐데…' 악플로 상처받은 걸그룹
멤버" ['It Would've Been a Pretty Group If Not for You…' Girl Group Member Who
Was Hurt by Malicious Comments]. *Joongangilbo*, April 8, 2017.
https://news.joins.com/article/21453277.

Chae, Hyeseon. "종현 유서 공개 "이만하면 잘했다고 고생했다고 해줘""
[Jonghyun's Will Revealed 'Tell Me I Did Well and That I Tried Hard
Now']. *Joongangilbo*, December 19, 2017.
https://news.joins.com/article/22215699.

Cho, Wooyoung. "[연예기자24시] 제2의 노예계약 분쟁, 터질 게 터졌다" [[24hour
Celebrity Reporter] the 2nd Slave Contract Dispute, Finally Breaks Out]. *StarToday*,
November 29, 2014.
https://www.mk.co.kr/star/musics/view/2014/11/1470775/.

Cho, Wooyoung. "제2의 노예계약 분쟁, 터질 게 터졌다" [The 2nd Slave Contract
Dispute, about Time It Happened]. *StarToday*, November 29, 2014.
https://www.mk.co.kr/star/musics/view/2014/11/1470775/.

Cho, Yoonsun. "'토크몬' 선미, 가슴 아픈 가족사 "父 돌아가신 후 이선미로 개명""
['Talkmon' Sunmi, Heart-Wrenching Family Story 'Changed Name to Lee Sunmi
after Father's Passing']. *Chosunilbo*, February 6, 2018.
https://www.chosun.com/site/data/html_dir/2018/02/06/2018020601095.html.

Chung, Chaewon. "How Female K-Pop Idols Suffer Gender Inequality and Are Held to
Different Standards: 'It's Totally Unfair'." *South China Morning Post*, February 22, 2020.
https://www.scmp.com/lifestyle/entertainment/article/3051389/how-female-K-Pop-
idols-suffer-gender-inequality-and-are.

Digital Issue Team. "10년간 데뷔 아이돌 436팀…1년에 한두팀만 남기도" [436
Idol Teams Debut within 10 Years… Even Only One or Two Left during One
Year]. *Chosun*, July 22, 2017.
https://www.chosun.com/site/data/html_dir/2017/07/22/2017072200936.html.

dingo music. "2018 Idol Dance Medley (G)I-DLE." April 20, 2018. Video, 1:58.
https://youtu.be/YkrS9kfFO_s.

Dingo. "걸그룹 데뷔를 앞둔 한 소녀에게 어마무시한 일이 일어났다?! 데뷔 전부터
살벌한(?) 신인 걸그룹 '아이들'!" [Something Scary Happened to a Girl Nearing a
Girl Group Debut?! Fierce before Debut, Rookie Girl Group 'Idle!']. April 26, 2018.
Video, 6:37.
https://www.youtube.com/watch?v=FoiDU23wjO4.

Gong, Se Eun. "'Stars Have Feelings. We Are Not Dolls': South Korea Mourns K-Pop Star Goo Hara." *NPR*, November 25, 2019. https://www.npr.org/2019/11/25/782567715/stars-have-feelings-we-are-not-dolls-south-korea-mourns-K-Pop-star-goo-hara.

Herman, Tamar. "Female K-Pop Stars Face Criticism for Seemingly Feminist Behavior." *Billboard*, March 26, 2018. https://www.billboard.com/articles/columns/k-town/8257777/female-K-Pop-stars-face-criticism-feminist-behavior.

Huh, Yoonsun. "아이돌을 만드는 사람들 <1>" [People That Create the Idols <1>]. *Allure*, May 14, 2016. http://www.allurekorea.com/2016/05/14/아이돌을-만드는-스타일리스트-안무가-디렉터/.

Huh, Yoonsun. "아이돌을 만드는 사람들 <2>" [People That Create the Idols <2>]. *Allure*, May 15, 2016. http://www.allurekorea.com/2016/05/15/아이돌-사진가-캐스팅-디렉터-보컬-트레이너/.

Hwang, Bosun. "아이돌을 만드는 사람들 ② 류재아" [People That Create the Idols 2) Ryu Jeah]. *Singles*, February 15, 2018. http://www.thesingle.co.kr/SinglesMobile/mobileweb/news_content/detail_news_content.do?fmc_no=599680&fsmc_no=599737&nc_no=696021&fsmc_nm=career.

Hwang, Jiyoung. "엑소에겐 없는 '마의 7년'" [No 7-Year Tribulation for EXO]. *Joongangilbo*, February 11, 2019. https://news.joins.com/article/23358683.

Im, Hyojin. "뉴이스트 'BET BET' 공중파 첫 1위 "러브에게 감사"" [Nu'Est 'Bet Bet' First #1 Win on Terrestrial TV 'Thanks to the Loves']. *SeoulEN*, May 11, 2019. https://en.seoul.co.kr/news/newsView.php?id=20190511500026&wlog_tag3=naver.

Im, Soojung. "보이밴드 '더이스트라이트' 폭행 묵인 기획사 회장 집유 확정" [Agency CEO Silent over Boy Band 'The Eastlight' Assault Is Confirmed House Arrest]. *Yonhap News*, March 26, 2020. https://www.yna.co.kr/view/AKR20200326082700004?input=1195m.

Jeon, Haeseung. "SM엔터테인먼트 오디션, 매주 500명 넘는 지원자 몰린다" [SM Entertainment Audition, Attracts over 500 Applicants Weekly]. *ChannelYes*, 2011. http://ch.yes24.com/Article/View/18106.

Jung, Hyeonmok. "전국에 '텔미' 열풍" ['Tell Me' Syndrome All over Nation]. *Joongangilbo*, November 6, 2007. https://news.joins.com/article/2937993.

Jung, Yeojin. "'뭉뜬' 트와이스 지효 "연습생 10년, 그만두려 회사 안 나가기도"" ['Moongddeun' TWICE Jihyo 'Trainee for 10 Years, Even Stopped Going in Order to Quit']. *Joongangilbo*, October 25, 2017. https://news.joins.com/article/22046089.

Kang, Myungseok. "아이돌 그룹, 이렇게 탄생한다" [Idol Group, This Is How They're Born]. *Hankookilbo*, May 27, 2015. https://www.hankookilbo.com/News/Read/201505271114342677.

Kang, Shinwoo. "[썸_레터] 치열한 '연습생 입시' 세계…"14살은 늦었어요"" [[Some_ Letter] The Fierce World of 'Trainee Entrance Exams'…'Age 14 Is Too Late']. *Seoul Gyeongjae*, June 3, 2019. https://www.sedaily.com/NewsVIew/1VJ9474B2O.

Kang, Youngwoon. ""섹시 강요당하는 여자 아이돌, 진짜 '아티스트'라는 걸 증명한게 가장 기뻐요"" ['I'm the Happiest about Proving That Female Idols Who Are Confined to Sexy Concepts Are Real 'Artists'']. *MK*, November 7, 2019. https://www.mk.co.kr/news/culture/view/2019/11/919238/.

Kim, Gunwoo. "아이돌 한명 키우는데 얼마? 데뷔활동만 5억원" [How Much to Raise One Idol? Debut Promotions Cost 500 Million Won]. *Joongangilbo*, October 2, 2015. https://news.joins.com/article/18779901.

Kim, Hayeon. "'YG 보석함', 방예담 속한 데뷔조 1순위 연습생 TREASURE A팀… "1 년에 최소 1억지원"" ['YG Treasure Box', #1 Priority Debut Group Treasure A Team Including Bang Yedam… 'Minimum 100 Million Won Support Yearly]. *Topstarnews*, November 16, 2018. http://www.topstarnews.net/news/articleView.html?idxno=526627.

Kim, Jinhee. "'꿀벅지'가 무슨뜻? '신조어' Vs '불쾌' 논란" [What Does 'Kkulbeokji' Mean? Controversy over 'New Word' vs. 'Discomfort']. *Joongangilbo*, September 23, 2009. https://news.joins.com/article/3789399.

Kim, Sookyung "BTS 같은 스타 되고 싶어 'K팝 유학' 옵니다" ['K-Pop Abroad Education' to Become a Star like BTS]. *Chosunilbo*, August 1, 2019. https://www.chosun.com/site/data/html_dir/2019/08/01/2019080100119.html.

Kim, Yeonji. "'배우 선언' 포미닛 전 멤버들, '현아와 아이들' 이미지 벗을까" ['Actress Declaration' 4Minute's Former Members, Can They Leave 'Hyuna and Girls' Image Behind]. *JTBC News*, March 7, 2017. http://news.jtbc.joins.com/article/article.aspx?news_id=NB11433750.

Korea Creative Content Agency (KOCCA). "2019 대중문화산업 실태조사보고서" [2019 Pop Culture/Art Industry Research Report]. Naju, KOCCA: 2020.

Korea Creative Content Agency (KOCCA). "대중문화 예술인 표준 전속 계약서" [Pop Culture Artist Standard Exclusive Contract]. KOCCA. Last accessed April 7, 2020. https://ent.kocca.kr/MW/UID/BBS/U007/contract.do.

Koreaboo. ""9 Muses of Star Empire' BBC Documentary." September 20, 2014. Video, 47:34. https://www.youtube.com/watch?v=4s3p15YAVF0.

KPOPALYPSE (blog). "Kpopalypse Interview - Kim Nayoon." April 8, 2020. Accessed April 23, 2020. https://kpopalypse.com/2020/04/08/kpopalypse-interview-kim-nayoon/.

Kwak, Donggun. "검찰, '프로듀스 101 순위조작' 안준영 PD에 징역 3년 구형" [Prosecution, 'Produce 101 Ranking Fraud' Demands 3-Year Sentence for Producer Ahn Joonyoung]. *MBCNews*, May 12, 2020. https://imnews.imbc.com/news/2020/society/article/5769633_32633.html.

Lee, Gayoung. ""YG·JYP 연습생 8년…38kg로 살빼고 男과 택시 탑승금지"" [YG, JYP Trainee for 8 Years… Reduce Weight to 38kg and No Riding in Taxis with Men]. *Joongangilbo*, April 8, 2019. https://news.joins.com/article/23434402.

Lee, Jungyeon. "억울한 JYJ…아직 끝나지 않은 전쟁" [Unfair for JYJ… the War Continues]. *DongA*, July 3, 2014. http://www.donga.com/news/article/all/20140703/64903119/4.

Lee, Sanghyun. "작성 이력 공개에 네이버 악플 급감…유튜브서도 가능할까?" [Naver's Malicious Comments Rapidly Decline upon Displaying User's past Comments… Will It Be Possible at YouTube Too?] *MK*, May 22, 2020. https://www.mk.co.kr/news/it/view/2020/05/526819/.

Lee, Sejung. "크레용팝 활동 재개? 엘린 "다시 태어나도 크레용팝"" [Crayon Pop to Resume Activity? Elin 'Crayon Pop Even after I'm Reborn']. *BizTribune*, December 23, 2019. http://www.biztribune.co.kr/news/articleView.html?idxno=230148.

Lee, Seulbi, Yoojin Sung, and Soojung Yoon. "하루 17시간 춤·노래 연습… '마음의 병' 돌볼 시간도 없다" [Daily 17-Hour Dance, Vocal Practice… No Time to Attend to the 'Heart's Disease']. *Chosunilbo*, December 20, 2017. https://www.chosun.com/site/data/html_dir/2017/12/20/2017122000253.html.

Lee, Yoojin. ""안 지켜도 그만"…허울뿐인 표준계약서에 멍드는 '연예인 인권'" ['No Worries for Noncompliance' … 'Celebrity Human Rights' Damaged over a Silhouette of a Standard Contract]. *Kyunghyang*, October 23, 2018. http://news.khan.co.kr/kh_news/khan_art_view.html?art_id=201810232130005.

Lin, Xi and Robert Rudolf. "Does K-Pop Reinforce Gender Inequalities? Empirical Evidence from a New Data Set." *Asian Women* 33, no. 4 (December 2017): 27-54.

MASHIHO, "아이돌 그룹이 공중파 음악방송 1위까지 걸린기간 2018 최신본" [The Amount of Time It Took for Idol Groups to Reach #1 on Terrestrial Music TV Programs 2018 New Edition]. T-Story, last modified 2018. Last accessed May 2, 2020. https://idolch.tistory.com/22.

Ministry of Culture, Sports, and Tourism (MCST). "대중문화 연습생 표준 계약서" [Pop Culture/Arts Trainee Standard Contract]. MCST: September 9, 2019.

No, Woori. "또 '연예인 스폰서' 폭로…달샤벳 백다은, '장기 스폰서 제안'에 "보내지 마"" ['Celebrity Sponsor' Exposed Again… Dalshabet Paik Daeun Sends 'Don't Send Me This' to 'Long-Term Sponsor Offer']. *Chosun*, September 11, 2018. https://www.chosun.com/site/data/html_dir/2018/09/11/2018091101234.html.

Online Issue Team. "'유재석·방탄소년단 RM'도 읽었다…'82년생 김지영' 페미니스트 논란" ['Yoo Jaesuk, BTS RM' Also Read It… *Kim Ji Young, Born in 1982* Feminist Controversy]. *AsiaKyungjae*, March 20, 2018. https://www.asiae.co.kr/article/2018032008485561584.

Park, Soyoung. "B.A.P, 월드투어에 소송과 복귀까지..7년 징크스 끝 결국 해체" [B.A.P, from World Tour to Lawsuit to Comeback… Eventual Disbandment after 7

Year Jinx]. *OSEN*, February 18, 2019.
http://osen.mt.co.kr/article/G1111083650.

Puzar, Aljosa. "Asian Dolls and the Westernized Gaze: Notes on the Female Dollification in South Korea." *Asian Women* 27, no. 2 (2011): 99.

Shin, Hyonhee and Hyun Young Yi. "K-Pop Singer Decries Cyber Bullying after Death of 'Activist' Star Sulli." *Reuters*, October 16, 2019.
https://www.reuters.com/article/us-southkorea-kpop/K-Pop-singer-decries-cyber-bullying-after-death-of-activist-star-sulli-idUSKBN1WV1L3.

Sung, Jinhee. "[HD인터뷰] 에이핑크 정은지, "보컬 트레이너? 이젠 가수로!"" [[HD Interview] Apink Jung Eunji, 'Vocal Trainer? Now I'm a Singer!] *Pickcon*, May 19, 2011.
http://pickcon.co.kr/site/data/html_dir/2011/05/18/2011051801977.html.

Yang, Seungjoon. "'비스트'를 비스트라 부르지 못하고… K팝의 그늘" [Can't Call BEAST 'BEAST'… K-Pop's Shadow]. *Hankookilbo*, February 26, 2017.
https://www.hankookilbo.com/News/Read/201702261550781855.

Yim, Hyun-su. "K-Pop Boy Bands Defy Traditional Idea of Masculinity." *The Korea Herald*, September 3, 2018.
http://www.koreaherald.com/view.php?ud=20180903000239.

Yoo, Jihye. "네이버 연예뉴스 댓글 서비스 폐지·댓글 이력 공개 한달, 어떤 변화 있었나?" [One Month since Banning Naver Celebrity News Commenting and Displaying past History, What Changes Have There Been?]. *DongA*, April 7, 2020.
https://www.donga.com/news/Entertainment/article/all/20200406/100528168/5.

Yoon, Sang-geun. "JYP, 차기 보이그룹 오디션 "2008년생까지 지원 가능"" [JYP, Next Boy Group Audition 'Allows up to 2008-Born Applicants']. *Starnews*, October 1, 2019.
https://star.mt.co.kr/stview.php?no=2019100114020764174&VBC.

PART 5 — THE MUSIC

"Super Junior Wins Best Featuring Award at Kids' Choice Awards Mexico 2018." *KBS World*, August 22, 2018.
http://kbsworld.kbs.co.kr/news/news_view.php?no=18556&sec=kpop&lang=eng&page=1&search_tag=Lo%20Siento&writer=.

"수능 금지곡: 헤어나올 수 없는 '수능금지곡' 탈출구 찾기" [Forbidden Exam Songs: Finding Escape Route for 'Forbidden Exam Songs' You Can't Escape From]. *BBC News Korea*, November 14, 2018.
https://www.bbc.com/korean/news-46189462.

Benjamin, Jeff. "Super Junior Debut on the Latin Charts with Leslie Grace & Play-N-Skillz on 'Lo Siento'." *Billboard*, April 24, 2018.
https://www.billboard.com/articles/columns/k-town/8377784/super-junior-lo-siento-leslie-grace-playnskillz-latin-charts.

Bruner, Raisa. "BTS Explains Why They're Not Going to Start Singing in English." *TIME*, March 28, 2019.
https://time.com/5560818/bts-singing-english/.

Cho, Chung-un. "K-Pop Still Feels Impact of Seo Taiji & Boys." *The Korea Herald*, March 23, 2012. http://www.koreaherald.com/view.php?ud=20120323001104.

Choo, Seunghyun. "[이주의 가수] 보아의 20년, '아시아의 별'은 여전히 찬란하다" [[This Week's Artist] BoA's 20 Years, the 'Star of Asia' Still Shines Bright]. *SeoulKyungjae*, August 29, 2020. https://www.sedaily.com/NewsVIew/1Z6RNE4GA0.

Cruz, Lenika. "BTS's 'Dynamite' Could Upend the Music Industry." *The Atlantic*, September 2, 2020. https://www.theatlantic.com/culture/archive/2020/09/bts-dynamite-international-pop-k-sensation-sunshine-rainbow/615928/.

Hwang, Soyoung. "방탄소년단, 'Black Swan' 전세계 93개국·지역 아이튠즈 톱송 1 위." *Ilgan Sports*, January 18, 2020. https://n.news.naver.com/entertain/article/241/0002997893?fbclid=IwAR0T-Huqoc1wkvtTBB7iSWokCjjy-HW8PzYzVwCoJ7VNKXL3iWBfwUg4VbM.

Jung, Hyejung. "가요계는 '2000년대 가수 앓이'중...박효신, 임창정, 젝키에 열광" [Korean Pop Industry 'Longing for Singers of 2000s'... Hype over Park Hyo Shin, Lim Changjung, Sechs Kies]. *KBS News*, October 24, 2016. http://news.kbs.co.kr/news/view.do?ncd=3366357.

Jung, Hyunmok. "멜로디·가사 반복 '후크송' 바람몰이" [Trendsetting 'Hooksong' with Repetitive Melody/Lyrics]. *Joongangilbo*, October 21, 2008. https://news.joins.com/article/3345249.

Kim, Eungoo. "K팝의 세계관 누가 만들까? A&R 주역 정병기(인터뷰)" [Who Creates K-Pop's Universe? A&R Lead Jeong Byung-Gi (Interview)]. *Edaily*, March 8, 2019. https://www.edaily.co.kr/news/read?newsId=01092246622421352&mediaCodeNo=258.

Kim, Eunwoo. "[미국음악일기] 케이팝 원조 SM을 이끈 '송캠프' 시스템" [[US Music Diary] 'Songcamp' System That Led K-Pop's Origins in SM Ent.]. *Bizhankook*, March 13, 2017. https://www.bizhankook.com/bk/article/12908.

Kim, Hyosook. "이수만 'SM만의 새로운 음악 공개 채널 'STATION' 공개...태연이 첫 주자'" [Lee Soo-Man "Presenting "SM's Newest Music Channel 'Station'... Taeyeon as Starter"]. *Seoul Kyungjae*, January 27, 2016. https://entertain.naver.com/read?oid=011&aid=0002793858.

Kim, Sungmin. 케이팝의 작은 역사 [K-Pop's Small History]. Seoul: Geulhangari Publishers, 2018. Adobe Digital Editions.

Lee, Daehwa. "SMP에 대하여" [About SMP]. *IZM*, August 2008. http://www.izm.co.kr/contentRead.asp?idx=19568&bigcateidx=15&subcateidx=17&view_tp=1.

Lee, Gyu Tag. 케이팝의 시대 [The K-Pop Age]. Seoul: Hanwool Academy, 2016.

Lee, Jaehoon. "엑소 'XOXO' 100만장↑ 대기록, 12년만의 밀리언셀러" [EXO's 'XOXO' Sets Huge Record of 1 Million+ Copies, Million-Seller after 12 Years]. *Joongangilbo*, December 27, 2013. https://news.joins.com/article/13499072.

Lee, Jinsub. "진지하게 '소녀시대' [I Got A Boy] 를 듣다" [Seriously Listening to Girl's Generation's [I Got a Boy]]. Korea Creative Content Agency. Last modified January 14, 2013. http://home.kocca.kr/mportal/bbs/view/B0000204/1780747.do;KCSESSIONID =dGp5YH1Tp57tkZvqQ7VnkJ1vwxmdt7bn1pPx9FvcCpJpSjHN01wv!1822035171!-218740271?searchCnd=&searchWrd=&cateTp1=&cateTp2=&useAt=&menuNo=2-01225&categorys=4&subcate=67&cateCode=0&type=&instNo=0&.

Leight, Elias. "How American R&B Songwriters Found a New Home in K-Pop." *Rolling Stone*, May 2, 2018. https://www.rollingstone.com/music/music-news/how-american-rb-songwriters-found-a-new-home-in-K-Pop-627643/.

Mendez, Blanca. "Seo Taiji & Boys Pioneered Socially Conscious K-Pop for Groups Like BTS." *VICE*, August 1, 2017. https://www.vice.com/en_us/article/7x95gz/seo-taiji-and-boys-pioneered-socially-conscious-K-Pop-for-groups-like-bts.

Noory, Diyana. "K-Pop Is Worldwide, but K.A.R.D Are the Idols Who've Already Started There." *VICE*, April 26, 2017. https://www.vice.com/en_ca/article/mgyxex/K-Pop-is-worldwide-but-kard-are-the-idols-whove-already-started-there.

Rolli, Bryan. "BTS Just Shattered a Major iTunes Record Formerly Held By Adele." *Billboard*, July 6, 2020. https://www.forbes.com/sites/bryanrolli/2020/07/06/bts-black-swan-itunes-record-no-1-adele/#1cb37c442d57.

Shin, Kiwon. "표절 시비로 저작수익 넘어간 노래 수두룩" [Many Songs' Royalties Lost Due to Plagiarism Scandals]. *Hankyung*, March 29, 2006. https://www.hankyung.com/life/article/2006032963738.

Song, Eunah. "요즘 가요 왜 영어가사 일색일까?" [Why Is *Gayo* Nowadays Full of English Lyrics?]. *Segye*, July 31, 2013. https://www.segye.com/newsView/20130731003851.

Sun, Mikyung. "헤이즈 만든 제이든 정이 말하는 A&R의 모든 것" [All of A&R Explained by Jaden Jeong Who Launched Heize]. *Chosunilbo*, June 15, 2018. https://www.chosun.com/site/data/html_dir/2018/06/15/2018061501456.html.

Yang, Seungjoon. "가요시장 콤비시대 지나고... 이젠 12명 '집단 창작' 시대" [Korean Pop Market past the Duo-Era... Now an Era of 12-Person 'Group Creation']. *Hankookilbo*, June 14, 2019. https://www.hankookilbo.com/News/Read/201906131646748087.

PART 6 – THE BUSINESS SIDE

"BTS Signs Contract with Def Jam Recordings." *The Korea Herald*, March 28, 2017.
http://www.koreaherald.com/view.php?ud=20170328000834.

"More K-Pop Artists Team up with U.S. Labels to Expand Careers." *YonhapNews*,
March 11, 2020.
https://en.yna.co.kr/view/AEN20200311008300315?section=culture/K-Pop.

"고양 K컬처밸리, 4만2000명 수용 공연장 들어선다" [Goyang K-Culture Valley,
Performance Venue for 42,000 People Coming]. *DongA*, August 11, 2020.
https://www.donga.com/news/Society/article/all/20200811/102405240/1.

"네이버, SM엔터에 1000억 투자..."글로벌 영상시장 공략" [Naver, Invests 100
Billion Won to SM Ent... 'Global Video Market Strategy']. *DongA*, August 3, 2020.
https://www.donga.com/news/Economy/article/all/20200803/102277722/1.

Benjamin, Jeff. "BIGBANG Earns 2nd Entry on Billboard 200 with Career-Defining
'Made' Album." *Billboard*, December 19, 2016.
https://www.billboard.com/articles/columns/k-town/7625656/bigbang-made-
billboard-200-charts.

Big Hit Labels. "Big Hit Corporate Briefing with the Community (2h 2020)." August
12, 2020. Video. 57:43.
https://youtu.be/MyGF8mFDMeI.

BT21. Accessed July 22, 2020.
https://www.bt21.com/.

Cho, Bernie. "The Hip Hype Reality of the Korean Wave." Lecture presented at
KAIST College of Business, Seoul, South Korea, October 6, 2020.

Dong, Sun-hwa. "EXO Becomes 'Quintuple Million-Seller'." *The Korea Times*,
October 31, 2018.
https://www.koreatimes.co.kr/www/art/2018/10/732_257915.html.

Eggertsen, Chris. "Billboard Announces New Chart Rules: No More Merch & Ticket
Bundles." *Billboard*, July 13, 2020.
https://www.billboard.com/articles/business/9417842/billboard-new-chart-rules-
no-more-merch-ticket-bundles?utm_source=twitter&utm_medium=social.

Elberse, Anita, and Lizzy Woodham. "Big Hit Entertainment and Blockbuster Band
BTS: K-Pop Goes Global." Harvard Business School Case 520-125, June 2020.

Fioretti, Julia, and Shinhye Kang. "K-Pop Superstars BTS's Agency Seeks up to $812
Million in IPO." *Bloomberg*, September 2, 2020.
https://www.bloomberg.com/news/articles/2020-09-02/K-Pop-superstars-bts-s-
agency-seeks-up-to-812-million-in-ipo.

He, Laura and Jake Kwon. "Big Hit IPO makes BTS millionaires and their producer
a billionaire." *CNN*, September 28, 2020.
https://www.cnn.com/2020/09/28/investing/bts-big-hit-entertainment-ipo/index.html.

Herman, Tamar. "For the K-Pop Industry, Merch Is as Important as the Music." *Billboard*, March 16, 2020. https://www.billboard.com/articles/deep-dive/K-Pops-merch-madness/9331910/for-the-K-Pop-industry-merch-is-as-important-as-the-music.

Herman, Tamar. "SM Entertainment A&R Chris Lee Talks 'Cultural Technology' & Creating K-Pop Hits." *Billboard*, August 5, 2019. https://www.billboard.com/articles/news/international/8526172/chris-lee-sm-entertainments-kpop-interview.

Hwang, Jiyoung. "SM, 수란 속한 밀리언마켓 레이블 흡수" [SM, Acquisition of Suran's Label Million Market]. *Joongangilbo*, October 2, 2018. https://news.joins.com/article/23014262.

JYP Entertainment. "JYP 2.0." July 26, 2018. Video. 24:51. https://youtu.be/o8257W8sdNs.

Kang, Insuk. "'BTS 유니버스 스토리' 3분기 글로벌 론칭" ['BTS Universe Story' 3-Quarter Global Launch]. *The Games Daily*, May 13, 2020. http://www.tgdaily.co.kr/news/articleView.html?idxno=220705.

Kim, Hyunyoo. "빅히트 엔터테인먼트의 영업이익이 SM·JYP·YG 합친 것보다 많아졌다" [BigHit Entertainment's Operating Profit Exceeds SM·JYP·YG Combined]. *Huffington Post*, March 31, 2020. https://www.huffingtonpost.kr/entry/big-hit-bts-profit_kr_5e82f51ac5b62dd9f5d51ba2.

Kim, Jongil. "[BTS 혁명] 'BTS 경제효과' 年 5.5조원" [[BTS Revolution] 'BTS Economic Effect' 5.5 Trillion Won per Year]. *Sisajournal*, February 21, 2020. http://www.sisajournal.com/news/articleView.html?idxno=196048.

Kim, Kyungmi. "아이유는 6000, 송가인은 3500 정말?... 트롯가수 vs 아이돌 행사 '몸값' 차이 얼마일까" [6000 for IU, Really 3500 for Song Ga-In?... Trot Singer V. Idol Haengsa How Big Is the Difference in 'Net Worth']. *Woman Chosun*, June 8, 2020. http://woman.chosun.com/mobile/news/view.asp?cate=C01&mcate=M1004&nNewsNumb=20200666931#_enliple.

Kim, Mooyeon. "CJ E&M, 다듀·크러시 속한 아메바컬처 마저 품는다" [CJ E&M, Harbors Even Dynamic Duo·Crush's Amoeba Culture]. *Edaily*, November 13, 2017. https://www.edaily.co.kr/news/read?newsId=02532166616125392&mediaCodeNo=257.

Kim, Soohyun. "[취재파일] 서울시향의 '빨간 맛'...SM이 왜 클래식을?" [[Report File] Seoul City's 'Red Flavor'... Why Is SM Doing Classical Music?]. *SBS News*, July 21, 2020. https://news.sbs.co.kr/news/endPage.do?news_id=N1005893421.

Kim, Sooyoung. "잘 나가는 빅히트·JYP, 주춤하는 SM·YG ... 희비 엇갈린 공룡엔터들" [BigHit and JYP Doing Well, SM and YG Setbacks... Bittersweet Dinosaur Entertainment Companies]. *Hankyung*, August 3, 2019. https://www.hankyung.com/life/article/201908017848H.

Kim, Sungmin. "연예계 빅4 분석…연봉 1위는 '방시혁 회사', 퇴사율 1위는?" [Entertainment Industry Top 4 Analysis… #1 Salary Is 'Bang Shi-Hyuk's Company', Who's Resignation #1?] *Chosun*, January 18, 2019. http://news.chosun.com/misaeng/site/data/html_dir/2019/01/18/2019011800690.html.

Kim, Youngdae. *BTS: The Review*. RH Korea, 2019.

Ko, Byunghoon. "지체할수록 독?'…빅히트 IPO 어디까지 왔나" ['The More Delay, the More Detriment?'… BigHit IPO So Far']. *Newsway*, May 14, 2020. http://newsway.co.kr/news/view?tp=1&ud=2020051414362921767.

Korea Foundation for International Cultural Exchange. *Hallyu Now - Global Hallyu Issue Magazine 2020 - 03+04 vol.35*. KOFICE, 2020.

Lee, Eunjung. "YG 새 걸그룹은 4인조 '블랙핑크'…"테디가 프로듀싱"" [YG New Girl Group Is 4-Member 'Blackpink'… 'Teddy Is Producing']. *Yonhap News*, June 29, 2016. https://www.yna.co.kr/view/AKR20160629067300005.

Lee, Hyerin. "[K-POP 제작소] 심은지, JYP에서 작곡가로 일한다는 것" [[K-Pop Production Lab] Shim Eunji, Working as a Songwriter at JYP]. *Chosun*, October 16, 2013. https://www.chosun.com/site/data/html_dir/2013/10/16/2013101601324.html.

Lee, Jiyoung. *BTS, Art Revolution*. Parrhesia, 2019.

Lee, Jungeun. "빅히트엔터테인먼트, 자회사 세워 방탄소년단 활용사업 확대" [BigHit Entertainment, Founds Subsidiary to Expand BTS-Applied Ventures]. *BusinessPost*, March 26, 2019. http://businesspost.co.kr/BP?command=mobile_view&num=120212.

Lee, Jungyeon. "'방탄소년단' 소속사 빅히트, '여자친구' 영입 왜?" ['BTS' Company BigHit, Why Recruit 'GFriend'?]. *DongA*, July 30, 2019. http://www.donga.com/news/article/all/20190729/96748986/4.

Maliangkay, Roald. "Defining Qualities: The Socio-Political Significance of K-Pop Collections," *Korean Histories 4.1* (2013): 27-38.

Mayfield, Geoff. "BTS Is Headed Straight to No. 1 with New Album 'Map of the Soul: 7'." *Variety*, February 27, 2020. https://variety.com/2020/music/news/bts-album-map-of-the-soul-7-number-one-projection-1203517980/.

Moon, Jaeyong. "K팝 키워놓고…공연수익 해외로 '줄줄'" [Despite Developing K-Pop… Show Revenues Heading Overseas One-after-Another]. *MK*, May 3, 2019. https://www.mk.co.kr/news/economy/view/2019/05/290414/.

Park, Pansuk. "'아이랜드' 글로벌 아이돌 엔하이픈 탄생..대단원 막 내렸다" ['I-LAND' global idol ENHYPEN is born…conclude with final results]. *JoongangIlbo*, September 18, 2020. http://www.koreadaily.com/news/read.asp?art_id=8668957.

Park, Soojin. "정부가 2019년 추진하는 '케이(K)' 관광 활성 방안들: '케이팝' 페스티벌, 경연, 전용 공연장" [The Government-Driven 2019 'K' Tourism Enhancement Measures: 'K-Pop' Festival, Competition, Special Venue]. *Huffingtonpost*, December 17, 2018. https://www.huffingtonpost.kr/entry/story_kr_5c172b1ee4b049efa753a308.

SBS PopAsia HQ. "A Beginner's Guide to NCT." *SBS*, July 9, 2018. https://www.sbs.com.au/popasia/blog/2018/07/09/beginners-guide-nct.

Sisario, Ben. "A *Billboard* No. 1 Is at Stake, So Here's an Album with Your Taylor Swift Hoodie." *New York Times*, June 9, 2019. https://www.nytimes.com/2019/06/09/business/media/billboard-charts-bundles.html.

Sung, Jungeun. "빅히트, 방탄소년단 캐릭터 '타이니탄'(TinyTAN)' 론칭" [BigHit, Launches BTS Character 'TinyTAN']. *Startoday*, August 10, 2020. https://www.mk.co.kr/star/hot-issues/view/2020/08/817677/.

Turnbull, James. "Just Beautiful People Holding a Bottle: The Driving Forces behind South Korea's Love of Celebrity Endorsement," *Celebrity Studies*, vol.8, no.1 (2017): 128-135.

Yi, David. "Meet Jeremy Scott's Muse: K-Pop Star CL." *ELLE*, March 21, 2013. https://www.elle.com/culture/celebrities/news/a15248/cl-2ne1-jeremy-scott-muse/.

Yoon, Sungyeol. "빅히트, 매출 5879억..전년대비 2배 "사업 다각화 결과"" [BigHit, Revenue 587.9 Million... Double the Previous Year 'Result of Diversified Ventures']. *Starnews*, February 5, 2020. https://star.mt.co.kr/stview.php?no=2020020516181146162&VBC.

PART 7 – THE FANDOM CULTURE

"방탄소년단, 유니세프에 26억 기부..'Love Myself Festa'도 함께 [BTS, Donates 2.6 Billion Won to Unicef... Also 'Love Myself Festa']. *The Korea Times*, October 25, 2019. http://sf.koreatimes.com/article/20191025/1276390.

Anderson, Crystal S. "K-Pop Fandom 101." *KpopKollective* (blog). December 8, 2013. https://kpopkollective.com/2013/12/08/K-Pop-fandom-101/.

Berbiguier, Mathieu, and Young Han Cho. "케이팝 (K-Pop)의 한국 팬덤에 대한 연구" [Understanding the Korean Fandom of the K-Pop]. *Korean Journal of Communication and Information*, Vol. 81 (2017): 273-297.

Bhandari, Aditi. "The Mobilizing Power of the BTS Army." *Reuters*, July 14, 2020. https://graphics.reuters.com/GLOBAL-RACE/BTS-FANS/nmopajgmxva/.

Bruner, Raisa. "How K-Pop Fans Actually Work as a Force for Political Activism in 2020." *TIME*, July 25, 2020. https://time.com/5866955/K-Pop-political/.

Bumsoo, "잡덕이면 안 되는 거야?" [Can't I Be a Multi-Stan?]. *Brunch* (blog). May 2, 2019. https://brunch.co.kr/@samonatzu/2.

Chang, WoongJo, and Shin-Eui Park. "The Fandom of *Hallyu*, a Tribe in the Digital Network Era: The Case of ARMY of BTS." *Kritika Kultura* 32 (2019): 260-287.

Choi, Annette. "The Parasocial Phenomenon." *PBS*, April 5, 2017. https://www.pbs.org/wgbh/nova/article/parasocial-relationships/.

Chung, Dahoon. "[콘서트 종합] 20주년 '신화' 뿐 아니라 '신화창조'도 현재진행형 " 젊게 살겠다"" [Concert summary] 20-year continuous progression for not just *Shinhwa* but also *Shinhwa Changjo* "Let's live young"]. *SeoulKyungjae*, October, 18, 2020. https://www.sedaily.com/NewsVIew/1S5UoILoWN.

Horton, Donald and R. Richard Wohl. "Mass Communication and Para-Social Interaction." *Psychiatry: Journal for the Study of Interpersonal Processes*, 19 (1956): 215–229.

Ingvaldsen, Torsten. "John Cena Matches BTS' Fans $1M USD Black Lives Matter Donation." *HYPEBEAST*, June 11, 2020. https://hypebeast.com/2020/6/john-cena-black-lives-matter-1-million-usd-donation-bts-army-match.

Jang, Wooyoung. "강다니엘 팬클럽, 소아암 환우 위해 기부...'선한 영향력 힘 믿는다'" [Kang Daniel Fanclub, Donates to Childhood Cancer Patients... 'Believe in Power of Positive Influence']. *Chosunilbo*, November 1, 2019. https://www.chosun.com/site/data/html_dir/2019/11/01/2019110100648.html.

Jenkins, Henry. "Confronting the Challenges of Participatory Culture: Media Education for the 21st Century (Part One)." *HENRY JENKINS* (blog), October 19, 2006. http://henryjenkins.org/blog/2006/10/confronting_the_challenges_of.html.

Jeon, Soyoung. "[팬덤에 빠진 대한민국①] 한국 대중문화 발전의 일등공신은 ' 빠순이'" [[Korea Immersed in Fandoms①] the 'bbasoon-ee (Fangirl)' Is the Most Meritorious for Korean Pop Cultural Evolution]. *Today Shinmun*, May 12, 2018. http://www.ntoday.co.kr/news/articleView.html?idxno=61282.

JoseOchoaTV. "BTS Send Heartfelt Message to Army! [*Billboard* Hot 100 No.1]." September 2, 2020. Video, 1:52. https://youtu.be/mlP2NJAF6j8.

Kang, Hongkoo. ""BTS 오빠들 덕에 행복해졌다"...'러브 마이셀프' 캠페인 파급력 기대 이상" ['Happier Thanks to BTS Oppas'... 'Love Myself' Campaign Exceeds Expected Ripple Effect]. *DongA*, May 2, 2019. http://www.donga.com/news/article/all/20190502/95358931/1.

Karasin, Ekin. "'You're Crazy' Terrified Chris Brown Hides as Crazed Fan Tries to 'Break into' His La Mansion and Yells That She's His 'Life Partner'." *The Sun*, March 29, 2020. https://www.the-sun.com/entertainment/605955/chris-brown-woman-break-into-mansion/.

KBStheLive. "The Real Reason Why BTS Hits No.1 on *Billboard*." September 4, 2020. Video, 8:41. https://youtu.be/HGgdl--y_Kg.

Kim, Hyoeun, and Hyekyung Cho. "월 100만원 쓰는 女사생팬 '알바·노숙 심지어…'" [Female Sasaeng Spends 1 Million Won per Month 'Part-Time Job, Homelessness, Even...']. *Joongangilbo*, March 15, 2012. https://news.joins.com/article/7621589.

Kim, Nam-ok and Suk Seunghye. "그녀들만의 음지문화, 아이돌 팬픽" [Shade Culture of Their Own: Idol Fanfics]. *Journal of Korean Culture*, Vol.37 (May 2017): 191-226.

Kim, Sungmin. 케이팝의 작은 역사 [K-Pop's Small History]. Seoul: Geulhangari Publishers, 2018. Adobe Digital Editions.

Kim, Youngrok. "'해투3' 간미연 '안티는 내 잘못…윤은혜, 나 때문에 실명할 뻔'" ['HappyTogether3' Kan Miyeon 'Antis Are My Fault... Yoon Eunhye Almost Went Blind Because of Me']. *Chosunilbo*, March 22, 2018. https://www.chosun.com/site/data/html_dir/2018/03/23/2018032300004.html.

Lee, Kyungran, and Inkyung Lee. "동방신기 독극물 테러범 '우발적 범행' 진술" [TVXQ's Poison Terrorist Alleges 'Accidental Crime']. *Joongangilbo*, October 15, 2006. https://news.joins.com/article/2476168.

Lee, Saeron. "앨범 안 내는 소속사에…팬 무시하는 아이돌에…'팬덤'이 뿔났다" [At the Company Not Releasing Albums... at Idols Ignoring Fans... 'Fandom' Is Angry]. *Yeongnamilbo*, August 21, 2017. https://www.yeongnam.com/web/view.php?key=20170821.010230800140001.

Lipshutz, Jason. "BTS Thanks Fans for Top Social Artist Win at Billboard Music Awards 2017: Watch." *Billboard*, May 21, 2017. https://www.billboard.com/articles/news/bbma/7801216/bts-video-top-social-artist-win-billboard-music-awards-2017.

Lorenz, Taylor, Kellen Browning, and Sheera Frenkel. "TikTok Teens and K-Pop Stans Say They Sank Trump Rally." *The New York Times*, July 11, 2020. https://www.nytimes.com/2020/06/21/style/tiktok-trump-rally-tulsa.html.

LOVE MYSELF. "Love Myself 캠페인 상세소개" [Love Myself Campaign Details]. Accessed May 2, 2020. https://www.love-myself.org/post-kor/campaign-post-kor/about-lovemyself/.

Lynskey, Dorian. "Beatlemania: 'The Screamers' and Other Tales of Fandom." *The Guardian*, September 28, 2013. https://www.theguardian.com/music/2013/sep/29/beatlemania-screamers-fandom-teenagers-hysteria.

Marshall, P. David. "The Promotion and Presentation of the Self: Celebrity as Marker of Presentational Media." *Celebrity Studies*, Vol.1, no.1 (March 2010): 35-48.

Merriam-Webster. s.v. "stan (n.)." Accessed April 13, 2020. http://www.merriam-webster.com/dictionary/stan.

Merriam-Webster. s.v. "stan (v.)." Accessed April 13, 2020. http://www.merriam-webster.com/dictionary/stan.

Min, Kyungwon. "방탄 국내외 팬들 관심사 달라...해외서는 젠더 이슈 주목" [BTS's Global Fans' Interests Are Different...focus on Gender Issue Abroad]. *Joongangilbo*, December 11, 2019. https://news.joins.com/article/23654581.

Moon, Ilyo. "“나이 스타 이름으로 착한 일 할래요" 유행처럼 번진 '팬덤 기부'" ['I Want to Do Something Good on Behalf of My Star' 'Fandom Donation' Trend Spreads]. *Chosunilbo*, January 18, 2020. http://futurechosun.com/archives/46254.

Noh, Kwang Woo. "YouTube and K Pop Fan's Tribute Activity." *The Journal of the Korea Contents Association*, Vol.15, No.6 (2015): 25-32.

Oh, Taeksung. "영화 '기생충' 오스카 수상...K-POP이어 K-FILM까지 세계 중심 '우뚝'" [Movie 'Parasite' Wins at Oscars... K-Pop and Also K-Film Stands Tall at Center of World]. *VoaKorea*, February 11, 2020. https://www.voakorea.com/korea/korea-life/parasite-oscar.

Park, Sungeun. "“잠 좀 자고 싶어요"...사생팬에 고통받는 연예인의 호소" ['I Want to Sleep'... Pained Celebrities' Cry Out against *Sasaeng* Fans]. *Yonhap News*, January 23, 2018. https://www.yna.co.kr/view/AKR20180122051400797.

PLEDIS. "Seventeen Official Fan Club 'Carat' 4기 모집 안내" [Seventeen Official Fan Club 'Carat' 4th Cohort Recruitment Announcement]. Accessed April 25, 2020. http://www.pledis.co.kr/m/html/artist/seventeen/KOR/notice?&view=1&idx=7808.

Rha, Hyojin. "트와이스 나연 스토커로 알려진 남성이 사과 영상을 올렸다" [Man Known as TWICE Nayeon's Stalker Uploads Apology Video]. *HuffingtonPost*, January 30, 2020. https://www.huffingtonpost.kr/entry/story_kr_5e32b729c5b611ac94d011d9.

Robinson, Sean. "Celebrity Role Models, Social Media, & LGBTQ Youth: Lady Gaga as Parasocial Mentor." In *Contemporary Studies of Sexuality & Communication: Theoretical and Applied Perspectives*, edited by Jimmie Manning and Carey M. Noland, 501-518. Dubuque: Kendall Hunt, 2016.

Ryu, Inha. "아이돌 팬덤문화 인기↑ 지하철 광고 문화 바꿨다" [Idol Fandom Culture Popularity↑ Changed Subway Ad Culture]. *Kyunghyang*, April 7, 2020. http://news.khan.co.kr/kh_news/khan_art_view.html?art_id=202004071122001.

Sebasi Talk. "BTS and Army Grow Together, Fighting Against Prejudice | JiYoung Lee, Professor." September 22, 2019. Video, 21:33. https://youtu.be/Rhjo1LbuwoI.

Seo, Jungmin. "방탄소년단, 한국인 최초로 그래미 시상...'다시 오겠다'" [BTS, First Koreans to Present at Grammys... 'We'll Come Back']. *Hangyeorae*, February 11, 2019. http://www.hani.co.kr/arti/culture/music/881618.html.

Shin, Kyujin and Heeyoon Im. "“해외 팬클럽과 왜 차별하나요"... 성난 팬덤, 일부는 '탈덕'까지" ['Why Do You Discriminate Us against Global Fanclubs'... Angry Fandom, Some Even 'Unstan']. *DongA*, July 27, 2019. http://www.donga.com/news/article/all/20190727/96718505/1.

Stokel-Walker, Chris. "What the Murder of Christina Grimmie by a Fan Tells Us about YouTube Influencer Culture." *TIME*, May 3, 2019. https://time.com/5581981/youtube-christina-grimmie-influencer/.

Sulway, Verity. "Miley Cyrus Obsessed Fan Desperate to Impregnate Her Arrested after Terrifying Threats." *Mirror*, September 24, 2019. https://www.mirror.co.uk/3am/celebrity-news/miley-cyrus-obsessed-fan-desperate-20165357.

Tiffany, Kaitlyn. "Why K-Pop Fans Are No Longer Posting about K-Pop." *The Atlantic*, June 6, 2020. https://www.theatlantic.com/technology/archive/2020/06/twitter-K-Pop-protest-black-lives-matter/612742/.

Whitehad, Mat. "What the Hell Is a 'Stan' and Where Does the Name Come From." *Huffington Post*, October 11, 2017. https://www.huffingtonpost.com.au/2017/11/09/what-the-hell-is-a-stan-and-where-does-the-name-come-from_a_23264113/.

Yim, Hyun-su. "K-Pop Ads Taking over Seoul Subway." *The Jakarta Post*, October 16, 2018. https://www.thejakartapost.com/life/2018/10/15/K-Pop-ads-taking-over-seoul-subway.html.

Yim, Hyun-su. "K-Pop Fans: A Diverse, Underestimated and Powerful Force." *The Korea Herald*, June 12, 2020. http://www.koreaherald.com/view.php?ud=20200612000721&np=1&mp=1.

Yim, Hyun-su. "Surprised at Seeing K-Pop Fans Stand up for Black Lives Matter? You Shouldn't Be." *The Washington Post*, June 11, 2020. https://www.washingtonpost.com/opinions/2020/06/11/surprised-seeing-K-Pop-fans-stand-up-black-lives-matter-you-shouldnt-be/.

Yim, Hyun-su. "Thai K-Pop fans trending #Dispatch to vent frustration at monarchy." *The Korea Herald*, March 30, 2020. http://www.koreaherald.com/view.php?ud=20200330000935.

Zaveri, Mihir. "BTS Fans Say They've Raised $1 Million for Black Lives Matter Groups." *The New York Times*, June 8, 2020. https://www.nytimes.com/2020/06/08/arts/music/bts-donate-black-lives-matter.html.

PART 8 – THE FUTURE OUTLOOK
1theK. "[MV] T-ARA - yayaya." November 26, 2013. Video, 4:49. https://youtu.be/sLfRdyqxXJk.

Beginagain. "[Full.ver] 제철소의 색다른 사운드로 재창조된 헨리(Henry) - Believer" [[Full.ver] Henry - Believer Recreated with Fresh Sounds of the Ironworks]. July 12, 2020. Video, 3:22. https://youtu.be/EU_JGT55vN0.

Herman, Tamar. "Holland on 'Nar_C,' Depicting LGBTQ Love Stories in K-Pop & Making His Own Way." *Billboard*, May 2, 2019. https://www.billboard.com/articles/news/international/8513142/holland-narc-lgbtq-K-Pop-interview.

MBCkpop. "H.O.T - We are the future, HOT - 위 아더 퓨처, MBC Top Music 19971122." June 19, 2012. Video, 3:36. https://youtu.be/Kir3HOZwZqM.

Ryu, Inha. "[인터뷰]'성소수자 신인가수 홀랜드입니다'" [[Interview] I'm LGBTQ Rookie Artist Holland]. *Kyunghyang*, February 4, 2018. http://news.khan.co.kr/kh_news/khan_art_view. html?artid=201802040927001&code=940100.

SBS NOW. "[스타킹] 모두를 놀라게 한 헨리(Henry Lau) 바이올린과 함께 춤을!! / StarKing' Review" [[Star King] Henry Lau Dancing with the Violin Surprising Everyone!! / StarKing' Review]. March 31, 2014. Video, 2:35. https://youtu.be/2mcPr8AonsQ.

CPSIA information can be obtained
at www.ICGtesting.com
Printed in the USA
BVHW091334201220
595724BV00005B/14